	DATE DUE		

2nd edition
FINDING FACTS
Research Writing Across the Curriculum

William L. Rivers
Stanford University

Susan L. Harrington

 PRENTICE HALL *Englewood Cliffs, New Jersey 07632*

Library of Congress Cataloging-in-Publication Data

RIVERS, WILLIAM L.
  Finding facts.

  Bibliography: p. 185
  Includes index.
  1. Report writing.   2. Interdisciplinary approach
in education.   3. Research.   I. Harrington, Susan L.,
(date).   II. Title.
LB2369.R56 1988   808′.02   87-17440
ISBN 0-13-316845-X

Editorial/production supervision and
  interior design: Lisa A. Domínguez
Cover design: Lundgren Graphics, Ltd.
Manufacturing buyer: Ray Keating

 © 1988, 1975 by Prentice-Hall, Inc.
A Division of Simon & Schuster
Englewood Cliffs, New Jersey 07632

Printed in the United States of America

10 9 8 7 6 5 4 3 2 1

ISBN 0-13-316845-X   01

PRENTICE-HALL INTERNATIONAL (UK) LIMITED, *London*
PRENTICE-HALL OF AUSTRALIA PTY. LIMITED, *Sydney*
PRENTICE-HALL CANADA INC., *Toronto*
PRENTICE-HALL HISPANOAMERICANA, S.A., *Mexico*
PRENTICE-HALL OF INDIA PRIVATE LIMITED, *New Delhi*
PRENTICE-HALL OF JAPAN, INC., *Tokyo*
SIMON & SCHUSTER ASIA PTE. LTD., *Singapore*
EDITORA PRENTICE-HALL DO BRASIL, LTDA., *Rio de Janeiro*

For Wilbur Schramm
With respect, admiration, and affection
—William L. Rivers

To my parents
—Susan L. Harrington

Contents

Preface

The first edition of this book, published over ten years ago, was dedicated to coalescing the research methods of English students, the sometimes haphazard methods of journalism students, and the systematic but sterile methods of the scientist—in a way that students could use in their papers.

There is still a need for such a synthesis, for traditionally students of English and history assess the human condition primarily by reading, while students of journalism and the social sciences assess it by observing human actions. But why restrict the students in English courses to themes they can explore only in their memories and in the library? And why not teach journalism students how to do careful research—and assign them to read books that can teach them more, instead of sending them out to learn by observation alone?

One book alone is not likely to persuade students, or their teachers in the various disciplines, that they must learn one another's methods. Fortunately, great teachers, such as Wilbur Schramm, professor emeritus of Stanford University, have demonstrated how researchers can make rich assessments by synthesizing several methods. After beginning his working life as a journalist, Schramm earned a Ph.D. in English and won the O. Henry Memorial Award for fiction, then became a social scientist whose research has brought him international renown. And some thoughtful students have learned that "What I Did Last Summer" is not necessarily a bad essay topic if they are equipped to use something besides their emotions to assess their experiences.

It would be impossible to list all those who have contributed their advice and expertise to the first and second editions of this book. The second edition, like the first, owes much to Wilbur Schramm's example, as well as his advice. The chapter on databases in this edition could not have been what it is without the information and advice given by David Langenberg, Data Services Librarian at Stanford University. The authors thank them, as well as the following professors, who gave much thoughtful advice: Duncan A. Carter of Boston University, Raymond N. MacKenzie of Mankato State University, Barbara Straus-Reed of Rutgers University, Paul Slater of the University of Cincinnati, Therese Brychta of Truckee Meadows Community College, Walter S. Minot of Gannon University, and Jon C. Hughes of the University of Cincinnati.

WILLIAM L. RIVERS
SUSAN L. HARRINGTON

1

The Aims of Researchers

In 1913 Frank Maloy Anderson, a history professor, began one of the most painstaking pursuits of a single fact in the annals of research—a quest that shows how demanding, yet how important, verifying a single fact can be.

Historians had puzzled for years over the authorship of "Diary of a Public Man," which had been published, unsigned, in four installments in the prestigious *North American Review* in 1879. They had reason for concern. As the only source of a detailed picture of President Lincoln's actions from December 28, 1860, to March 15, 1861—the important winter of Secession—the dairy had been mined for information, much of which was used in many volumes of history. Historians could not resist the diarist's richly detailed notes, which included close descriptions like this one of Lincoln's Inauguration: "A miserable little rickety table had been provided for the President, on which he could hardly find room for his hat, and Senator Douglas, reaching forward, took it with a smile and held it during the delivery of the address. It was a trifling act, but a symbolic one, and not to be forgotten, and it attracted much attention all around me."

Was this anecdote authentic, or was it an ingratiating bit of color in a narrative that was pure hoax? Identifying its source seemed crucial. Professor Anderson started down a trail of identification that was to wind through thirty-five years of research.

His first efforts were discouraging. The editor of *North American Review* had refused to name the author when the diary was published in 1879. Professor Anderson searched the files of fifty leading newspapers and magazines of the period to determine whether they had tried to identify the diarist. Nothing.

Then he began to analyze the diary. He found that the entry for February 20, 1861, had been written in New York. But the author described himself as a man of "long experience in Washington." A senator? A representative? Professor Anderson combed the *Congressional Globe* to determine which members of Congress had not participated in congressional proceedings on February 20. None of the absent senators had been long in Washington, and 54 absent representatives were eliminated for one reason or another. The representatives were unlikely possibilities in any case, because no entry in the diary referred to proceedings in the House.

But Professor Anderson's analysis of the diary drew a clear picture of the writer:

> He had prestige. His advice was sought by people who conferred with Lincoln.
> He was tall. Lincoln had once asked him whether he had ever matched backs with towering Charles Sumner.
> He was a deft writer who knew French.
> He was urbane. He had been amused that Lincoln wore black gloves to the opera.
> He had many influential friends.
> He was devoted to the Union, but he knew the South well.
> He had met Lincoln twice, once in 1848 and again in 1861.
> He was especially interested in tariff, patent, and postal issues and problems.
> He often attended Senate sessions.
> He was a friend of William Seward and Stephen Douglas.
> He was an intimate of several leading citizens of New York and knew the city well.
> He was in New York on February 20 and in Washington on twenty other days during the period covered by the diary.

Using this picture to reduce a long list of possibilities, Professor Anderson settled on Amos Kendall (who had been so influential a member of Andrew Jackson's "Kitchen Cabinet" that one congressman had declared: "He was the President's thinking machine, his writing machine, aye, and his lying machine"). To the delight of the researcher, Kendall was a perfect fit for every detail of the picture— with one possible exception. Had he been in New York on February 20? The search for this elusive clue demonstrated Professor Anderson's passion for certainty.

Returning to the newspaper files, he searched the lists of hotel arrivals in vain. When he learned that Kendall usually stayed at the Astor House during trips to New York, he tried to trace the hotel register, which was then more than fifty years old. A woman who worked in the Morgan Library was related to the last manager of the Astor. Professor Anderson tracked him down only to learn that the man had no idea whether the register still existed. Then Anderson remembered hearing years earlier that hotel journals had been published in nearly every large city. He located the files of the New York journal, *The Transcript*, and found in the issue for February 20, 1861, the name of a guest at the Astor who had apparently registered as "J. Kendall." Had this actually been "A. Kendall" in some indecipherable script in the register? Professor Anderson was never able to determine.

To establish beyond doubt that Amos Kendall could have been the diarist, Professor Anderson next tried to ascertain that Kendall had been in Washington during each of the twenty days when diary entries had been written there. This investigation dissolved his theory. On two of the days, news accounts made clear, Kendall could not have been in Washington.

This information was not quite as disappointing as it might have been, for the longer Professor Anderson studied the diary, the more he doubted its authenticity. He did not consider it pure fiction for only one reason: writers of pseudo-fact commonly make at least one statement that is demonstrably false, but the diarist had not.

Professor Anderson decided that the diary was a combination of fact and fiction, a skeleton of fact that had been fleshed out with fancy. It was suspicious, for example, that the prose was polished, unlike the fuzzy sentence structure in most diaries, and was vague on exactly the points a diarist might be expected to describe precisely. Also, for such a short period, the diary seemed to carry entirely too many revealing anecodotes about Lincoln and pungent remarks by him. Moreover, the diarist seemed to be judging the leading men of the time with uncommon insight, causing Anderson to suspect that the man was recalling an earlier period and judging with hindsight rather than writing his impressions of events at the time they occurred. For these and similarly persuasive reasons, Professor Anderson concluded that he was seeking a fabricator, not an authentic diarist.

This description only sketches Anderson's dedication; he wrote a 256-page book[1] that traces all his labors. Although few researchers are so dedicated to single projects, Professor Anderson's work illustrates strikingly how a painstaking researcher attacks a complex problem.

FACTS

I grow daily to honor facts more and more, and theory even less.

—Thomas Carlyle

Professor Anderson's work also demonstrates that pursuing facts is almost always inseparable from interpreting them. The diarist's prestige, height, and urbanity, for example, are interpretations that Anderson drew from the diary. On the basis of probable facts and reasonable interpretations, Anderson then pursued the facts he needed: Was Kendall at the Astor House on February 20, 1861? The information he collected led to the interpretation that the diary combined fact and fiction. This interpretation was based on facts that could not have been substantiated without previous interpretations based on other facts.

A "fact" is indeed a slippery matter. *Webster's New Collegiate Dictionary* defines a fact, in part, as "a piece of information presented as having objective reality." Another perhaps less complete definition is that a fact is that which can be apprehended by the five senses. However, "objective reality" is itself a matter for definition, and our five senses often deceive us. It is a fact that concrete, lead, and steel are solid. But all are made up of molecules and of atoms—and the distance between the nucleus of an atom and its electrons may be roughly comparable to the distance between an aphid sitting on the goal line of a football field and a ladybug at the 50-yard line. Does an atom sound solid?

By the same token, it is a fact that a man five feet tall is "short." But this is actually an interpretation derived from comparison. To a Pygmy in the Ituri Forest of Zaire, a man five feet tall would be a towering figure.

So it is with "facts." They are relative and must be interpreted in the light of other facts. In short, there is seldom a real distinction between gathering facts and expressing ideas. As it has been put, "most of the facts we gather come dripping with ideas."

There are, of course, facts that delight the collector of trivia but that have neither purpose nor meaning, including some that were reported from Vietnam during the long years of American action there. Desperate to report something new in periods when one action seemed much like another, American correspondents joked among themselves about "the left-handed battalion commander syndrome." The effort to develop a "first," or "most," or "least" in the lead of a newspaper article caused them to surmise that "for the first time" a left-handed commander led a battalion into battle. Although this observation would be a fact on interpretation, identifying one commander by comparison with others, such trivia suggests why Claude Bernard has said that a mere fact is "nothing. It is only useful for the idea attached to it, or for the proof that it furnishes."

Though all researchers pursue facts, they differ on the ways in which to use them. Ultimately, the aims are basic: to understand ourselves and to understand the world in which we live. There are different methods of attaining that understanding, however. Natural scientists quantify data and perfect theories that can be demonstrated in experiments—a highly analytical approach. Poets, however, might agree with the great French writer Pascal, who argued against logic and for a spirit of subtlety and finesse—*esprit de finesse* over *esprit de géométrique*—holding that the heart as well as the mind has its reasons. T.S. Eliot made a similar point in his pageant play *The Rock*:

> Where is the wisdom we have lost in knowledge? Where is the knowledge we have lost in information[2]?

Wisdom—understanding what is true, right, and lasting—is not reserved for poets, sages, and prophets, and the methods of scientists are not to be disdained. Information (or facts) interpreted judiciously become knowledge, and knowledge is the foundation of wisdom.

The aims of the literary researcher nonetheless reflect the poet's view. The goal is to enlighten, and an individual fact works almost as a shaft of light to illuminate the topic of research. The historian, too, like Professor Anderson, seeks out individual, crucial facts, analyzing history.

If the historian or literary researcher has a theory to prove, that researcher could conceivably be accused of "interpreting facts" to suit his or her theory. To a natural scientist, though, refining the theory is the critical thing. The "facts" that support theories are experiments, and the individual experiments are not necessarily of much importance. For example, there are many ways to "prove," or at least demonstrate, the theory of gravity—so many, in fact, that scientists have elevated the theory to the level of a "law." Far from being unique, like the "fact" the historian seeks, the results of an experiment must actually be repeatable to be considered valid.

A theory is a system of explanation—a coherent body of general propositions that explain relationships and events. A body of theory enables a researcher to hypothesize and then to test hypotheses to determine whether they should be added to, or substituted for, existing theory, which is always tentative. A hypothesis directs the search for order among facts, and careful scientists accept hypotheses only after vigorous attempts to refute them have failed.

Historians and literary researchers have become more accustomed recently to working in terms of theory and hypothesis. But journalists have not—at least not consciously. Ben Bagdikian, now the dean of the Graduate School of Journalism at the University of California at Berkeley, tells of a social scientist who excitedly announced a discovery: "You guys don't have any hypotheses!" As Bagdikian points out, the journalist must not have a hypothesis—or must appear not to have one. The efforts of the journalist revolve around facts themselves—gathering them, checking them, and reporting them. Of course, an article must place the facts in context, and to a certain extent must interpret them too, explaining their significance to the reader if the reader will not otherwise understand them. Good journalists actually do *have* hypotheses, of varying strengths in varing situations, as to how things work, but they have a professional prejudice against them. Ideally, a journalist tries to report verifiable fact and avoid presuppositions.

Pursuing and interpreting fact is not a single process. Indeed, even Professor Anderson's long and involved research illustrates only part of a single approach—and there are many. An examination of the approaches of literary researchers, journalists, historians, natural scientists, and social scientists can indicate their range.

THE LITERARY RESEARCHER'S APPROACH

Diligence is the mother of good fortune.

—Miguel de Cervantes

Literary research, like historical research, works with facts, but its aim is to aid intuitive understanding. In *The Art of Literary Research*, Richard Altick speaks lovingly of the scholar's work: "the sheer joy of finding out things that have previously been unknown and thus of increasing, if but by a few grains, the aggregate of human knowledge." Literary research is, to Altick, the "enlightenment of criticism," and he sees a second goal as well: the discovery of the soul of a past society expressed in its language.[3]

The first aim is an aesthetic goal: to facilitate commentary, analysis, comparison, and generally a greater understanding of a literary work as art. This is literary criticism. The second is historical, almost sociological in nature: to understand a society whose personality and character have been lost to time and can be recaptured only through an understanding of its art. To do so, the literary researcher seeks out facts, compares them, analyzes them, and attempts to find out the truth from among the forest of details.

The methods of the literary researcher are similar to those of the historian, but the questions are often different. Literary researchers may be curious about the personality and background of an author—why the author thought, felt, and wrote in just such a way. To understand authors, some literary researchers turn to psychological interpretations of their works. Others analyze handwriting; it is not unusual for the editors of an anthology to add a photograph of a page from a handwritten diary, for example. One of the most magnetic personalities for research is the elusive William Shakespeare. Charles Hamilton searched for forty years for a scrap of Shakespeare's handwriting, for the purpose of understanding better the personality of the poet and thus facilitating the interpretation of his works. In June 1983 Hamilton found what he sought. He compared Shakespeare's handwritten will to the six known Shakespeare signatures and found to his astonishment that the handwriting matched. To establish authenticity beyond a doubt will be yet another challenge.

Another question for the literary researcher has to do with different versions of literary works. Stephen Crane's *The Red Badge of Courage* and some of William Faulkner's works were severely edited before they were published. James Joyce wrote and rewrote parts of *Ulysses* throughout its printing process. The interesting question is the *why* of the revisions. What did the second, third, and fourth versions say in comparison with the first? What shades of meaning did the author leave behind in favor of some other, more pointed wording? The answers can help the researcher understand the work better; in short, the process is the enlightenment of criticism.

Sometimes a researcher may find outright major errors in a published book. When the first American edition of Henry James's *The Ambassadors* appeared in 1903, there was a real whopper: Chapters 28 and 29 were transposed. Moreover, the mistake was not caught for 47 years. In 1955 the publishers announced that they had produced a corrected version; to their embarrassment, the book appeared with the chapters still transposed. The order was not set right until 1957.[4]

Literary researchers may also trace the truth of an anecdote, the real person behind a fictional character, or the identity of a person referred to by nickname in a letter. They may search out forgeries, such as the alleged diaries of Adolph Hitler sold to *Stern* magazine a few years ago.

Literary research, like historical research, involves building answers from an avalanche of data. In *The Scholar Adventurers*, which preceded *The Art of Literary Research*, Altick points out that the literary scholar must have a lively imagination as well as a devotion to truth because he or she confronts a vast jigsaw puzzle made up of countless fragments of fact, but some pieces are missing and others are fitted into the wrong places. The researcher must tidy up a sector of the puzzle, finding new pieces and rearranging old ones.

> To interpret the significance of this material in terms of literary art, he must recreate in his mind, in as minute and faithful detail as possible the social, intellectual and literary conditions of a past age, and make himself, as well, an intimate spectator of the inner life of a great artist. A Chaucerian must train himself to think according to medieval patterns of thought; a specialist in Hawthorne must recapture Hawthorne's special mood and outlook upon life. [5]

Research in literature, then, like research in history, illuminates the past and is based on traces of the past. Literary researchers also place the work of the artist in the context of his or her intellectual, social, and artistic milieu. Finally, like most historians, most literary researchers analyze written documents intuitively, shunning the scientists' leaning toward quantifying. As the next section will show, the journalist's research also aims to illuminate history—but it is the history of the future, the chronicles of the present.

THE JOURNALIST'S APPROACH

> There has never been a greater need for calm, journalistic voices.
>
> —Wes Gallagher

More often than any other serious researcher, the journalist pursues facts for their own sake. The journalist may explain the background of events, but interpretation of the facts traditionally takes second place to reporting them. A reporter can seldom know whether an event will be banal or significant, nor can he or she always judge its value in the moment of its occurrence. This limitation is inevitable, at least for those journalists who face daily deadlines. Indeed, the reporter may never know the significance of the events related in a story; the value of many of the events can be judged only by specialists. One of the criteria of newsworthiness is the extent to which the event will excite the passing interest of the public, and thus much of the journalistic mission of *enlightening* the public comes to little.

If most journalism produces merely a mass of information, however, it is still true that journalists pursue significances as well as trivialities. It would be odd if this were not true, for the journalist has entrée to great events and to decision makers ("a right to butt in," one has called it) seldom granted to any other researcher.

Because journalists and not the general public are so often the eyewitnesses to history, most of us must depend on the mass media for current information. Newspapers and magazines, radio and television tell us most of what we know about public figures and public affairs. Most of our facts come to us at second hand rather than through our own experience and observation.

We get only occasional firsthand glimpses of government by catching sight for a moment of a presidential candidate or a senator, by doing business with the field offices of federal agencies, by dickering with the Internal Revenue Service. We may also glean information at secondhand from friends and acquaintances who have some contact with officialdom. Yet this is sketchy stuff, and it adds only patches of color to the mosaic. Most of our knowledge of public affairs comes from the mass media. There simply are no practical alternatives to living in a world we hear about primarily from others.

A distinguished political scientist, Harold Lasswell, urged his colleagues to collaborate with journalists rather than merely use their reports, because a journalist often sees firsthand the events of the day and has the expertise with which to find out facts about them.

> Attuned to the immediate, he is impatient of delay. Accustomed to coping with tacticians of deceit, he is a sophisticated assessor of false witness. A journalist is also aware of who knows what, since his dramatizing imagination often perceives the relationship of every participant to the central action, recognizing potential informants who would otherwise be overlooked.[6]

The journalist most often pursues fact by interviewing and observing, processes that are treated in detail in other chapters. Here we will focus on another important aspect of journalism: how raw, unevaluated facts are reported for the sake of timeliness.

The assassination of President Kennedy in 1963 is an excellent example. Dozens of reporters were in the motorcade with the president when he was shot. Hundreds of others descended on Dallas a few hours after the shooting. In the inevitable confusion, the accounts varied alarmingly.

Item.   The rifle from which the bullets came was found by the window on the second floor of the Texas Schoolbook Depository Building. Or it was found in the fifth-floor staircase. Or it was hidden behind boxes and cases on the second floor. Ultimately, all reports agreed that it had been found on the sixth floor.

Item.   The rifle was first reported to be a .30 caliber Enfield. Then it was a 7.65mm Mauser. But it was also an Army or Japanese rifle of .25 caliber. Finally, it became an Italian-made 6.5mm rifle with a telescopic sight.

Item.   There were three shots. But some reports mentioned four bullets: one found on the floor of the President's car, one found in the President's stretcher, a third removed from Governor Connally's left thigh, and a fourth removed from the President's body. There was even one report of a fifth bullet, which was said to have been found in the grass near the side of the street where the President was hit. Finally, there was general agreement that there were only three bullets.

Item. The first reports of the President's wounds described a "bullet wound in the throat, just below the Adam's apple" and "a massive gaping wound in the back and on the right side of the head." The position of the President's car at the time of the shooting, 75 to 100 yards beyond the Texas Schoolbook Depository Building, explains the head wound. But how does one account for a bullet in the throat?

Item. The shots were reported to have been fired between 12:30 and 12:31 P.M., Dallas time. It was also reported that Lee Oswald, who was accused of the shooting, dashed into the house at Oak Cliff where he was renting a room "at about 12:45 P.M." Between the time of the assassination and the time of his arrival at the rooming house, Oswald reportedly (1) hid the rifle, (2) made his way from the sixth floor to the second floor of the building, (3) bought and sipped a Coke (lingering long enough to be seen by the building manager and a policeman), (4) walked four blocks to Lamar Street and boarded a bus, (5) descended from the bus and hailed a taxi, and (6) rode four miles to Oak Cliff. How did he accomplish all this in fourteen minutes?

The confusing array of misleading reports is easily explained. *Reporters* did not say on their own authority that a bullet had entered the President's throat; they quoted Drs. Malcolm Perry and Kemp Clark of the Parkland Memorial Hospital in Dallas, who turned out to have been wrong. The Dallas police first identified the rifle as a .30 caliber Enfield and a 7.65mm Mauser. A Secret Service agent said he thought the weapon was .25 caliber Army or Japanese rifle. The housekeeper at the Oak Cliff rooming house said that Oswald had come dashing in at about 12:45. And so on.

The most that one can charge the journalists with is haste, which gave equal status to everything posing as fact. Some errors were inevitable. Texas Governor John Connally said that the President's car had just made the turn at Elm and Houston Streets when the firing began. Mrs. Connally said that the car was nearing the underpass—220 yards beyond the turn. Both cannot be right. In fact, the consensus of other observers indicates that both were wrong; the car was about midway between these points.

Such discrepancies mar the work of the reporter who is on a deadline. He observes what he can and relies on authorities, or purported authorities, for the rest. The nature of journalism makes it obvious that although such methods cannot be supplanted, they can be refined to yield closer approximations of fact—for example, by reporters' choosing authorities more wisely.

Increasingly, another kind of journalism seeks to go beyond reporting random facts. More and more journalists are linking, combining, and interpreting facts to paint coherent pictures. These *interpretive reports*—also known as *news analyses*—are a step beyond straight news. They usually focus on an issue, problem, or controversy. Here, too, the substance is verifiable fact—not opinion, but instead of presenting facts in straight news or depth report fashion and hoping that they will speak for themselves, the interpretive reporter clarifies, explains, analyzes. The interpretive report usually focuses on *why*: Why did the President make that trip, appoint that bureaucrat, make that statement? What is the real meaning of the event?

Although journalists cannot have the long perspective that is available to most historical writers, the effect and value of their work is much like that of historians. In a few cases, journalists employ the methods of survey research developed by behavioral scientists. Again, systematic research enables the journalist to pursue and report relevant information.

THE HISTORIAN'S APPROACH

> A dwarf standing on the shoulders of a giant may see farther than the giant himself.
>
> —Robert Burton

The speech, "Everyman His Own Historian," delivered by the late Carl Becker when he was president of the American Historical Association, argues that

> . . . the natural function of history . . . running hand in hand with the anticipation of things to be said and done, enables us, each to the extent of his knowledge and imagination, to be intelligent, to push back the narrow confines of the fleeting present moment so that what we are doing may be judged in the light of what we have done and what we hope to do.[7]

"Mr. Everyman," then, must be a historian. Becker provided a homely example, showing that in the course of paying a fuel bill one may recall incurring the debt, consult personal records, call upon the creditor who in turn consults records—all these actions a miniature of historical research.

There is an essential difference between the layman and the professional historian, however, although a layman may develop either a personal or a professional interest in some aspect of the past—and may then study it thoroughly and become an authority—the historian's work consists entirely of analyzing the past. Because the past can be examined only through its traces, the historian is devoted to studying them: coins, stamps, art objects, buildings, and especially documents.

How the historian examines the past is indicated in part by the sketch of Professor Anderson's work earlier in this chapter. We can discover that a particular detail in a document is false by comparing that detail with facts established in other studies. Those facts, in turn, were first examined to determine whether they corresponded to other facts that had previously been established by careful examination. It is thus not oversimplifying to say that the writing of history is based on correspondences—on the degree to which not-yet-proven evidence corresponds with established fact. Essentially, historians work in probabilities, although many are little in doubt that their factual basis is unquestioned. For example, no one living today was a firsthand observer of the signing of the Declaration of Independence, and we cannot *know* that it was signed on the second of August; however other facts that make the date probable are so well established that it is not to be doubted.

Many "facts" asserted by some historians are less certain because they have been challenged by other historians. Revisionist historians—known variously as *new historians, radical historians,* and *leftist historians*—have challenged beliefs that are widespread because they are found in standard histories. Professor Jesse Lemisch of Roosevelt University has said that town meetings in colonial New England were not, as it has been widely believed, democratic. He and others have conducted studies that show that powerful figures in New England towns often used devices to control the meetings, such as exile of "political, ideological, and social deviants, as well as many of the poor. Thus, the apparent consensus within the town meeting reflects the exclusion from the town of those who didn't fit the consensus."[8]

It is always disturbing to find that the "facts" historians have long used are actually myths, but historians are accustomed to seeing cherished probabilities destroyed by examinations of the past that yield findings that are more probable. Even a book like David Hackett Fischer's *Historians' Fallacies,*[9] which is one great, and highly readable, catalog of error, does no more than persuade the historian that the method of research must be refined. Fischer's book, which is subtitled *Toward a Logic of Historical Thought,* was a major step toward that refinement.

THE NATURAL SCIENTIST'S APPROACH

Genius has been defined as a supreme capacity for taking trouble.

—Samuel Butler

It is an uncomfortable experience to have one's theory overturned by an awkward fact. But natural scientists are not dismayed (except in a limited or particular sense) when they discover that a once-trusted "fact" is really not true. Indeed, correcting a fact or theory is a cause for rejoicing. Theories that can be trusted depend on a foundation that can be trusted; researchers must work on solid ground instead of quicksand. The knowledge that "The Diary of a Public Man" was a suspect source enabled historians to make their theories more reliable. Similarly, the discovery that an atom is not a solid substance but a miniature solar system with electrons orbiting around an almost inconceivably small sun enabled physicists to proceed from the true rather than the spurious.

In a central sense, however, the methods of the scientist and those of the historian are not all alike. The scientist is ever seeking to systematize knowledge by stating general laws; some may be amended by discoveries, but the substance of science is a body of *general* propositions rather than the *particular* truths of the historian. Scientists are interested in the particular only as an instance of a universal principle. They aim to write sentences that begin with an expression of certainty: "Whenever," "If ever," "Any," "No," "All." Many historians and other scholars have attempted to assert and prove "laws," but only the natural scientists have succeeded. They alone can *predict* with any degree of certainty. Scientists themselves hold that no theory is better than the facts that support it, but scientific prediction is reasonably certain.

How do scientists work? Volumes would be required to describe all the individual methods, so we must be content with the brief summary given by James Bryant Conant after he talked with a number of scientists:

> (1) a problem is recognized and an objective formulated; (2) all the relevant information is collected; (3) a working hypothesis is formulated; (4) deductions from the hypothesis are drawn; (5) the deductions are tested by actual trial; (6) depending on the outcome, the working hypothesis is accepted, modified, or discarded. [10]

This process may seem no more complicated than Everyman's method of meeting everyday problems. In fact, it is not an uncommon way to solve common problems. A student might realize that he is often sick with colds and decide he needs to improve his health. He realizes he is living on hamburgers and french fries, rarely exercises, and often keeps himself awake by drinking coffee. The student hypothesizes that he is getting sick because he does not take care of himself. He tests out the theory by eating more vegetables, sleeping more, and exercising more for a month or so. He discovers that he feels much better and decides that his hypothesis was correct. Such a student might be surprised to find that he was using a facsimile of the scientific method—much like the character in Molière's comedy who discovered that he had been speaking prose all his life without knowing it. He might decide that he had been an unwitting scientist.

The professional scientist, however, differs from the student in at least one respect: The professional can select all the relevant informaion, test deductions, and evaluate the result in the light of many facts or general propositions that bear upon it.

The depth and range of the knowledge that a scientist may bring to a problem is suggested by Henri Poincare:

> Suppose we have before us any machine; the initial wheel work and the final wheel work alone are visible, but the transmission, the intermediary machinery by which the movement is communicated from one to the other, is hidden in the interior and escapes our view; we do not know whether the communication is made by gearing or by belts, by connecting rods or by other contrivances. Do we say that it is impossible for us to understand this machine because we are not permitted to take it to pieces? You know well that we do not, and that the principle of conservation of energy suffices to determine for us the most interesting point. We easily ascertain that the final wheel turns ten times less quickly than the initial wheel, since these two wheels are visible; we are able thence to conclude that a couple applied to the one will be balanced by a couple ten times greater applied to the other. For that there is no need to penetrate the mechanism of this equilibrium and to know how the forces compensate each other in the interior of the machine. [11]

On a much higher level, this kind of reasoning about hidden mechanisms led to the law of gravity, the theory of organic evolution, and the theory of relativity.

THE SOCIAL SCIENTIST'S APPROACH

Patience, diligence, painstaking attention to detail—these are the requirements.

—Mark Twain

Sketching the approach of the social scientist follows naturally the approaches of historians and natural scientists, for fact finding in the social sciences leans in both directions. Some sociologists, anthropologists, psychologists, political scientists, and communication specialists are drawn to the research techniques of the historian, some to the methods of the scientist (and a few historians are beginning to apply scientific methods). Given the rapid growth of the leaning toward science, however, it seems obvious that those who think of themselves as social *scientists* are winning the day—or at least the most attention. They can be distinguished from the others because they describe themselves as *behavioral scientists*.

Behavioral scientists seeking to construct methods like those used by natural scientists face a critical problem: If the distinguishing feature of science is the ability to state general propositions—Galileo's laws of falling objects, for example—how are they to state the *laws* of human action? Kenneth Colby tells an apocryphal story of an object that reaches Earth from outer space and defies the efforts of physicists and astronomers to analyze its composition, structure, or function. At last, a social scientist asks, "What's your name?" and the object answers, "Ralph." The fable is designed to suggest that the nature of the behavioral scientist's work allows him research techniques denied to natural scientists. But, of course, the techniques create infinite problems.

The mission of all social scientists is to examine humankind, and not only have they found it impossible to establish a universal proposition, or law, for any human behavior, but the prospect for establishing one is nowhere in sight.

From time to time a behavioral scientist will claim to have established a universal; Clark Hull published in *The Scientific Monthly* an article titled "A Primary Social Science Law,"[12] which states that human responses to physical and verbal stimuli, diminish with increasing distance from the point of stimulation. For example, if an aunt lives with or near a mother and assists the mother in caring for a child, the child will regard the aunt as a mother, and less so—or not so at all—if the aunt lives at a distance. Like the other "laws" of human action that are occasionally set forth, however, this one has not been accepted by behavioral scientists.

Yet human behavior does take on patterns. Mail a dollar bill in an envelope with no return address to an American, and the recipient is almost certain to spend it. Mail a dollar under the same conditions to an Australian aborigine; the recipient may convert it to Australian currency, discard it, or burn it. However, even the American's behavior is not predictable—he or she may give the dollar away, keep it, even frame it. Nonetheless, a pattern is discernible.

Behavioral scientists cannot begin their sentences, as natural scientists do, with "Whenever," "If ever," "Any," "No," and "All," but they can sometimes assert with confidence that in given circumstances most people will usually react in a predictable way. In some instances, the behavioral scientist can also explain why most of the others react differently.

It is no more possible to explore in a short space all the methods through which the behavioral scientist makes judgments than it is to treat adequately the methods of the historian, the literary researcher, or the natural scientist. Increasingly, behavioral scientists are using content analysis, a research technique that enables them to study written works systematically and quantitatively. For example, psychologists Richard Donley and David Winter of Wesleyan University analyzed the inaugural addresses of twelve U.S. presidents to try to measure the need for power versus the need for achievement of each president. The researchers considered words indicating strong action, aggression, persuasion, and argument as showing need for power. Words such as "good," "better," "excellent," and "high quality" were analyzed as showing a need for achievement. Theodore Roosevelt and John F. Kennedy were judged to have the strongest need for power. The inaugural addresses of each contained 8.3 power images per 1,000 words. Only three presidents were judged to have a greater need for achievement than for power: Herbert Hoover, Lyndon Johnson, and Richard Nixon. (A few historians and literary researchers occasionally use this kind of content analysis, but most continue to rely on intuition, which is usually better suited to most of the questions they try to answer by analyzing documents.)

Most behavioral investigation is based on two methods: *survey research* (commonly called *polling*, which is based on interiews, questionnaires, or both) and *experiments*. Both depend on two techniques: *asking questions* and *observing actions*. Both methods are so common in *all* research involving humans that they are treated in detail in the chapters on "Observing" and "Interviewing."

Research in the social sciences cannot be nearly as tidy as the experiments of a natural scientist. Perhaps the greatest obstacles the researcher encounters are, first, that survey findings may tell *what* is being thought or done by the interview subjects, but not *why*; and second, that all field work is so little subject to control that it seldom yields rock-solid results. As one researcher put it, "The real world is a messy place."

By contrast, a researcher *can* control human subjects in a laboratory experiment, but the laboratory itself distorts the experiment by taking the human beings out of real-life situations:

> As long as we test a [broadcast] program in the laboratory we always find that it has great effect on the attitudes and interests of the experimental subjects. But when we put the program on as a regular broadcast, we then note that the people who are most influenced in the laboratory tests are those who, in a realistic situation, do not listen to the program. The controlled experiment always greatly overrates effects, as compared with those that really occur, because of the self-selection of audiences.[13]

Another example of how experimental work can lead to misinterpretation of facts is the Hawthorne effect, which took its name from a classic study of the effect of various working conditions on rate of output at the Hawthorne plant of Western Electric Company. The experimenters varied the number and length of rest periods and working days over several weeks for six women, expecting that doing so would determine which kinds of conditions promoted work and which interfered with it. Regardless of conditions, however, the women worked harder and more efficiently with each succeeding experimental period. The most important reason was their feeling that, having been chosen for an experiment, they were special people and should perform exceptionally.

In experiments, researchers try to control and manipulate some factors, called *variables*, so that they can focus on the effect of one or more specific factors. In research with monkeys, rats, or pigeons, for example, it is simple enough to make sure the animals have identical cages, food, light, temperature, and so on, and the researcher can alter one of these variables in order to observe the result of the change. The researcher may put certain rats in larger cages to see if the cage size affects the rats' behavior. If the rats in the bigger cages behave differently than the rats in the smaller cages, the scientist can use that evidence to support a hypothesis.

Researching human behavior is a more difficult matter. The problems that spring from studying people who are aware that they are being studied—in the field as well as in the laboratory—have led some behavioral scientists to devise techniques that allow unobtrusive investigation. The best summary of them is a readable book entitled *Unobtrusive Measures*[14] by Eugene J. Webb and three colleagues. To ask visitors to the Museum of Science and Industry in Chicago which exhibit they prefer, for example, would undoubtedly cause many to name one that might confer distinction on them (just as unbelievable numbers of respondents in surveys claim to read prestigious but not widely read magazines like *Harper's* and *The Atlantic*). A research committee that was formed to set up a psychological exhibit at the museum learned, however, that vinyl tiles around the exhibit containing live, hatching chicks had to be replaced every six weeks or so; tiles in other areas of the museum went for years without replacement. The conclusion is obvious.

Unobtrusive Measures carries hundreds of other examples of studies that avoid the most evident difficulty in human research: the act of measuring may change the measurement. Such methods are valuable but somewhat limited. Behavioral scientists must continue to refine their methods of studying the subjects who are all about them.

To set forth briefly some of the similarities and differences among research approaches:

To Summarize: Different Varieties of Research

1. Literary researchers and historians analyze traces of the past, usually written documents, and they usually pursue particular truths. They try to establish probable truth by determining how the facts they find correspond with other facts that have been established. They work by accretion, adding a bit here and a piece there. They ordinarily analyze facts that cannot be proven except in relation to other, established facts.

2. Journalists usually pursue facts that may or may not be part of a large and coherent design. Although they try to select interview subjects judiciously, in reporting what the subjects say journalists assert *that it was stated*, not necessarily that the statement is true. Journalists do assert the truth of their reports of actions that they observe.

3. Natural scientists are chiefly concerned with stating general laws. They work from theory and hypothesis and are usually able to control their experiments.

4. Some social scientists use methods that are more like those of historians and literary researchers than like those of scientists. Behavioral scientists adapt the methods of natural scientists. They are unable to assert laws with assurance, however, since they are dealing with human behavior, it is more difficult for them to control experiments. They often try to analyze behavior by interviewing and observing.

At no point in this chapter have we spoken of *the* method of research, nor even of *the* scientific method, a familar phrase. As Abraham Kaplan points out in his useful book *The Conduct of Inquiry,* "there is no one thing to be defined."[15] Speaking of the method of research is like speaking of the method of baseball. There are many ways of pitching, hitting, running bases, catching and throwing the ball, devising strategy, and developing myriad skills and tactics. One can state a kind of method succinctly—to score runs if you are batting and to prevent them if you are not—but that is only a sketchy and unsatisfIying description of the goals.

We have touched on some of the many methods used in various disciplines to pursue facts that can be translated into knowledge and theory. Succeeding chapters will cover strategies for weighing and assessing facts and will prescribe ways of recognizing and avoiding pitfalls in research that involves human behavior.

EXERCISES

1. Which research approach—literary, historical, journalistic, natural science, or social science—will work for finding out the following facts? (Note: There may be more than one answer.) Which is best?
    a. Finding out what kind of entertainment sophomores at a given college like best.
    b. Finding out who left a bundle of carnations and a handwritten poem on a student's door on Valentine's Day.
    c. Finding out whether a disputed student election was rigged.
    d. Finding out who threw a sofa out the window during a fraternity party.
    e. Finding out who, or what, is keeping one from getting to sleep at night.
    f. Finding out whether a book missing from the library shelves was checked out, stolen, misshelved, or simply unshelved.

2. Identify the research method reflected in each of the following situations.
    a. A student makes a point of trying out every dish served in the residence hall cafeteria. She then moves off campus.
    b. An instructor tallying the final grades for a course notices that seven students have precisely the same scores for all three of their tests. She retrieves the tests and compares the answers. They match. The instructor suspects that the seven students cheated.

c. A student asks a friend what he did during his Christmas vacation. He draws his friend out, asking questions on many aspects of the friend's holiday trip.

d. A freshman tries to decide where to live during his sophomore year. Should he stay in Dry Gulch Flats or Ground Around Townhouses? He meanders over to both places and sits by the swimming pool at each one, watching people come and go. He engages a few people in conversation about the landlord and the neighbors and the noise. He decides on Ground Around Townhouses.

e. A student arrives home from the grocery store and unpacks her food. She notices that she has an extra package of cheese that she did not want. She pulls out the receipt and double-checks. She has not been charged for the cheese. She *has* been charged for a roll of color print film that she neglected to bring home. She thinks back to the scene at the checker's stand and remembers how crowded the counter had been. She concludes that the shopper behind her in line has her film and that she has the other shopper's cheese.

f. A student develops a rash on his face and chest. He is sure that he has an allergy, but he prefers to avoid the student health center, so he decides to find out what he is allergic to. For two days he avoids the school cafeteria, but the rash stays. He changes the blankets on his bed, replacing them with pure wool blankets. No change. He sends his roommate's pet cat on a vacation to a neighboring apartment. Still no change. Finally, he changes his soap. Voilá! No rash. He decides never to use deodorant soap again.

3. Which kind of research described in this chapter corresponds to the activities of the following researchers?

a. An anthropologist who lives in remote areas for months, seeking out demographic data on the people who live there, listing the crops they grow, and observing the way they live.

b. A linguist who compares the grammatical structure of sentences, sound of syllables, and meanings of suffixes and prefixes of three languages and announces that two of them are from the same language family.

c. A student who takes a Meyers-Briggs personality test, then compares his or her personality type with the personality types of people in various careers in order to decide which career will be the most satisfying choice.

d. An advertising or marketing researcher who monitors circulation figures and the demographic breakdown of major magazines to determine which ones will be the best vehicle for advertising, say, jeans, hamburgers, Japanese subcompacts, or power saws.

e. A business executive who uses a mathematical computer program for calculating the risks of a business decision.

f. A factory manager who experiments with productivity by asking one group of workers to exercise at break time while another group rests and drinks coffee.

4. Was it worthwhile for Professor Anderson to wind through 35 years of research just to find a single fact about the identification of a diarist? Write an argument of at least two pages that would convince the editor of *North American Review* to tell you who wrote the four-installment "Diary of a Public Man."

5. Which of the research approaches described in this chapter do you prefer? Why? (a) "Literary research is the enlightenment of criticism." (b) "Journalists pursue signifi-

cances as well as trivialities." (c) "Historians work in probabilities." (d) The natural scientists' way of conducting research by formulating a working hypothesis. (e) The social scientists describe themselves as behavioral scientists.

Choose one of the approaches and write a paper of at least two pages.

FIGURE 1

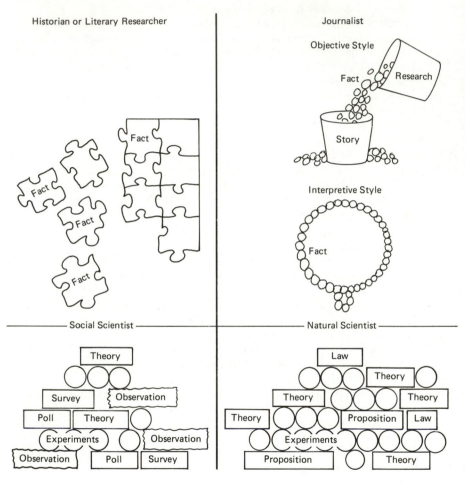

2

Evaluating Facts ___

THE HUMAN FACTOR

When Gary Taylor decided, as a matter of "duty and thoroughness," to double-check the manuscript sources of a book he was editing, he had little idea he would discover the first candidate for addition to the known Shakespeare writings since the seventeenth century.

Taylor, a Kansan in his eighth year of editing a one-volume collection of Shakespeare's works for Oxford University Press, was merely following up on details long waiting for attention at the Bodleian Library at Oxford. Twice—once in 1895 and once in 1969—the printed catalogs at the Bodleian had noted that an old volume of manuscripts contained a poem attributed to Shakespeare. The 1969 listing even gave the first line of the poem. But either no scholar had noticed or none had thought to double-check before Taylor took to turning pages. What Taylor found was a nine-stanza poem beginning:

Shall I die? Shall I fly?
Lovers' baits and deceits,

Before making his finding public, Taylor ran several tests on its authenticity. First he checked the authenticity of the volume itself. The manuscript proved to be no modern forgery and, furthermore, the volume had proven accurate in its attributions of other authors' poems. Taylor then checked the phrases and words in the poem against a Shakespeare concordance, a book containing an index of every word used in Shakespeare's works so that scholars can see the frequency and location of each. In the concordance Taylor found what he felt was corroboration for the claim that the poem was truly Shakespeare's.

The instant the news spread, the debate began. Other scholars immediately claimed that the poem could not possibly be written by Shakespeare, if only because it was so poorly written. "It's clumsy, inept. It's a clunker. It's quite clear to anyone who doesn't have a zinc ear that this is not a poem written by Shakespeare," said Edward W. Tayler of Columbia University. Another scholar looked more closely into the style of the poem and commented, "True, Shakespeare wrote some bad poems, but the way this one is bad is not similar in any fashion to the way Shakespeare was bad."[1]

Taylor's concordance check was called in doubt, too. The phrases Taylor had marked as similar to those in *Romeo and Juliet* were tagged as conventions of the time, and one word, *scanty*, came to light almost fifty years after Shakespeare died. Taylor's response was that Shakespeare was an innovator and he was experimenting with the language.

The need to check, double-check, and triple-check sources is the inescapable shadow of a researcher's work. When the document is as dear to the hearts of researchers as a poem by Shakespeare, the double-checking never ends. Modern books, however, are less often scrutinized; all too often, the second and third look take place only when inaccuracy threatens to lead to a lawsuit. There was no little flurry of fact checking after C. David Heymann's biography of heiress Barbara Hutton was published a few years ago, but the publisher's double-checks evidently began only after Hutton's personal physician threatened to press a libel suit.

In his defense, Heymann claimed that the spirit of the book was true to the spirit of its heroine. However, the mistakes were genuine: The physician, whom Heyman portrayed as a "Dr. Feelgood," was only fourteen years old the year that Heymann's book said he became Hutton's personal physician.

Nor was it Heymann's first indiscretion. One of his previous books had proven to be filled with mistaken dates. Another book, on Ezra Pound, drew from what Heymann claimed was an original interview, but one critic hinted that it was drawn from a similar interview that had been published in a obscure journal.

James Fallows and Robert Samuelson have both pointed out a far more insidious error than a misattributed poem or a sloppily researched biography: In a 1985 article Fallows claimed that some academic soothsayers were basing their predictions about the American economy partly on wrong reckoning of 1979 U.S. Census data. In 1979, Fallows said, the Census Bureau started splitting the $25,000 to $50,000 income classification into finer gradations. As a result, the Census Bureau should have reclassified older Census data so that comparisons could be made between previous and current censuses. Fallows wrote:

> One way to do so would have been to run all the original Census tapes back through the computers, but that would have been time-consuming and expensive. . . . The

bureau had a well-established routine for estimating income distribution by fitting the data to statistical curves, and the results were usually correct.

Those statistics indicated that 10 percent of American households had dropped from the middle-income to the lower-income category in 1979. Economists immediately seized upon the evidence as support for the idea that the American middle class is shrinking, leading to a two-tier society in which the rich become progressively richer and the poor poorer. According to Fallows, when two researchers obtained the Census tapes and actually ran them through a computer, they found that income category changes were, as Fallows put it, "remarkably constant through the years." But the reinterpretation had never been fully recognized: the "analysis never seemed to catch up with the fast-moving "fact.""[2] Thus, one simple misinterpretation was the source of numerous theories and subtheories, all of which were warped because of the incorrect underlying data. Even the most solid of "facts" may be wrong, and for that reason, the researcher must be constantly on guard.

In short, it has been well said that the price of truth is eternal vigilance and eternal skepticism, for without it, major and minor errors continue to creep into published documents and, from there, into the work of researchers. The point can be summarized in the old adage that "just because it's in print doesn't mean it can be trusted." No "fact" is utterly trustworthy.

THE IMPOSSIBLE OBJECTIVE

"Where shall I begin, your majesty?" he asked. "Begin at the beginning," the king said, gravely, "and go on till you come to the end: then stop."

—Lewis Carroll

Any researcher whose work involves human behavior must seem at a tremendous disadvantage: all his or her perceptions are in doubt.

No researcher has it all that easy, however. Not even dedicated and dispassionate physicists deal with a world of truly "hard" facts. In 1927 a German physicist named Werner Heisenberg demonstrated the uncertainty principle, which showed that every attempt to describe nature is marred by uncertainty. The more accurately one measures the position of a particle, the less able one is to measure its velocity at the same time, and vice versa. According to Heisenberg's principle, every intervention in nature affects it unpredictably. This is, of course, much like the Hawthorne effect: Merely observing human beings when they know they are being observed is enough to distort their behavior.

Moreover, the inescapable fact is that scientists are human. Not only is a scientist's work shaped to some degree by human desires—to win a Nobel Prize, to publish a learned paper or an admired article, to earn a promotion, or simply to make a point—at bottom, it is impossible by definition for a human to be objective, to be like a machine or a rock or a mathematical equation, without thoughts or beliefs.

Journalists (like historians, natural scientists, and other professionals) have long worked to develop formulas that will help ensure objective reports. Because, unlike most other professionals, journalists tend to pursue unadorned facts, attempting to report rather than evaluate events, and because journalists often have no stake or interest in the events they report, it might seem that "straight" or "objective" reporting actually *is* objective. Lester Markel, the late Sunday editor of the *New York Times*, once pointed out the error in this judgment:

> The reporter, the most objective reporter, collects fifty facts. Out of the fifty he selects twelve to include in his story (there is such a thing as space limitation). Thus he discards thirty-eight. This is Judgment Number One.
>
> Then the reporter or editor decides which of the facts shall be the first paragraph of the story, thus emphasizing one fact above the other eleven. This is Judgment Number Two.
>
> Then the editor decides whether the story shall be placed on Page One or Page Twelve; on Page One it will command many times the attention it would on Page Twelve. This is Judgment Number Three. This so-called factual presentation is thus subjected to three judgments, all of them most humanly and most ungodly made.[3]

What happens is suggested by the varying news stories about a simple report on gifts to Stanford University during one fiscal year. The university-published *Campus Report* headed its story:

HIGHEST NUMBER OF DONORS
IN STANFORD HISTORY

The *San Francisco Chronicle* headline said:

STANFORD AGAIN RAISES
$29 MILLION IN GIFTS

The *Palo Alto Times* story was headed:

DONATIONS TO STANFORD
LOWEST IN FOUR YEARS

The student-published *Stanford Daily* announced:

ALUMNI DONATIONS DECLINE:
BIG DROP FROM FOUNDATIONS

These headlines accurately reflected the stories—and the stories were also accurate. Stanford did have more donors than ever, as the *Campus Report* story said. It did raise more than $29 million for the fourth consecutive year, as the *Chronicle* said. Donations were the lowest in the past four years, as the *Palo Alto Times* reported. The total was lower than in the preceding year and it included less foundation money, as the *Stanford Daily* said.

The fact that we cannot be objective in the ultimate sense, does not mean that we should simply throw up our hands and surrender to subjectivity, following wherever it leads. Doing this leads too many toward the rationale expressed by Ray Mungo in his book *Famous Long Ago:*

> *Facts* are less important than *truth* and the two are far from equivalent, you see, for cold facts are nearly always boring and may even distort the truth, but Truth is the highest achievement of human expression. . . . Now let's pick up a 1967 copy of the Boston *Avatar*, and under the headline "Report from Vietnam, by Alexander Sorenson" read a painfully graphic account of Sorenson's encounter with medieval torture in a Vietnam village. Later because we know Brian Keating, who wrote the piece, we discover that Alexander Sorenson doesn't exist and the incident described in *Avatar*, which moved thousands, never in fact happened. But because it has happened in man's history, and because we know we are reponsible for its happening today, and because the story is unvarnished and plain and human, we know it is *true*, truer than any facts you may have picked up in the *New Republic*.[4]

No "truth" can spring from fiction *disguised* as fact (although great fiction presents truths about the human condition). Instead of throwing up our hands, we must analyze our human failings and allow for them to the high degree that is now possible so that our evaluations of fact lead to the best that we can attain: probable truth.

"Probable truth" may seem vague, somehow unsatisfying, to a researcher with high standards in the quest for understanding. Remember, though, it is probable truth on which natural science itself is based: on theories that may, at any moment, be altered or discarded to help explain a new fact. Such probable truth has put human beings in space and on the moon and brought them safely home again; it has revolutionized medicine; and much more. Indeed, to seek "probable truth" is to follow a high ideal.

WHO AM I?

I grow daily to honor facts more and more, and theory even less.

—Thomas Carlyle

A great English scholar, Sir John Clapham, once noted: "Thirty years ago I read and marked Arthur Young's *Travels in France*, and taught from the marked passages. Five years ago I went through it again, to find that whenever Young spoke of a wretched Frenchman I had marked him, but that many of his references to happy or prosperous Frenchmen remained unmarked."[5]

Honest observers find such biases creeping in despite their best efforts, but they can still balance their biases somewhat by cold self-examination. Note that Clapham discovered his own bias. What if Clapham had analyzed his biases, as he read *Travels in France* for the first time? He might then have placed a proper focus on the happy Frenchman.

To balance our bias, we must first become aware of three processes that affect what evidence we notice and what evidence we disgard: exposure, perception, and retention.

- *Exposure.* We tend to expose ourselves to information with which we agree. Thus, Republicans tend to read and hear more information they perceive as favorable to Republicans than to Democrats. Businessmen tend to read articles they perceive as favorable to businessmen, doctors read articles favorable to doctors, and so on. An atheist is likely to seek out articles that cast aspersions on Bible-belt evangelists; fundamentalist Christians are likely to read magazines written specifically for Christians.
- *Perception.* It is not possible, of course, to avoid all information that opposes our beliefs. A Democrat is certain to be exposed, at least occasionally, to the views of President Reagan, and a doctor who dislikes the policies of the American Medical Association (AMA) is nonetheless exposed to them. When that happens, we tend to swing into a second unconscious strategy for protecting our biases: When we are exposed to information with which we disagree, we tend to perceive the points in it that will not disturb our established attitudes and beliefs. Thus, the partisan Democrat may sneer at a Republican president's statement regarding love of country as pietistic flag-waving (while the partisan Republican calls it fervent patriotism), and the idealistic doctor is likely to focus on the aspects of AMA policy that show that doctors place respect for human life above money.
- *Retention.* Finally, we have a third way to defend our biases: We tend to remember the evidence that supports them. A Republican may remember a Democrat's statement that had a false ring to it: a Democrat remembers the well-put point made by a fellow Democrat. The idealistic doctor who dislikes the AMA may remember an AMA policy that benefits doctors financially; a doctor who backs the AMA unequivocally might gloss over that point and remember a statement that shows the AMA to be greatly concerned with serving patients.

The researcher who makes himself or herself aware of these processes and tries to gauge their effects has taken a long step toward countering them.

There is another strategy for lessening one's bias that is a form of role playing. The researcher imagines that the information with which he or she disagrees actually came from a source of which he or she approves. If the partisan Republican tries to imagine that the Democrat's statement came from a Republican's speech, and if the idealistic doctor tries to imagine that the policy announced by the AMA was put forth by his or her own group, Doctors for Society, they can see better whether it is the statement or the source that brings on the sense of disagreement. If the imagining yields nonsense—if a Republican could not make that statement, if Doctors for Society could not have announced that policy—that fact is significant.

There is a lesson in the story of the Californian who was outraged by Robert Donovan's report of a peace march in Washington. Donovan worked for the *Los Angeles Times*, and the reader telephoned to complain that the report would encourage young dissidents. But when the reader found out that Donovan was 57 years of age, had served in the infantry in World War II, and had a son who was about to be commissioned into the Army through ROTC, his attitude changed. If readers only knew, the man said, that Donovan was neither young nor unpatriotic, they would read his reports quite differently. The reporting, then, mattered less than the reader's assumptions about the author.[6]

Another way to minimize bias is to deliberately seek out information that challenges one's personal opinions. The conservative might subscribe to the *New Republic*, the liberal to *National Review*. The middle-aged might listen to rock music, the young to the songs of the 1930s and 1940s. Mere exposure can produce results, but of course a conscious effort to appreciate the other's viewpoint is more effective. The aim is not to change one's opinions. Many studies show that changing an opinion is such a complicated process that merely exposing oneself to different opinions is highly unlikely to make the difference.

The suggestions given here do not require us to pretend we think things we do not think, nor do they produce a bewildering array of ideas that stupefy one into indecision. Rather, these suggestions tell us how to combat our own ignorance. When the Puritans settled Massachusetts, the Narragansett Indians reasoned that the English must have burned all the firewood in their homeland. That would have been one of the Indians' principal reasons for moving to a new home.[7] Similarly, if we judge only from the base of our own understandings, our evaluations will remain narrow and biased.

WHO IS HE? WHO IS SHE? WHO ARE THEY?

Imagination is a warehouse of facts, with poet and liar in joint ownership.

—Ambrose Bierce

In judging the evaluations offered by others, we must know who the others are. When a speaker warned in 1972 that the pressures of the clean-environment movement endanger the economic health of the nation by requiring too much of industry, it was naturally important to know that the speaker was an industrialist. Even this information is not conclusive; one may suspect self-interest, but the speech may have been accurate. The speaker cited U.S. Department of Commerce figures that "show that 210 plants last year were forced to shut down primarily because of economic pressures." The Department of Commerce, which is directed by former businessmen, has a certain affinity for the business viewpoint; its findings, too, may be suspect. But Gladwin Hill of the *New York Times* reported that the speaker's words "were untrue," that Commerce records show no such thing.[8]

The next question, of course, is whether Gladwin Hill and the *Times* are suspect sources. Any newspaper is basically a human institution, and humans err, even those who work for an institution as august as the *Times*. Either the speaker or the reporter treated the truth casually, and the evidence points to the speaker. He had a strong self-interest (one that led him to err unintentionally), and the likelihood was slender that anyone in the college audience he addressed would know the Department of Commerce data. Gladwin Hill, on the other hand, had no apparent self-interest, and he had to take greater care than the speaker; many *Times* readers are armed with accurate information about the effects of pollution control. Thus the weight of probability is that the *Times* report should be trusted.

In addition, because the *Times* is a business, its reporting of information that injures business might be considered a strong indication of probable truth: an argument against self-interest. Hill and the *Times* were right.

This example illustrates one of the central concerns in deciding whether to accept an evaluation: Who says so? In many cases, it is not possible to learn everything we need to know about individuals (although Chapters 6 and 7 of this book provide a guide to reference books that will help). More often, one must judge the individual by the groups to which he or she belongs. It is not certain that an individual will share group values in all things, and everyone belongs to many groups. But the group process has been studied rigorously, and nearly everything we know about it indicates that a member of a group is usually lured into sharing the opinions of the other members, both because it is usually in the person's self-interest and because he or she wants to be liked, accepted and respected by the others. Were the speaker's words automatically suspect because he was an industialist? No, but they needed to be examined by one who did not share that group's values.

It would be misleading to leave the impression that groups are no more than propaganda machines with little purpose other than promoting their own interests. Understanding other aspects of groups is important.

Groups have standards, and as the late H. L. Mencken observed, a man wants the approval of his colleagues, those who know what he is doing and are expertly equipped to judge his work. It follows that knowing the standards of a group helps to gauge the worth of an evaluation.

Consider the leading scholarly journals listed in Chapter 7. Almost all are published by associations of specialists who reach their conclusions on the basis of generally accepted standards of research. The articles are published, as a rule, only after they have been reviewed and criticized by other specialists. This does not mean that the specialists agree with the conclusions; the range of opinion is wide. Furthermore, some articles are published to test ideas, to put them in the marketplace of expert opinion for debate and refinement. It is also true that some members of almost any scholarly association consider most of its publications inconsequential. The point is not that scholarly publications carry ultimate truth but that they do not publish random observations.

One must be aware of dubious standards as well. When a politician is nominated for the U.S. presidency and announces that the vice-presidential running mate is the politician most capable of succeeding him, no one who is politically astute believes that Richard Nixon chose Spiro Agnew in 1968, claiming that Agnew was the best successor, but Agnew was selected primarily because he was governor of a border state, Maryland, and might be able to draw votes from border states and the South. Gerald Ford, who succeeded Nixon as President when Agnew had resigned, was a special case. The discrepancy between the claim and the actuality was hardly worth pointing up by the Democrats, who also tried to balance *their* ticket. The standard of political discourse is to claim the ideal. That is understood in politics, and it should be understood by anyone who tries to interpret political action.

Group standards may be set forth in a code of ethics, but that code sometimes has no meaning. Item 7 in "The Code of Professional Standards for the Practice of

Public Relations" rules that "A member shall not intentionally disseminate false or misleading information and is obligated to use care to avoid dissemination of false or misleading information." But members of the Public Relations Society of America, which framed the code, often set up front organizations for their clients to make it seem that persuasive information comes from those who have no vested interest, and they are neither reprimanded nor expelled. In such cases, a group rarely honors with leadership positions or awards members who are unethical—except a group in which devious practice is itself a kind of ethic.

One can, of course, share the attitudes of one group for a time, then share the quite different attitudes of another group. There was not much doubt, for example, that Professor Theodore N. Beckman of the College of Commerce and Administration of Ohio State University had changed his consumer-group attitudes after he appeared before a Senate committee to oppose truth-in-lending legislation as a consultant for the National Retail Merchants Association.

"At no time," Professor Beckman said, "have I been motivated solely or primarily by pecuniary considerations on matters of this kind because all of my adult life has been devoted to teaching and research at the university level, and thus in a constant search for truth." But Senator Paul Douglas of Illinois placed in the hearing record excerpts from Professor Beckman's book *Principles of Marketing*, which supports truth-in-lending by noting that "few consumers know just how to determine the rates paid by them on a per annum basis, and yet such knowledge is indispensable in making intelligent comparisons with respect to alternative methods of financing."

Beckman hastily explained that he was preparing a new edition of the book: "In that edition, I am treating the subject with greater maturity, with much more knowledge, a great deal more sophistication, and you will not find me making statements of that character."[9]

Fearing that sharp practices may bring public condemnation or government regulation or both, some groups that cannot exclude applicants or expel members, such as doctors, publicize standards or tests that may have similar effects. When the American Association for Public Opinion Research (AAPOR) set up the National Council on Polls to issue guidelines for examining poll results, the effect was to stigmatize pollsters, including some AAPOR members, whose work could not stand that kind of examination. Lawyers, of course, can be disbarred.

When specialists (scholars, politicians, industialists, plumbers, or whoever) communicate with a general audience, any one of three influences is likely to distort the presentation—sometimes all three. First, the specialists may distort in their own interests or in the interests of their groups. Second, they may distort through oversimplification because they are convinced that the audience cannot grasp the fine points. Finally, they may distort because they do not believe that anyone in the audience will catch the distortion.

Ideal conditions are so seldom available that one can sometimes only wish for them. The ideal condition for learning what people really believe often requires hearing or reading the communications within a group: a presidential candidate consulting with party leaders about a suitable vice-presidential candidate, industrialists discussing among themselves the probable effects of pollution control, scholars talking or writing to other scholars.

A lay person seldom has the time or the entrée for firsthand observation or access to documents and must usually rely on publications. Some are comprehensible to anyone with intelligence, but many are not because specialists are communicating among themselves. They share a fund of knowledge and experience that confounds the lay person, and they use a language that may seem to resemble English only because it uses an occasional familiar connective. It is small consolation to be told that the jargon is both concise and precise. A social psychologist who says, "That was because of the Hawthorne effect," has communicated long paragraphs of information, but only to those who know the language. In such circumstances, the layperson who is not sufficiently interested to devote the time to becoming a knowledgeable amateur must usually rely on journalists, many of whom make a mission of translating specialties into everyday English.

Journalists also usually have a vantage point, or can arrange one, that is denied to most others. When American troops in Vietnam invaded Cambodia in 1970, Governor Raymond P. Shafer of Pennsylvania was a member of a team of dignitaries who visited the troops at a site called Shakey's Hill. He climbed atop a sandbagged bunker manned by three soldiers and asked, "What do you feel the attitude is of our men with reference to coming into Cambodia?"

Knowing the answer he wanted, the soldiers squirmed and glanced nervously at one another. Then one said, "They feel it might help end the war, so they came, you know."

"Well, I've been talking to men everywhere and I find they think it should have been done sooner," the governor said. "Is that your attitude too?"

"Yes, sir," said the first soldier. "That's what I think too."

"Do you all agree to that?" the governor asked the others.

"That's right, sir. Yes, sir." They nodded emphatically.

"That's good," the governor said. "I think Americans sometimes get a distorted picture, and I'm here to find out the real facts."

The governor then strode off to join the other fact finders. An Associated Press reporter stayed at the bunker long enough to hear the first soldier breathe deeply and say, "Jeez, I hope none of the guys heard us."[10]

SAMPLES—AND SAMPLERS

The truth is never pure, and rarely simple

—Oscar Wilde

The story is told of a scientist who published an astonishing generalization about the behavior of rats. When a colleague asked to see the records of the experiments on which the judgment was based, the scientist pulled a notebook from a pile of papers and said, "Here they are." He pointed to a cage in the corner and added, "There's the rat."

Nearly everyone thoughtlessly generalizes from samples that are too small. Anyone who has had two or three bad experiences with car salesmen is likely to decide that all of them are crooks. Still we tend to suspect the conclusions of those who make a profession of sampling human behavior and generalizing about it, since most of us feel that people are much too individual and erratic for safe prediction. It is right to be suspicious, but necessary to be suspicious for the right reasons. Instead of questioning whether there are patterns in human behavior that are sufficiently sharp and distinctive for investigation—which is quite clearly true— one should question the methods and conclusions of the investigators. The man who said there were three kinds of lies—lies, damned lies, and statistics—could easily have applied his words to polls.

A classic example of shoddy sampling was the effort of the now-defunct *Literary Digest* to forecast the 1936 presidential election. The sample was large: more than 10 million ballots were mailed, more than 2 million were returned. The returns led the *Digest* to predict 370 electoral votes for the Republican, Alfred Landon, and 161 for Franklin Roosevelt. In fact, Roosevelt won 523 electoral votes, Landon only 8. The error in the *Digest's* methods was using mailing lists derived from telephone directories, automobile registration lists, and magazine subscriptions. The pollsters may have accidentally received ballots from an adequate sample of voters with telephones, automobiles, and magazine subscriptions, but these were hardly representative of the general population in the depression year of 1936.

Since then, pollsters have developed techniques to ensure randomness in finding interview subjects. The word "random," however, is misleading: it may imply that pollsters choose their interview subjects in a way that is arbitrary or even whimsical. A better term might be "representative sampling," because the methods for ensuring randomness are carefully designed to reach as accurate a cross-section of the population as possible. In addition, pollsters choose the number of interviews on the basis of a statistically derived "margin of error." The margin of error tells a pollster how accurate the results of a poll should be. If 1,000 people are chosen at random and interviewed, the error margin is usually considered to be 3.1 percent. That is, if the pollster's results say that 60 percent of a random sample of 1,000 people think that the governor is doing a good job, the actual number could range from 56.9 percent to 63.1 percent. (The 3.1 percent figure, in turn, is based on a 95 percent "level of confidence," which means that the pollster is 95 percent confident that the results are accurate to 3.1 percent. The margin of error differs at different levels of confidence: at the 99 percent level of confidence, the margin of error for a random poll of 1,000 people is 4.1 percent.)

The margin of error can be important. For example, if poll results for a presidential race show 51 percent in favor of candidate A and 49 percent in favor of candidate B in a certain district, an error margin of 3.1 percent could mean that candidate B is actually in the lead. The alert poll watcher should be aware of the margin of error, and poll reports should give it along with the poll results.

The margin of error is only one of the many considerations to take into account in evaluating polls. By the time of the presidential campaigns of 1948, the leading pollsters knew that it was essential to ensure response from voters at random. Nonetheless, they wrongly predicted victory for the Republican, Thomas Dewey, over the Democrat, Harry Truman. Why? Primarily because their surveys during the early stages of the campaign showed Dewey leading so decisively that they stopped polling. Truman's campaign gathered momentum in the last days; Dewey's stagnated. (It is important to realize that no matter how close to an election one conducts a survey, it is *prior* to the election. It may show accurately how most voters are leaning at the time of the survey, but at least a few are certain to change their minds by election day.) The pollsters also learned in 1948 the importance of intense political convictions. A respondent who is certain about his preference is much more likely to vote than one who expresses a vague leaning.

The National Council on Public Polls once issued guidelines aimed at political polling that are useful for testing other kinds of surveys.

1. *Who paid for the poll?* Obviously, if someone who has a vested interest in the results sponsored the poll, that fact should be known.

2. *When was the poll taken?* Changes caused by events are so common that it is important to know, for example, whether the voters favoring the 1972 Democratic presidential candidate, Senator McGovern, were asked their preference *before* it became known that the first running mate he chose. Senator Thomas Eagleton, had undergone psychiatric treatment, *immediately after* that fact became known, or *after* McGovern had chosen a new running mate.

3. *How were the interviews obtained?* Telephone interviewing is relatively inexpensive, but, as George Gallup has pointed out, it has a built-in bias toward middle-and upper-income groups and older people. In mail surveys, it is important to know how many letters were mailed and how many were returned. If the percentage of return was small, the sample may be heavily biased.

4. *How were the questions worded?* Questioning his constituents by mail, one congressman asked, "I publicly proposed an extra tax credit for parents of college students. Are in favor of such a tax exemption as presently gaining bipartisan support in Congress?" The answer the congressman wanted, and toward which he steered his constituents, is obvious.

5. *Who was interviewed?* A front-page story on the Vietnam War in the *New York Times* was headlined 54 Per Cent In Ohio Poll Assert U.S. Role In War Is Mistake. Readers who went no further were misled. As the story made clear, Congressman Charles Mosher had sent a mail questionnaire to constituents in his 13th Ohio District, not to the entire state. It is important to know not only the area sampled but also the demographic breakdown of the sample.

6. *How large was the sample?* The response to Congressman Mosher's questionnaire was 3.5 percent. Because Gallup, whose work is widely respected, uses a sample of only 1,500 in his monthly opinion index (some pollsters use only 1,200 in national surveys), and more than 1,500 responded to Mosher's questionnaire, it might seem that Mosher was safe in generalizing. Size is important—a survey of 36 voters in a city of 300,000 is too small—but random distribution is vital. Certainly, those in the 13th Ohio District who respond to congressional surveys are not randomly distributed. In fact, many mail surveys are biased because those who have the ability, the confidence, and the inclination to respond are seldom representative. (Those with little education

may have the ability to respond to a simple mail survey, but many are not accustomed to writing and lack the confidence to respond.)

7. *What was the base of the data if it is based on part of a total sample?* One of the subtlest tricks in polling is to use partial data as though it represented the entire sample. For example, if a politician surveys 1,500 people and reports that among Jewish voters he is nine times as popular as his opponent, the reader of the report is likely to believe that 1,500 Jewish voters were surveyed. In fact, only forty Jews might be in the sample.

Stephen Isaacs formerly of the *Washington Post*, who devised the "Jewish voter" example above, has written:

> Many other points can be useful in evaluating a poll. These include whether inter-viewers had any discretion as to whom they interviewed (in a pure probability survey, they have no choice—each respondent is chosen mathematically); what time of day interviews were conducted (most professional men, obviously, aren't home at 2 in the afternoon); how the interviewers were supervised and whether their work was "vali-dated"—checked to determine whether they actually did the interviews they reported and whether they reported the interviews truthfully; whether any "weighting" was done to bring the actual interviewees into line with the demographic makeup of the electo-rate, and so forth.[11]

In summary, the evaluation of facts is a tricky business. Whatever truth lies beneath the facts is clouded by interpretation—that of the fact gatherer, the writer of the report, and the reader. The overriding concern for the researcher who hopes to evaluate facts with accuracy, then, is this: Take into account the nature of facts. Be aware, and be wary.

EXERCISES

1. Compare the information given in different reference sources in the library by looking up the same topic in several. Which one seems to give the most complete and objective information? Are there discrepancies? The following are some suggestions for topics.
   a. Look up a specific person—Winston Churchill, Homer, Duke Ellington, Daniel Webster, Sylvia Plath—in several different biographical reference sources listed in Chapters 6 and 7.
   b. Compare the figures on population density, annual rainfall, and topographical features such as altitude or infant mortality for several different nations. Atlases and yearbooks are good sources for this type of information; try to find others as well.
   c. Look up "platypus" or "mammals" in several encyclopedias and field guides.
   d. Look up "Notre Dame" in an encyclopedia, an architectural reference, and a history reference listed in Chapters 6 and 7.
2. Compare three or four different newspapers' coverage of a particular news story. Describe the biases reflected in each newspaper's coverage, including the words that are used in the story, the lead sentences, and the space given each story.
3. Find a report of an opinion survey. Check to see how carefully the pollster has reported the results. Does the report give the number of people interviewed and the margin of

error? Does the pollster say the poll was random? Evaluate the report according to the guidelines given in this chapter.

4. Listen carefully to several TV commercials, for products that you use daily: cars, toothpastes, cereals, and the like. Judge whether the claims are in conformity with your own experience. Write a one-page report, analyzing whether the commercials were telling the truth or exaggerating the facts.

3

Reporting on Research ____

Every week or so a young woman who works evenings in a New York City public library is confronted by a man sent by a group of blue-collar workers who have been arguing in a bar a few blocks away. She knows before he speaks that he will ask a question that will send her to the reference shelf for *Famous First Facts*, the *World Almanac*, *The Guinness Book of World Records*, or a similar book.

One evening he asked, "Didn't Walt Frazier lead the New York Knicks basketball team in scoring and assists in 1971?" When she found the answer, the man took the book to a photocopying machine located in a library alcove, copied the relevant page, then returned to the bar, where his friends were waiting to learn who had won the bet that had grown out of the argument.

This incident reflects three basic methods of research: interviewing, observation, and ultimately, nailing down evidence through library research. The man who visited the library had once heard an assistant coach of the New York Knickerbockers say that Walt Frazier was the most valuable Knick player because Frazier always led the team in scoring and assists. But another barroom patron argued that he had *seen* all the Knick's home games in 1971 and was certain that Willis Reed was the leader. Other patrons of the bar were drawn into the argument. A bet was made, and the men decided to conduct their usual research in the nearby library.

The lessons of this incident could be spelled out almost endlessly, but consider a few that are central. The casual conversation with the assistant coach was not a useful interview. Unless one sets out to find particular facts, what is asked, answered, heard, and remembered during a general conversation is so likely to be distorted by interviewer and interview subject that the results are probably useless. The observations of the man who watched the Knicks play were equally useless. Observers who are emotionally involved in what they see, especially if they are not then trying to focus on particular facts, are poor witnesses. The concluding act in the bar, however, can be trusted: In the best tradition of research, the man who visited the library consulted an authority and reported his findings with documentary evidence.

This example suggests what is worth reporting. Vague memories are suspect; verifiable facts are not. Unfortunately, a few research projects are so simple. Instead of finding one fact that speaks for itself, a researcher must usually gather scores—if not hundreds or thousands—choose among them, and stitch them together in an informative report.

RESEARCH

> Research is to see what everybody else has seen, and to think what nobody else has thought.
>
> —Albert Scent-Gyorgy

Researchers who limit their exploration of a topic to reading books and periodicals are always in danger of writing one-dimensional papers. Instead of using the living world as a source, they use only what is in print. It is true that the authors of books and articles have captured much of the world and have expressed its essence. It is also true that thoughtful students who base their writing on what has appeared in print are not actually limiting themselves to it. Because they bring to their reading selves that have seen and heard and acted, their writing is invariably informed by their experiences. One can grant all this, however, and still argue that researchers who choose a topic, then explore it in the living world as well as in the library, are much more likely to describe and analyze reality. (They are more likely too, to prepare themselves for challenging careers. Most interesting work involves asking intelligent questions, observing accurately, and reading analytically.)

Although some topics can be researched thoroughly in the library alone, it should be obvious that most lend themselves to exploration in the living world as well. Everyone who is able to conduct research has abilities that can be employed, improved, and refined in the living world. Why not use them?

THE ACADEMIC RESEARCH PAPER

William James once said that there is only one kind of scholarly report: the research paper. If the paper is short, it is an article; if long, it is a book. Established scholars can talk off-handedly with one another about the length of their writing; most of it is article or book length. But unless they are having trouble trimming an article to size for publication or deciding whether to devote another year to expanding a long article into a book manuscript, they regard discussions of the length of their work as little more than cocktail party talk.

Unfortunately, the proper length seems to be the principal concern of students. Most seem to resemble the amateur writer who called a publisher and asked, "How long is the average novel nowadays?"

"Oh, between 75 and 90 thousand words."

"Well, then, I've finished!"[1]

Perhaps he had actually finished, perhaps he should have written more—or perhaps he should never have written a word. In any case, length was not the proper criterion. There is no appropriate length for novels in general. Ernest Hemingway's *The Old Man and the Sea* is fewer than thirty thousand words. Tolstoy's *War and Peace* is more than three hundred thousand. Similarly, student research reports should cover the subject, whatever the length.

The trouble is, of course, that students are accustomed to having the lengths of their reports prescribed—or at least the minimum length. That is probably inevitable. Ideally the instructor in any course would have to do no more than say that he expected a research paper. Each student would soon become so caught up in the substance of the course that he would read widely, noting how, and at what length, different researchers treated different topics. Then the student would say, "The topic that intrigues me is this, and I can treat it that way if I do this and that." By the middle of the term each student would be able to outline his or her topic; the instructor would do little more than nod approvingly to encourage each student to develop his or her excellent idea. One student's report would cover twenty pages, another ten, another fourteen—each an appropriate length because it suited the topic and the purpose of the assignment.

But an instructor is fortunate to find one or two such students in the average course. As a result, the instructor must assign topics and lengths to everyone and encourage those who are caught up in their own ideas to develop them. An instructor may sigh and assign the students to prepare for more demanding work by writing finger exercises: papers that do not demand the time, the attention, or the sophisticated understanding of research and writing that go into a research paper.

The Importance of Focus

Take care of the sense and the sounds will take care of themselves.

—Lewis Carroll

A fun-loving professor once gave a class a list of topics for a research paper, all but one of which were reasonable. That one was:

Describe the history of dramatic poetry from its origins to the present, concentrating especially but not exclusively on its social, political, religious, and philosophical impact on Europe, Asia, America, and Africa.

To the professor's dismay, most of the students considered that to be seriously intended as a topic. Three chose to write on it. Perhaps nothing else could have demonstrated more clearly that the students did not understand the goals and limitations of research. Unless a teacher explains them in some detail, few students ever seem to understand, if one judges accurately by the many who sigh, "I have to write a paper tonight," as though a research paper represented only meaningless hard labor that actually could be completed properly in one night.

Considered as a negative example, the grotesque topic quoted above shows the goals and limitations of research papers. The most important point is that the topic is impossibly broad. If it can be undertaken successfully, only a specialist should try it, one who is prepared to spend years—probably decades—writing several volumes. A student could do little more with it than pull scraps of information from several books, quote several passages and paraphrase several more, then use a few of his or her own sentences to string the hodge-podge together.

That approach points up flaws common to many research papers that cover reasonable topics. Written by a student who does not understand what he is about, even a paper on a topic narrow enough to provide a suitable foundation for research and writing is likely to be made up of pieces of the findings and ideas of others. This process can be described as transferring bones from one graveyard to another. Instead, the student should *use* the writings of others, but should produce a research paper that bears the clear mark of his own thoughts. That is the scholar's way.

Why should a student who cares not at all about becoming a scholar imitate one? The answer lies at the center of learning. To mingle the works of others in a form whose only claim to originality is that no one has ever placed them in quite the same order is to learn nothing of much value. But a student who *analyzes* the research and insights of others and tries to take them a step further is engaged in the best kind of education.

A student may undertake research paper after research paper in course after course without reading anything or developing any ideas that will seem in later life to have practical value. That goal is much less important than the real value: learning to think. Gail Thain Parker, who became president of Bennington College when she was 30, said that "The best ideas I have about college administration came from courses in nineteenth-century novels. They taught me to think."

Choosing and Developing a Topic

The student must first choose a topic that interests him or her, for without interest, research and writing are drudgery. Choosing should be a long process, in part because one must be sure that the topic actually is narrow enough to be explored—not just touched on—in the length assigned. The idea is to develop a *thesis statement* or *topic sentence*, and a concise beginning that shows the direction the paper will take.

An unimaginative student may sidestep original thinking by using the well-worn overview-of-history approach. In a few cases of historical research, a writer should begin by tracing the beginnings of the subject; that suggests to readers that the topic the writer will examine *is* history, but it is usually both the simplest and the dreariest way to begin. Most research papers should use history for illumination but should begin by focusing on something other than the history of a topic.

The student's aim should be to reach the blank page with *one* argument and its supporting ideas and evidence. The student can usually accomplish this when doing research by asking over and over again: What aspects of this topic am I writing about? What is my opinion on this topic? Does my opinion have evidence to back it up? One should make it one's business to know what one is trying to prove.

The first rule of developing a topic is to get away from the most general statements of it. A student who chooses love, crime, the Russian Orthodox church, communism, or philosophy is in bad shape. The scope is simply too broad. To move to the next step, the student can simply ask the first question on the list above: What aspect of this topic am I writing about?

No one approaches a subject with a completely clean slate. One's background knowledge on the topic, one's ideas, and one's personal experiences will build up to a certain prior opinion, or at least a bias. These are the starting points for developing a topic. Preliminary ideas, then, will be the student's first guide. First, the student should examine what he or she *knows* about a topic, then what he or she *thinks* about it.

Suppose the paper is to be about today's journalism. Journalism is as broad a subject as can be found. The first step is to apply the question: What aspect of this topic am I writing about? There are a tremendous number of possibilities. Will the paper be about the profits of today's newspaper industry? The shrinking number of daily newspapers? The implications of broadcast journalism for the American public? Today's journalist compared to yesterday 's legendary tough-talking crusading muckrakers? Or the future of newspapers?

Suppose the student is interested in newspaper journalism. In fact, suppose the student has an even more practical interest: Suppose he or she wants to be a newspaper reporter but harbors anxiety about the future of the industry. The student then has a compelling reason to choose the future of the industry as the topic.

The student has now focused to a narrower topic, but it is still not narrow enough. There are compelling questions: What kind of planning are newspaper owners doing? Are people reading newspapers any more? What do they like about their newspapers?

Now the student has a better sense of direction. He or she heads for the periodical room to see what the hot topics are in the industry. As the student leafs through issues of the *Columbia Journalism Review, Editor & Publisher, Presstime,* and other periodicals, articles on technology seem to leap out of the page. There is an article on videotex in this magazine, an article on teletext in that. The articles pique the student's curiosity. He or she begins to take notice.

Videotex, it seems, is newspapers on a screen—delivered over the telephone lines from the newspaper office to a special computer in the subscriber's home. Teletext, like videotex, is words on a screen or pictures, but it is broadcast in a sort of piggyback fashion along with regular television signals. What would it be like to read a newspaper like that? the student thinks. Why would anyone prefer them to a paper newspaper?

With these questions in mind, the student begins to look into the uses of both media. On teletext, it seems, it takes up to several minutes for a screenful of information to "build" on a screen. There are different teletext stations, but the viewer has little choice of reading matter: just as with a regular television broadcast, the broadcaster controls the material.

That anyone should prefer teletext to paper newspapers makes no sense at all to the student. Not only does the viewer have to read a wiggly wavy screen, but he or she has no choice of article. The only advantage, it seems, is that the broadcasts cost nothing. Even then, the television set has to be adapted before it can be used. The student thinks hard to find what teletext would be good for. Weather reports? Hourly headlines? Advertising? The student mulls it over and decides that teletext is no substitute for print newspapers.

At this point the student could junk teletext as a topic and start researching videotex alone, applying the same kinds of questions. A sharp student however, will simply set the ideas aside for a bit: the evidence and perspective might be useful later.

Videotex offers a lot more to the viewer, the student learns. Every videotex newspaper starts with a table of contents called a menu. From there, the viewer can move into a certain subject, then choose another, more specific subject with the next menu and the next. Finally, there are headlines to choose from. In short, the viewer has a choice about what news appears on the screen.

The student is interested. This seems to be something that would work for some readers. But who? Who has the money to subscribe to such a service, which the student has found out is quite expensive? Is there advertising to help pay? The student meanwhile takes notes, not only on evidence and sources of evidence, but on ideas. He or she notes carefully the informed opinions of industry watchers; they will be useful for giving different sides of the issue later.

The student continues researching the main idea: the paper will compare videotex and teletext with newspapers in regard to what readers seem to want. Readers want to get their news fast, according to readership surveys in communication journals and industry publications. Circulation figures show that "soft" news newspapers are gaining readers, while newspapers with long, interpretive articles are losing ground. Surprisingly, viewers seem to like advertising. Although advertising appears on both videotex and teletext, with teletext the viewer is essentially stuck with the advertisement until it disappears from the screen.

The student eventually concludes that videotex is better than teletext but that neither of them is a match for print newspapers in reader choices, cost, or convenience. That becomes the thesis: Today's electronic newspapers are no match for paper ones.

Woven through this process are research and thought, note taking, more research, more thinking, more notes. Research and note taking are skills that a student must develop by experience, but learning them will be much less painful if the student heeds the advice of the following sections.

Selecting Sources

Whatever the topic, there are several different sources of basic information. A researcher should always seek *primary sources* (firsthand information) rather than *secondary sources*, which are one step removed from the original. For example, William Faulkner's writings are primary; analyses of them by a literary critic are secondary. A president's book on his administration is primary; a critical review of it is secondary. Firsthand observation is primary; a summary of observations or a newspaper report is secondary. A painting or any other artistic production is primary; a description or analysis of it is secondary. An interview is primary; a personality profile from a magazine is secondary.

Most authorities define primary sources differently. A researcher examining a book by William Faulkner is not consulting a primary source. The original manuscript is the primary source. The book is a secondary source because editors and others probably produced a book that is at least slightly different from the manuscript. Similarly, a researcher must examine the original of a painting—not a reproduction—to use a primary source.

Although these are important distinctions for many scholars, for the present purpose the examples in the first paragraph of this section may provide the most useful distinction. To analyze the printed works of Faulkner or the President or to examine a good reproduction of a painting is to avoid relying on what *someone else* has written about the works. The important matter is that the researcher must make an original analysis rather than depending on someone else to do the thinking. In practice, the researcher considers the analyses of authorities and examines them independently. The ultimate value of a research paper pivots on the writer's own thoughts.

Taking Notes

The order of the sections of this chapter—first choosing a topic, then selecting sources and taking notes—may suggest that all research projects, proceed step by step: choosing the topic, reading, note taking, outlining, and writing following upon one another in marching order. Few projects are so neat, however. In fact, a researcher who can make a work march along crisply is either extraordinarily well organized or produces sterile papers, or both. In many cases, one chooses a topic, begins reading, develops a vague notion for an outline while taking notes, rejects the first topic and chooses a related one, reads more and takes more notes, starts outlining, reads again and revises the outline, reads, changes the focus of the topic in a way that requires additional reading, note taking, and outlining, and so on.

Chaotic as this may seem, it is a kind of a map of the mind at work. The research cannot take each step mechanically; thinking—having new and different thoughts—is central to reading, taking notes, outlining, and writing. The researcher sometimes takes one step forward and two steps back. Even when he steps backward, he should consider taking with him what he picked up along the way. He should not, for example, automatically discard his notes when he decides to undertake a new topic. The new is likely to be related to the old and may even be a different version of it.

All seasoned researchers seem to agree that a researcher must make as many complete notes on three-by-five cards as time and temper allow. The typical card should give as much information as possible—the idea or the quotation, and always, the author, title, page numbers, dates, and other data that will later be needed for the footnotes and bibliography (Figure 1). Perhaps nothing is more irritating in research than discovering that more of a quotation is needed than one has copied, or that one has not noted some of the facts needed for footnotes, and bibliography.

Researchers are also nearly unanimous in believing that a photocopy machine is no substitute for handwriting. The researcher who writes out an important quotation or set of facts rather than merely making a photocopy of the relevant page fixes it in mind, giving it a central place that will help later in writing. Furthermore, this system facilitates the organizing of the notes later, when the outline is being formed. The writer can simply shuffle and reshuffle the data to fit.

Many modern researchers both write notes and photocopy pages. They may find later that they use only the notes, but having the photocopy at hand enables them to refer to the context in which the notes appear. If this seems to be a curious duplication of work, consider a similar journalistic practice. Some journalists both take notes *and* tape record interviews and news conferences, then in most cases refer only to their notes, using the tape recording occasionally for checking and for providing the context of a quotation. To rely on the recording alone would require struggling through so much extraneous material that the reporter might not be able to fix on the highlights that had seemed to shine during the event.

By the same token, the library researcher who does not take notes but relies on photocopies of many pages that include both primary and secondary points may discover during a shuffle through them that he or she has forgotten the point that had prompted the photocopy. This page was photocopied because it carries this quotation that must be used because I was thinking then that—What *was* that point?

Photocopying is more useful than this analysis indicates, of course. In the past many researchers used three-by-five cards for short quotations and notes, and larger cards for summaries as paraphrases of long passages. Many now continue to use the three-by-five cards for the brief material but photocopy passages that are to be summarized or paraphrased, thus doing away with the larger cards.

Photocopying may also enable the researcher to consider a much wider range of material for writing. If the focus of the topic should shift, material that was once considered secondary is now at hand, not back in the library. Even if the topic remains the same, the many photocopied pages may be useful because they give the researcher the benefit of being able to select from much material rather than little. To avoid being overwhelmed by a jungle of photocopied pages, however, a researcher should organize them by jotting down notes about them on cards. If this multiple use of cards seems to build the stack of cards alarmingly, the researcher should remember again the basic value of cards: No other form of writing is easier to organize.

Outlines

There are compelling arguments for and against making outlines. Setting down a full outline before beginning a short piece of writing is usually useless, but some form of outline is valuable in writing longer pieces. Even in lengthy writing, the full, formal outline that uses I-II-III-A-B-C-1-2-3-a-b-c cuts a precise pattern before writing begins that can bear little resemblance to what one will produce in shaping sentences that grow out of one another during the writing process.

That is a strong argument against outlines for almost *any* form of writing. For a research paper, however, a full outline of some kind is often useful in planning, because the writer usually depends heavily on many sources. It is foolish to begin to write an ambitious paper after making a plan no more precise than arranging note cards in a semblance of order.

Cards can be used to help shape an outline; then the outline helps the researcher reorganize the cards. Consider the most common kinds of outlines.

The *scratch outline*, which is usually made up of notes scribbled on one or two pages, is a preliminary survey of the research the writer has assembled and his or her thoughts about it. Before writing, one should consider making the scratch outline more organized and detailed. Some researchers use the scratch outline to develop one of the more formal outlines described below.

A scratch outline for the article on electronic newspapers might run like this:

—Story of hypothetical reader trying to read a teletext "newspaper" while eating breakfast.
—Statement: Today's electronic media are no match for print newspapers.
　　—hard to read
　　—No choice of articles
　　—Difficulties of advertising
　　—Inconvenient
　　—Costs more than print newspapers
—True for both videotex and teletext. Videotex better, but not much so.
　　etcetera, on to more detailed descriptions of all the items listed above.

The *topic outline* is ordinarily made up of both the topics and the subtopics that will form the bulk of the paper. Although designed to show general relationships—topics are more important than the subtopics under them—the topic outline does not usually represent the full shape of the paper. Again, some researchers are content to write from a topic outline, and others use it to build a more formal outline.

A topic outline might resemble the following example:

—Intro anecdote
—Videotex—describe
—Teletext—describe
—But they are no match for print
—Reason: Not as good for readers

The *sentence outline* is full-fleshed, with each item written in the form of a complete sentence, and with the relationship of each item to the others made clear by symbols: Roman numerals identify sentences on topics, capital letters those on the most important subtopics, Arabic numerals those on the next most important subtopics, lower-case letters those on the least important.

Sentence outlines take much more effort than scratch or topic outlines, but students who do them often find their writing the quickest of all. Here is a section of such an outline, based on the scratch outline given above.

I Story of reader
  Flips on TV to teletext channel. Chooses channel arbitrarily.
  Sits down to breakfast of bacon and eggs. Watches screen form.
  Finishes eggs and bacon. Lifts coffee to lips, blows, sets cup down. "This is boring," he thinks.
II Teletext and videotex

So might it be on a morning with teletext, one of today's new electronic newspapers.

A. Brief description of teletext—
  1. A form of television.
  2. Broadcast piggyback with regular television programming.
  3. It is "decoded" via a special attachment to the television.

Whatever the form of outline one uses, it should be considered a guideline, not an unchangeable set of rules. The important point is that research material must be organized in some systematic way before the writing and must be reorganized as the work progresses. Because individuals are different, the form most useful to one may not be to another. Moreover, a form that is most useful in one case may not be the best for the same researcher in another. A good general rule is this: The longer and more complex the research paper, the fuller the outline.

WRITING THE PAPER

Good writing, like a good house, is an orderly arrangement of parts.

—Mortimer Adler

At one time most research papers were written in a formal tone and a rigidly formal structure. Some are still written that way, with the writer stating the subject and goals at the beginning, laying out his or her findings at length, then summarizing the whole—all in heavy detail. Many modern teachers and students sneer at the tone of such papers and ridicule the structure with, "Yeah, first you tell 'em what you're gonna tell 'em, then you tell 'em, then you tell 'em what you told 'em."

However, those who overreact to the formality may forget that it is essential to steer the reader, to say near the beginning of the paper where the researcher is going and how he or she expects to get there. Doing this is especially essential when one reports complex research at length. Without direction, readers will become lost in thickets of facts and ideas.

Perhaps the most critical structural guideline for a research paper is that it should begin in a way that indicates where the paper is going. The structure is illustrated by the following, the first four pages of "The Abortion Dilemma," a short research paper written by a student, Diane Norburg.

COMMENTS

This paper is designed to argue a case as well as to describe and analyze. The writer wisely begins with a definition so that readers will know the basis of the argument as well as that of the description and analysis. Similarly, the focus of the argument is defined: morality.

Note that the writer manages at the outset to define the subject (abortion) and her topic (the morality of abortion) even as she provides a brief overview of the attention both receive.

Just as the writer has put first things first above, she does so here by recognizing that not every question can be answered readily, if at all.

Throughout this passage, the writer is calling upon an amalgam of information and ideas. To try to cite sources in these paragraphs would be futile. The mixture of what she knew before she began research for the paper is so mixed with her reading since she began it that singling out this source or that one is not possible.

In a more extensive paper, a writer would be careful to cite sources for several points that crop up from point to point in this passage. For example, a source that discusses the limitations of science would be in order, even a general source that does not discuss science in connection with the problem of abortion.

PAPER

Abortion is the deliberately induced miscarriage of a potential

human being in the embryonic or fetal stages of its growth. The purpose

of this paper is not to outline the various procedures employed to effect

an abortion, but rather to concentrate on the morality of the issue.

Abortion is one of the most widely discussed contemporary controversies.

Many organizations and religious and ethnic groups have felt a pressing

need to formulate positions which indicate who they believe should be

allowed to receive abortions and what stipulations must be met for the act

to be justifiable. These statements rely in part on the laws drafted by

the American Law Institute and encompass forced impregnation, age and

marital status of the woman, medical evidence that an abortion is advisable,

and criteria for the proper and legal performance of the abortion.

However, the vast majority of position papers fail to state an answer

to the question which lies at the heart of the abortion controversy--Where

does one draw the fine line between "murder" of a living human and abortion

of a potential human? In short, the question is, "When does life begin?"

The reason for this omission is obvious. The answer cannot be deduced,

even with the aid of elaborate modern science. First, one must realize

that science is merely a human construct to aid in interpreting our

environment; therefore, any "scientific definitions" are necessarily

arbitrary. The men of science draw their own lines; they do not suddenly

discover Almighty Truths which describe the natural world.

It is doubtful that science will ever be able to pinpoint the exact

moment when life begins by choosing one hypothesis from among the several

in existence today. When and if they do, the abortion decision will be

COMMENTS

Having stated her beliefs, the writer is now concerned to make it clear that they are not based on pure emotion but grow out of reasoning based on research. This is central in research papers that state a position and argue a case. Although a writer need not ordinarily show that the position taken and the argument reflect the opinions of most authorities, the position and the argument are not likely to be persuasive if they are not solidly grounded.

This passage and most of the others are artfully constructed. The writer is simultaneously arguing and informing. Readers who might reject her argument can nonetheless learn from her research—enjoyable learning because the information is not presented woodenly but is entwined in the context of her argument.

PAPER

-2-

removed from the individual and be regulated by the penal codes of the world. Until that unlikely time, however, the question of abortion will remain a personal and moral one and will continue to comprise one of the greatest issues in science and religion which mankind labors to solve.

It is the contention of this paper that until the debate regarding the beginning of life is brought to a close, one must regard the issue of abortion in the light of <u>potential</u> human life. The welfare and rational desires of the future mother must be weighed against the right of the original fertilized zygote to grow and experience life after birth. Therefore, the abortion decision rests solely upon individual conscience.

It would appear reasonable, however, to assume that no person has the right to deny existence to one who was created just as he was, unless the reasons for so doing are such that <u>all</u> those involved in the considered abortion could not function healthfully and normally if the pregnancy were carried to term.

In order to include the beliefs and present viewpoints which aided in the formulation of this opinion it is necessary to begin with the existing laws.

One draft of the Model Penal Code (1962), set forth by the American Law Institute, treats justifiable abortion in Section 230.3. It reads,

> A licensed physician is justified in terminating
> a pregnancy if he believes there is substantial
> risk that continuance of the pregnancy would
> gravely impair the physical or mental health
> of the mother or that the child would be born
> with grave physical or mental defect, or that
> the pregnancy resulted from rape, incest, or
> other felonious intercourse (Society of
> American Friends 105-106).

The Institute also requires that two physicians certify in writing "the circumstances which they believe to justify the abortion" (Society of American Friends 106).

COMMENTS

The kind of information presented here *does not call for a citation because it is general. Should the writer have cited the source of the information on spontaneous abortions of nature? That depends on a writer's judgment of the needs of readers—which is sometimes faulty. Surely most readers would accept that as a verifiable fact without documentation. It probably need not be footnoted. (But researchers must always keep in mind that a few readers are not likely to accept important information on faith, and perhaps at least one reader would wish that a source had been cited so that he could read more about it.)*

Like the other facts drawn from sources cited by the writer, the information on the AMA platform is valuable. It supports the writer's argument, and it provides facts that will interest anyone who cares enough about the topic to read this paper. Moreover, the writer would have been at fault had she not done research on the AMA platform. The leading association of physicians is one of the most obvious and important sources on a subject involving human life.

PAPER

-3-

Different states have adopted liberal or conservative variations on the rules in the Model Penal Code. Only one state, California, does not list the possibility of an imperfect child as a justifiable cause for abortion. This paper holds the omission to be laudable. In the light of recognizing the sanctity of human life, potential or actualized, one must look to the existence of those handicapped individuals already born, many of whom have made valuable contributions to society. To have denied them life would have been barbaric and not in keeping with the idea of everyone's right to life. Few people, born deaf because their mother contracted rubella in the early weeks of her pregnancy, would opt for death simply because of their handicap. Yet, some people would have had them aborted.

Nature spontaneously aborts one in six babies conceived. Thus, selection is canalized to the development of only those fetuses which have the best chance for survival. When modern obstetrics and gynecology find a fetus to be grossly malformed, the question of euthanasia might vie with that of abortion to determine whether the deformity is so severe that life would not be a gift. Once again, it is doubtful that even the most sophisticated experimentation could set up a value scale to make such a determination. One can call to mind the renowned thalidomide babies of a few years ago. Now, many of them are excelling in school and enjoying the company of their playmates. Especially noticeable is the fact that they all, without regard to the extent of their deformity, have been an addition of love to their families, just as any normal child would have been.

The platform of the American Medical Association parallels the law quite closely. In their policy adopted in June, 1967, they opposed induced abortion except in the following instances:

COMMENTS

The writer did not cite a source for this information on the number of illicit abortions because it had become common knowledge by the time she wrote.

Although it was not essential that the writer follow the progression from law to medicine to religion—the order depends on the structure of the paper, which might have placed them in another order—all three are certainly essential to any cogent discussion of abortion, which has obvious legal, medical, and religious qualities.

PAPER

-4-

> 1. when there is a threat to the health or life
> of the mother,
> 2. when medical evidence indicates deformity in the
> fetus,
> 3. when two competent physicians concur in writing,
> 4. when rape or incest cause a mental or physical
> threat to the mother,
> 5. when abortion is performed in an accredited
> hospital (Society of American Friends 99).

A look at these criteria, coupled with a look at the actual statistics on abortions, shows that the majority of abortions do not legally fit into one of these categories. In spite of leniency in respect to the clause concerning the mental health of the mother, most abortions remain illicit. Many women seek abortions because the child was conceived out of wedlock or because they already have enough children and another would be too great a financial burden. If they are denied aid through legal channels, they can receive the help they want elsewhere. This situation once again points to the undeniably personal and moral aspects of abortion. In the final analysis, the lawyers and doctors have little part in the decision.

Because of the moral nature of abortion, many religious groups have formulated guidelines for their members to follow. The most outspoken criticism of abortion comes from the Roman Catholic Church. Papal encyclicals have repeatedly stressed that the only legal abortion is an <u>unintentional</u> one, in which the fetus is incidentally killed during attempts to save a mother's life. The 1968 encyclical, <u>Humanae Vitae</u>, issued by Pope Paul, states,

> We must once again declare that the direct
> interruption of the generative process
> already begun, and above all, directly
> willed and procured abortion, even for
> therapeutic reasons, are to be absolutely
> excluded as licit means of regulating
> birth (Society of American Friends 96). ...

Diane Norburg ended her paper with this paragraph:

> So also must abortion be available in instances in which it offers the best choice. Lest this paper seem to imply an unequivocal support of abortion when social, psychological, and economic pressures call for one, it might be wise to conclude with a saying promoted by the "Chance of a Lifetime" group in Washington: "Abortion is not healthy for children and other living things" ("Anti-Abortion Campaign").

CREDITING SOURCES

Many students are depressed by the very word "notes," in part because using them requires assembling dull details in a form that has no color or flavor. Perhaps more important, many dislike notes because they worry almost endlessly about *what* to note.

To a casual reader, notes *are* dull details. They are not likely to disappear, though, because many serious readers value them and can use them most easily in the economical form in which most notes appear. The best one can do to reduce note worry is to try to understand why notes are valuable and how one should decide which items deserve them.

Plagiarism

Notes are an explicit means of expressing debts to other writers. A writer must avoid any form of plagiarism, including paraphrasing the ideas of another and passing them off as original. At the 1980 *World Book Encyclopedia* put it: "A work need not be identical to the original to be a plagiarism. But it must be so similar that it has obviously been copied."

Plagiarism can be anything from lifting a clever sentence from a newspaper article, to altering a few words and using a well-written sentence from some source, right up to blatant copying. Virtually all students know that copying is a heinous offense, but some draw the line a little too leniently. For example, a student might read the following passage from a magazine article, describing the "macho man" handshake:

> The best defense is a good offense: grab his hand toward the base of the palm, cutting down on his fingers' leverage, and start your grip before he starts his. Of course, if he's strong enough and macho enough, it won't work, and he'll bond your individual digits into a single flipper for trying to thwart him.

A student who writes the following passage without citing the source is plagiarizing:

> Our football coach's handshake is enough to make you wince. I figured, finally, that my best defense is an offense: I grab his hand toward the base of the palm, hoping to cut down on his fingers' leverage, and start my grip first. But this coach is strong enough and macho enough that I'm afraid he'll bond my individual digits into one huge flipper for trying to thwart him.

Even the making of the statement, "Then the coach bonded my individual digits into one huge flipper for trying to thwart his macho man handshake" is plagiarizing for the purposes of a student paper. Such literary sleight-of-hand is unacceptable.

Retrievability

Because scholars want readers to have confidence in their published work, they ordinarily cite those important aspects that are not common knowledge. They also cite important aspects to enable readers to retrieve them. This is a second important reason for crediting sources in a research paper.

Who deserves credit is not usually difficult to determine, but how do scholars know what to cite to give readers confidence? How do they know what readers will want to retrieve? They can usually judge fairly accurately because they know their readership. Academic journals are read primarily by those who teach much the same courses, so the writer has some sense of the knowledge they share and thus can judge what aspects of the research must be cited. A professor of English, for example, shares a common fund of information with most other professors of English who specialize in the same field.

No scholar or journal editor, however, can really judge *precisely* what readers know and would like to know. Thus a reader occasionally writes to an author or to a journal editor, irritated because an article was not properly noted. In some cases, *many* readers are irritated by inadequate citations and related matters.

A student's strategy in citing sources should be similar to a scholar's. The student should use notes to express debts, to establish confidence, and to help readers retrieve information. Like the scholar, too, the student must consider the knowledge and needs of those who read the journal. In the absence of any such well-defined readership, it is probably best to try to write for fellow students. Whatever the readership, the writer uses citations to serve it.

The student is likely to make mistakes, even while following the guidelines of scholarship. But few will make the absurd mistake of the student who, acting on the naive principle that the more notes one provides the better the research paper, cited a biography to make the point that George Washington was the first president of the United States.

Types of Documentation

There are several note styles that are widely used. The purpose in citing sources is not to observe rules but to enable readers to find basic information readily. To avoid confusing readers, however, a writer must use one style throughout the research paper. If the instructor does not prescribe a style, any that provides information briefly can be used. Most teachers of English seem to prefer the style recommended by the Modern Language Association, the MLA Style Sheet; some prefer that developed by the University of Chicago Press. Many psychologists and other social scientists have adopted the quite different style—remarkable for brevity—developed by the American Psychological Association.

Most styles are alike in basic prescriptions. They require, for example, that an article or book be identified fully the first time it is cited, briefly in succeeding notes. The various styles also prescribe that one should underline titles of periodicals and books but use quotation marks for titles of items published in periodicals. There are different basic styles for social sciences, natural sciences, and humanities papers. Social sciences references sometimes follow natural science style, sometimes humanities style. Because most of the readers of this book will be working on humanities papers, we will demonstrate the MLA style in this chapter; students who need a natural science style should consult their instructors.

Works Cited.   The most common MLA format for citing sources that were used in the research paper is *Works Cited*. Like the standard bibliography, it is listed in alphabetical order. The author's last name is written first. When there is no author, the entry is listed according to the first important word (not A, *An, The,* etc.) of the title. The text reference to the citation is in parentheses and consists of the author's last name—or a shortened title, if there is no author—and the year of publication. The Works Cited form is the one that was used in the student essay on abortion.

Endnotes.   An alternate MLA system of documentation is the endnote format. Endnotes are similar to footnotes but appear after the text rather than at the bottom of the page. They are numbered and appear in the order in which they are referred to in the text. The text reference is a superscript number. The endnote style is the style that is used for the notes in this book and is the one that will be described in detail in this chapter.

Works Consulted.   Some sources are not actually quoted in a research paper but have provided a significant amount of information for it or have influenced the writer's thinking. These *Works Consulted* lists enable the paper's readers to find more narrowly focused articles, which may in turn carry bibliographies leading to still other articles.

A book or article one has merely scanned or thumbed through has no place under Works Consulted. Even works a researcher has examined should not be listed unless they are reflected in the paper. The purpose is not to persuade readers that one has been industrious but to list useful works. The temptation to list too much is likely to be so strong that it is probably better to err on the side of omission.

Documentation Form

Most students are aghast at the thought of writing notes, but they need not be. For a student with even the slightest grasp of detail, it is quite simple to put such references in a style once he or she has grown accustomed to using it.

The following examples relating to Diane Norburg's paper on abortion, illustrate both Works Cited and endnotes in Modern Language Association style. Look at them as carefully as possible, because the better the researcher impresses a standard style on his or her brain, the easier it will be to use:

Endnotes

[1]Society of American Friends, *Who Shall Live? Man's Control over Birth and Death* (New York: Hill and Wang, 1970) 105-106.

[2]Society 106.

[3]Society 99.

[4]Society 96.

[5]John T. Noonan, *The Morality of Abortion* (Cambridge: Harvard University Press, 1970) 9.

[6]Daniel Callahan, *Abortion: Law, Choice and Morality* (London: Macmillan, 1970) 414.

[7]Virgil C. Blum, "Public Policy Making: Why the Churches Strike Out," *America* 6 March 1971: 224

[8]"Anti-Abortion Campaign," *Time* 29 March 1971: 73.

Works Cited

"ANTI-ABORTION CAMPAIGN." *Time* 29 March 1971: 70-73.

BLUM, VIRGIL C. "Public Policy Making: Why the Churches Strike Out." *America* 6 March 1971: 224-225.

CALLAHAN, DANIEL. *Abortion: Law, Choice and Morality*. London: Macmillan, 1970.

EDMISTON, SUSAN. "New York City—Abortion Capital." *San Francisco Chronicle* 21 April 1971: 21.

FRIENDS, SOCIETY OF AMERICAN. *Who Shall Live? Man's Control over Birth and Death*. New York: Hill and Wang, 1970.

GRANFIELD, DAVID. *The Abortion Decision*. New York: Doubleday, 1969.

NOONAN, JOHN T., ed. *The Morality of Abortion*. Cambridge: Harvard UP, 1970. (essays used for reference include those by Paul Ramsey, James M. Gustafson, Bernard Haring, and Noonan)

OLDS, SALLY. "What We Do and Don't Know About Miscarriages." *Today's Health* Feb. 1971: 42-45.

Citing Books

[1]JEAN MCGARRY, *Airs of Providence* (Cambridge, Mass.: Johns Hopkins UP, 1985) 33.

Edited Book

[2]STEVEN H. CHAFFEE, ed., *Political Communication: Issues and Strategies for Research* (Beverly Hills: Sage, 1975) 170.

A Book by Two or Three Authors

[3]MARGERY RESNICK and ISABELLE DE CORTIVRON, *Writers in Translation: An Annotated Bibliography, 1945-1980* (New York: Garland, 1981) 117.

Book Written by More Than Three People

[4]EVERETTE DENNIS et al., *New Strategies for Public Affairs Reporting: Investigation, Interpretation, and Research* (Englewood Cliffs, NJ: Prentice-Hall, 1977) 101.

Book Edited by More than Three People

[5]ITHIEL DE SOLA POOL et al., eds., *Handbook of Communication* (Chicago: Rand McNally, 1973) 102.

Reference to an Article in the Same Book

6WILLIAM J. MCGUIRE, "Persuasion, Resistance, and Attitude Change," *Handbook of Communication*, ed. Ithiel de Sola Pool et al. (Chicago: Rand McNally, 1973) 217.

Translation

7MIGUEL DE CERVANTES, *Don Quixote*, trans. Tobias Smollett (New York: Farrar, Straus & Giroux, 1971) 219.

8WILLIAM R. PARKER, trans., *Milton*, (Oxford: Clarendon, 1968) 204.

Book Published as Part of a Series

9RUTH WALLERSTEIN, *Richard Cranshaw: A Study in Style and Poetic Development*, University of Wisconsin Studies in Language and Literature 37. (Madison: U of Wisconsin P, 1975) 14.

Book With Corporate Authorship

10Special Task Force to the Secretary of Health, Education and Welfare, *The Second Newman Report: National Policy and Higher Education* (Cambridge: MIT: 1973) 201.

Anonymous Book

11*Literary Market Place: The Directory of American Book Publishing, 1986* (New York: Bowker, 1985) 203-313.

Note Citing More Than One Book

12ROBERT L. COLLISON, *Indexing Books*. (New York: DeGraff, 1962); Sina Spiker, *Indexing Your Book* (Madison: U of Wisconsin P, 1964); and *The Chicago Manual of Style* 13th ed. (Chicago: U of Chicago P, 1982) 399-430.

Citing Articles (Magazines, Journals, Newspapers)

Journal Article with Continuous Pagination

1WOLFANG MIEDER, "Modern Variants of the Daisy Oracle 'He Loves Me, He Loves Me Not," *Midwestern Journal of Language and Folklore* (1985): 66-114.

Journal Article in Which Pages
Are Numbered Separately in Each Issue

2JOHN R. FREY, "America and Her Literature Reviewed by Postwar Germany," *American-German Review* 20.5 (1974): 4-6.

An Article from a Monthly or Bimonthly Periodical

GAY TALESE, "Looking for Hemingway," *Esquire* July 1963: 44.

An Article from a Weekly or Biweekly Periodical

TZVETAN TODOROV, "Stalled Thinkers," *The New Republic* 13 April 1987: 26.

Book Review from a Magazine

[3]RAYMOND SOKOLOV, rev. of *Marina and Lee*, by Priscilla Johnson MacMillan, *Newsweek* 31 Oct. 1977: 105.

Anonymous Article in a Magazine

[4]"SMITHSONIAN HIGHLIGHTS," *Smithsonian* Nov. 1977: 167-171.

Signed Article in a Newspaper

[5]DALE RUSSAKOFF, "Many Winners, Losers in Senate Tax Overhaul," *Washington Post* 11 May 1986, final ed.: 3-4.

Unsigned Article in a Newspaper

[6]"Simple Elegance: Minimalist Look Maximizes Luxury with Dark Colors," *San Jose Mercury News* 14 May 1986, final ed.: 1-4.

Note that in all the periodical citations, the page numbers of the entire article, not just the quoted page, are given.

Citing Pamphlets

Signed Pamphlet

[1]TERRY CHRISTENSEN, *Reliable Sources: A Handbook for Political Research in San Jose and Santa Clara County* Calif. 33.

Citing Other Documents

Public Documents

The U.S. Constitution is published so widely that it need not be identified beyond citing the article and section.
[1]U.S. Constitution, Art. II, Sec. 1.

However, referring to a book devoted to spelling out the meanings of the U.S. Constitution, one would use the following form:

[2]JAMES THOMAS NORTON, *The Constitution of the United States: Its Sources and Application* (New York: Committee for Constitutional Government, 205 East 42nd Street, 1943).

When citing among the many hearings conducted by legislatures or the U.S. Congress, use the following:

[3]United States. Cong. *Hearings on the Failing Newspaper Act before a Subcommittee of the Senate Committee on the Judiciary.* Part 1. 90th Cong., 5, Rept. 291. 1st Sess. Washington: GPO, 1967.

Dissertations

[4]ERIC L. GANS, "The Discovery of Illusion: Flaubert's Early Works, 1835-1837," diss., Johns Hopkins, 1967. 12.

Shortening Notes   After the first reference to a given book in a list of notes, the full information does not need to be given again. For example, here is a first entry:

[1]LEE T. LEMON, *Approaches to Literature* (New York: Oxford UP, 1973) 71.

The second, third, and fourth notes would look like this, if the reference is to the same page as the first note.

[2]Lemon.

If the second citation comes from the same book, but from a different page, use the following:

[3]LEMON   93.

When there have been two previous notes citing different books by the same author, the second note for either book must specify which of the previous books it is. The title may be shortened, as in the following:

[11]LEMON,   *Counterplot* (New York: Oxford UP, 1978) 89.

Although Latin abbreviations are used less often today, researchers run across them in many older works and should know what they mean. Following are some of the more commonly used ones.

anon.   Anonymous.
c. or *ca.* (*circa*)   This refers to an approximate date when the actual date cannot be determined.
cf. (confer)   Compare.
et al. (*et alii*)   And others, an abbreviation often used for works by several authors. The first author is named, the others referred to by *et al.*
f. or *ff.*   One or more pages following the page indicated.
infra   Below.
passim   In various places, or here and there. Used to indicate that information appears on several pages.
supra   Above.

PREPARING CLASS PAPERS

Unless you are given other instructions, observe these rules:

For handwritten essays, use 8½ by 11-inch paper, with double-spaced lines to allow room for corrections. Write on only one side of the paper, leaving wide margins (at least one inch at each side), and use blue or black ink. If your handwriting is small and cramped, or large and sprawling, make a conscious effort to slow your pace to improve legibility.

For typewritten essays, use standard-weight typing paper (8½ × 11 inches); onionskin paper is suitable only for carbons. Type on only one side of the paper, using a black ribbon, double-spacing between lines, and leaving wide margins. Leave two spaces after a period and other forms of end punctuation (question marks, exclamation marks, and colons). To indicate a dash, use two hyphens, without spacing at either side.

Your cover page should look like this. It may also include additional information required by the instructor.

```
                    Smith, John
                    English 1
                    October 3, 1985
                    Instructor:  Mr. Doe
                    Class Essay 2
```

The first page should look like this:

```
                              ↑
                    margin    |    2 inches
                              |
                              |
   (Capitalize the title)     ↓          (Center the title)

                        THE QUEST FOR HISTORY

   (Paragraphs indent)

       5 spaces The time for starting a quest for history is now.  When you
   margin                                                              margin
   ←────→  attempt it, remember the words of George Washington:        ←────→
   1 inch      10 spaces Just as Thomas Jefferson said when he was writing   1½ inches
     5 spaces his manuscript on history...

              (Indent and single space quotations and case histories)




                  (Use no page number on the first page.
                   Number all other pages at the center
                   or right-hand corner with Arabic numerals)

                               ↑
                    margin      |  1 inch
                               ↓
```

EXERCISES

1. Take an essay by a well-known writer—George Orwell, E. B. White, Lewis Thomas, or any essay in a book of essays—and outline it to discover the progression of the author's argument. List the main points, and then mark *ideas* presented by the author, *evidence* to back them, and *illustrations* to clarify them. Then critique the essay on the basis of the outline, answering the following questions:
   a. Do the points follow one another in a sensible order? If so, is it the most logical order the author could have used? If not, how did the author link the points of the argument? By a clever transition? By an analogy? By a new heading?
   b. How much evidence does the author give to support each point? Two or three bits of evidence? Does he or she use facts, details, and numbers that can be verified, or examples and stories?
   c. Where are the weak points in the logic, and how has the author obscured them?
   d. Where in the essay does the author present the single main point of the essay? Is it presented more than once?

2. Take a 4- to 6-page paper that you have already written for any class, and outline it as you did the essay in Exercise 1. Compare your outline by the same criteria. Does your argument make sense? Did you inadvertently leave gaps in the logic? Are there places where a clever transition substitutes for a missing bit of evidence? Finally, answer this question: How could you have written a more effective paper? Write a new and better outline for your paper. Note: You can also do this exercise by trading papers with a classmate.

3. Practice the steps for developing a topic for a paper using the guidelines given in this chapter. Write down each of the following steps:
   a. Brainstorming. Come up with a half dozen ideas for a brief research paper. (This can be on virtually any topic, serious or frivolous, but a wise student will choose a topic that may later be used for another class.)
   b. Selecting one of the ideas. Give several reasons why you chose the idea you did. Complete these sentences:

   This topic is of interest to me because . . .

   I hope to learn the following from this paper . . .
   I think this is a workable topic for a paper because . . .

   c. List what you know about the topic already—briefly.
   d. List your preliminary ideas on the topic—briefly.
   e. Write down a half dozen ideas that you may want to research. Choose one or two.

3. List several reference sources that you will consult for your research. List what you hope to find in each one. (Note: You may choose references that will give background information.)

4. Put the following footnotes in the style described in this chapter.

   [1]*News from Nowhere* by Edward Jay Epstein. New York: Random House, p. 81, 1973.
   [2]Alfred Werner: "The Angry Art of Chaim Soutine." *The Progressive,* vol. 37, 1973, p. 43.
   [3]Alfred Werner: "The Angry Art of Chaim Soutine." p. 43.
   [4]James McCartney. "Vested Interests of the Reporter." In *Reporting the News,* edited by Louis Lyons—Cambridge: Belknap Press of Harvard University Press, published 1965, quoted from p. 98.
   [5]*News from Nowhere.* Edward J. Epstein. New York: Random House. p. 27. 1973.

5. Write a short paper, about two pages, explaining what plagiarism is. Refer to at least three different sources, which may be as simple as encyclopedias.

6. Which of the following should have an endnote? For each, answer

    I would (never) (always) (sometimes) have a note for this.
    I would have a note for this for a paper for a _____ class.

    a. The year Charles Dickens was born.
    b. The total population of the United States.
    c. The quote, "Fourscore and seven years ago. . . ."
    d. The quote "All but three of the approximately seventy-five American semiconductor firms are located in the Santa Clara Valley in California."
    e. The list of members of the European Economic Community in 1980.
    f. The last year a clipper ship went "round the horn."

FIGURE 1   Sample note cards

Bibliographic Note

Cry of the People by Penny Lernoux.
Harmondsworth, Middlesex, England:
Penguin Books, 1982. First published by Doubleday
& Co., Inc., 1980.

Bibliographic notes should be as complete as possible on note cards, but they can be put in proper footnote style later. Sometimes it is helpful to put bibliographic notes on colored cards so they are quick to identify when the footnotes are being typed up.

Quotations and Information Notes

Subject note—
spell out completely
on the first
card.

> Agency for International Development (AID)
>
> Lernoux says AID backs US business in Latin America.
>
> "In addition to low-interest loans to U. S. companies, AID funds paid for 50 percent of their pre-investment surveys, which often, and particularly in mining, saved these companies large sums."
>
> Page number
> of reference   Lernoux p. 208

Subject note

> AID
>
> Sen. Jacob Javits says AID helps "smaller companies get into private investment. Lernoux says these companies include United Fruit, Kaiser, Allied Chemical, American Metals Climax, and Standard Fruit."
> Page number
> of reference   Lernoux p. 208
> (Info. taken from Michael Klare, War Without End. See p. 489, Lernoux.)

Background
information in case
further info. will
be needed.

4

Using
Libraries

Researchers who do not know their libraries are crippled; they bypass vast bodies of information that they could find easily. Some rely merely on *Encyclopaedia Britannica, Reader's Guide to Periodical Literature,* and *Who's Who in America.* Others simply make a beeline for the card catalog. Those researchers who can find their way in a large library can find a profusion of facts, often quite quickly.

Even the professional researchers—journalists—often neglect to use the library as well as they might. Neale Copple, now dean of journalism at the University of Nebraska, used to tell of a newspaper editor who was proud of spending $250 on telephone calls to run down the background facts for an important story. The editor had his reporters call cities all over the United States to gather figures on street-paving costs. It would have been a model of research in depth except that, as Copple observed, even better figures were available in the reference room of a library ten blocks away.

Researchers who bypass library research not only waste time and money, they also sacrifice accuracy. Nearly every specialist has at some time been asked by a researcher for information, when that same information that has already been set down clearly, accurately, and completely in books, articles, and reference works. Even the specialist who has written on a subject often wishes that interviewers would consult the published works rather than asking questions that have already been answered in print. No specialist can remember everything—perhaps not even the most important details in a work that was written years earlier.

CLASSIFYING KNOWLEDGE: THE DEWEY AND
LIBRARY OF CONGRESS CLASSIFICATION SYSTEMS

I was eyes to the blind . . . .

—Job 25:15

Many researchers simply do not understand how libraries work. Some know little more about libraries than the freshman who is attempting to write his or her first ambitious research paper. The late Douglas Southall Freeman, a respected newspaper editor who wrote several distinguished volumes on George Washington, knew the Washington documents in the Library of Congress so well that the librarians often consulted *him*. Freeman became so knowledgeable about his specialty that he actually forgot some basics of library research. Once, when he went to the Library of Congress for information on another subject, he had to ask a novice librarian for help in using one of the keys to all libraries, the card catalog.

So it is with most of those who are undertaking library research. Perhaps in grade school or junior high they listened to a librarian explain the card catalog system. But if the explanation went beyond first principles, it was of so little use at that age that few retained anything more than "Dewey Decimal System," "Library of Congress System," and the fact that both use letters and numbers.

Perhaps because of such unhelpful early experiences, many students approach a card catalog with a sense of stress. Locating *all* the cards they might use seems hopeless, so they decide to go for the minimum; though dimly aware that each card is a mine of information, they are sure it will be incomprehensible.

Is it possible to learn to like card catalogs? Perhaps. Any researcher should know that the card catalog was a tremendous step in intellectual progress. Great minds—among them Aristotle, Francis Bacon, and Thomas Jefferson—brought all their intellectual power to bear on the problem of classifying knowledge. The importance of the problem is suggested by the fact that until Linnaeus developed a classification system for botany and zoology in the eighteenth century, research in those fields was almost at a standstill. In devising his system, Linnaeus enabled researchers to order and organize their own work, build upon the work of others who had made similar observations and performed similar experiments, and thus push back the frontiers of knowledge about plant and animal life.

Librarians were long faced with a similar but much larger problem: how to order and organize—*classify—all* recorded knowledge. The systems devised by Aristotle, Bacon, Jefferson and others proved unworkable as knowledge expanded. Then in 1876 Melvil Dewey introduced the Dewey Decimal Classification. Although it has been revised often, the basic system held sway for years, and it is still used in many small libraries. It divides all knowledge into ten major groups or classes:

1. A class of general works—among them encyclopedias and general periodicals—which contain so many different kinds of information that they do not fit into any other class
2. Philosophy (conduct of life)

3. Religion (nature and meaning of life)
4. Social Sciences (man's relations with his fellows)
5. Language (human communication)
6. Pure Science (observation of man's environment)
7. Technology (manipulation of man's environment)
8. Arts (enrichment of life)
9. Literature (thoughts about life)
10. History (examination of the past)

Each of these ten classes is further divided into ten classes for a total of 100 each of which is still further divided by ten for a total of 1,000. Adding decimal points and numbers after the first three digits creates thousands of other subdivisions.

The subdivisions for American Literature illustrate how the classification system works

810 General American literature
811 American poetry
812 American drama
813 American fiction
814 American essays
815 American oratory
816 American letters
817 American satire and humor
818 American miscellany
819 Canadian English literature

The decimal point adds yet more subdivisions, as the classification for zoology, 591, illustrates:

591.1 Animal physiology
591.2 Animal pathology
591.3 Animal maturation
591.4 Animal morphology
591.5 Animal ecology
591.6 Economic zoology
591.8 Microscopic zoology
591.9 Zoogeography

Although the Dewey Decimal System has long been used throughout the United States, many larger libraries now use the Library of Congress classification system. Introduced in 1897, the Library of Congress system was so obviously valuable that many large university libraries adopted it quite early. Some large libraries now combine the two systems: Library of Congress classification for newer books, Dewey Decimal system for books already catalogued under that system. This is a brief outline of the Library of Congress classification system:

A	General Works
B-BJ	Philosophy, Psychology
BL-BX	Religion
C	Auxiliary Sciences of History
D	History: General and Old World (Eastern Hemisphere)
	History: General and Old World (Eastern Hemisphere)
E-F	History: America (Western Hemisphere)
G	Geography. Maps. Anthropology. Recreation
H	Social Sciences
J	Political Science
K	Law (General)
KD	Law of the United Kingdom and Ireland
KE	Law of Canada
KF	Law of the United States
L	Education
M	Music
N	Fine Arts
P-PA	General Philology and Linguistics. Classical Languages and Literatures
PA Supplement	Byzantine and Modern Greek Literature Medieval and Modern Latin Literature
PB-PH	Modern European Languages
PG	Russian Literature
PJ-PM	Languages and Literatures of Asia. Africa. Oceania. American Indian Languages. Artificial Languages
P-PM Supplement	Index to Languages and Dialects
PN, PR, PS, PZ	General Literature. English and American Literature. Fiction in English. Juvenile belles lettres
PQ, Part 1	French Literature
PQ, Part 2	Italian, Spanish, and Portuguese Literatures
PT, Part 1	German Literature
PT, Part 2	Dutch and Scandinavian Literatures
Q	Science
R	Medicine
S	Agriculture
T	Technology
U	Military Science
V	Naval Science
Z	Bibliography Library Science

The system is almost infinitely expandable. The principal branches of knowledge represented by the list are subdivided further by the addition of second letters. For example, in section P, Philology and Literature, the additional classifications from A to Z include:

PN	General literature
PR	English literature
PS	American literature
PZ	Fiction and Juvenile Belles Lettres

Each category is further subdivided by the addition of numbers from 1 to

9999. In the category PS, American literature, a partial list of categories is the following:

301-325	Poetry
330-351	Drama
360-379	Prose
400-408	Oratory
409	Diaries
410-418	Letters
420-428	Essays
430-438	Wit and humor. Satire
451-478	Folk literature
501-688	Collections of American literature
530-536.2	By period
537-574	By region

Even further subdivisions are added by the use of a decimal point and more letters and numbers. In PN, General Literature, subcategory 6231, Collections on Special Topics, includes the following headings:

.A24	Accounting
.A28	Adultery
.A3	Advertising
.A4	Aeronautics
.A45	Alphabet
.A5	Animals
.A7	Artisans
.A73	Astrology
.A76	Australia
.A764	Austria

The list continues on to Birds, Blue glass, Boredom, Bundling, and on and on. In fact, the entire list of subject categories covered by the Library of Congress classification system is so vast that it is published in over 30 volumes—enough to take up a good two shelves in any reference collection. The categories are constantly being updated, revised, and refined.

Despite the complexity of the subject listings, the Library of Congress system is quite easy to use when it comes to locating books in the library stacks. A call number such as PN.6110.H8 practically pinpoints a book on the library shelves. All you need to know is what floor PN is shelved on.

USING THE CARD CATALOG

The worst cynicism: a belief in luck.

—Joyce Carol Oates

With a few exceptions, no matter how vast the holdings of any library, no matter how many branches and subdivisions it has, the card catalog is the key to understanding and using it. At Stanford University well over 5 million books and other materials are housed in the main library and some 20 branch and coordinate libraries. Yet the card catalog on the first floor of the main library, together with Stanford's online catalog system, records nearly everything in all the libraries except the one maintained by the Stanford Linear Accelerator Center.

Although nearly all library systems differ from each other in some way, the similarities are so obvious and pronounced that one who masters the card catalog system of one large library is well equipped to use the others with little additional effort. Nonetheless, students should make a point of finding the method used in the libraries they use most often; research will be that much easier.

Author, Title, and Subject Cards

Books are ordinarily listed under one of three headings--author (Figure 1), title (Figure 2), or subject (Figure 3). Often all three kinds of cards are filed in one huge listing; in many other libraries they are separated into author/title and subject catalogs.

The author cards may tell more about a specific book than any other entries in the card catalog, so a search by author is often the best bet. One note, though: authors are usually individuals, but some books are listed by companies, institutions, or government agencies.

A search for a subject listing will be more fruitful the more specific the topic is. For example, look under "astronomy" rather than "science," or even "sun" or "stars." Major headings, like "science," usually have subheadings as well, such as "science—history" and "science—biography" (for important scientists). When looking up topics that involve geographic areas, it is usually best to look up place names first, such as "Tanzania—history" rather than "history—Tanzania." Proper names are sometimes filed as subjects, and one is better off looking for information on, say, Karl Marx by looking up "Marx, Karl" than by looking up "*The Communist Manifesto*" or "Political theory—Communism."

Some libraries catalog series, such as the example in Figure 4. Such series usually include a number of fairly short scholarly books called monographs. Books in such a series may be catalogued under both the name of the individual monograph and the series name.

Sometimes a student will find it simply impossible to locate a subject. This is not difficult to explain, nor is it difficult to solve. Cards in card catalogs may have been written up decades ago, and terminology has often changed since then. For example, to find information on nuclear weapons, the student must look under "atomic." Before World War II some cards on World War I were filed under "The Great War." Furthermore, listings are determined by the Library of Congress subject listings, which may or may not use terms that the student will find familiar. The answer is to look through the Library of Congress listings—not necessarily down to the "blue glass" and "bundling" level, but enough to get some idea of the terms used. For example, what student will look up slang under "cant" unless he or she has been steered there by the Library of Congress listings?

Alphabetizing

As strange as it may seem, there are a good many complexities involved in the alphabetizing of card catalog entries (as well as in the entries of reference books). Here are some of the idiosyncrasies of a typical cataloging system:

1. *By word or by letter.* Two systems of alphabetizing are most often used in catalogs and reference books: word-by-word and letter-by-letter. The difference between them is illustrated by the following example:

Word-by-word	*Letter-by-letter*
News report	Newspapers
News service	News report
News wire	News service
Newspapers	News wire

   In the word-by-word system all the "news" entries are grouped and alphabetized together, but the letter-by-letter system alphabetizes the words as if there were no word divisions. Although letter-by-letter seems simpler at first glance, it actually tends to be more difficult to use than the word-by-word system. Most library card catalogs use word-by-word, but it is worthwhile to double-check.

2. *Abbreviations.* Abbreviations are usually alphabetized as if they were spelled out. That is, "St. Sebastian" appears after "sail" and before "spaghetti." The same holds true with abbreviations such as "Mt.," "Dr.," and "Mr."

3. *Initial articles.* Book titles that begin with "A," "An," and "The," are usually cataloged by the second word of the title.

4. *Foreign-language letters.* Those fascinating letters like *ä, ö, ü, å,* and *ø* may be filed as if they were, *ae, oe, ue, aa,* and *oe.*

5. *Name prefixes.* Names that begin with *Van, Von, de, L',* and so on are often filed as if the prefix is not separated from the main part of the name. *Mac* and *Mc* are sometimes alphabetized as if both were spelled *Mac;* sometimes, all *Mc-* names are alphabetized first, followed by *Mac-.*

The important thing to remember is that if you do not find an entry where you expect to find it, try again. The system of alphabetizing may be the problem.

ENJOYMENT OF FACT

I still find the English dictionary the most interesting book in our language.

—Albert Jay Nock

Even those who have solved the mystery of the card catalog are likely to consider reference collections a hazard, and perhaps a bore. They may be surprised to learn that some people are fascinated by reference books. The late James Thurber once confessed that he enjoyed reading dictionaries. Seán O'Faoláin, the famous Irish writer, wrote of one reference book:

> The most soothing book I know is *Whitaker's Almanack*. When I have spent weeks struggling with a recalcitrant short story; when the Ecumenical Council seems to have lost itself in a Roman fog; when the bottom seems to have fallen out of sterling; or when the Congo, Cyprus, Vietnam, Tibet, Pakistan and Malaysia make me feel that I never again want to hear the word *insoluble*—what a relief to wander among such undeniable facts as that Stoddart hit 485 for Hampstead in 1886, whereas Bradman only hit 452 for New South Wales in 1929–30; to establish the number of theatres in London or the number of colleges in Oxford; to note that in 1918 the Derby was run at Newmarket and not at Epsom; to know where Ammaputtaland is and who runs the magisterial province of Babanango.
>
> For other men a bit of fox-hunting or hot squash would do just as well, but at my advanced age I agree with that famous old lexicographer, Walter William Skeat, that the most pleasant, bloodless sport in life is to hound an innocent fact to its lair. . . . Out-of-the-way knowledge you may sniff? Beneath a writer, you may add? Utterly unimportant, you may conclude? But such minutiae are the very stuff of biography, and, indeed, of science, to which no knowledge is unimportant until we examine it. Had Max Planck not been idly inquisitive enough to wonder (on no evidence whatever) whether radiant energy may come out not in a stream but in bits, like shot-gun pellets, we might never have had the Quantum Theory—or TV.[1]

Writers and trivia buffs are not the only ones who enjoy reference works. Many baseball and golf addicts explore sports record books and the sports sections of general references. *The Guinness Book of World Records* is a continuing best-seller in America as well as in England (where it is published as *The Guinness Book of Records*). Indeed, anyone with a special interest may enjoy poring over a few favorite references.

But such dedication is selective, and librarians are right to complain that most reference books become dusty with disuse. That would not be true if researchers would try to become *whole* researchers, at home with reference sources and with interviews and questionnaires as well, capable of finding facts in a variety of fields and disciplines. Many do not because they feel that only expert reference librarians can pick their way through the vast reference collection confidently. The next section will show that the reference section is not, after all, an insoluble mystery.

HOW TO USE REFERENCE SOURCES

Beware lest you lose the substance by grasping at the shadow.

—Aesop

This chapter emphasizes finding individual facts, a small but essential step in developing knowledge.* The nagging problem in most fact research is that the researcher often does not know how simple the task may be. Surprisingly enough, general sources should often be consulted first. Too many researchers look for the hard-to-find specialized reference when a general source would yield the informa-

---

*This section owes much to the work of Will Rogers, a former reference librarian, and especially to the work of William Allan of the General Reference Department of Stanford University Libraries.

tion more rapidly. All too often one who looks for a fact assumes that no one ever *had* such a research problem before. He or she begins a wild search—and sometimes stumbles upon the answer. More often, the researcher becomes frustrated and gives up. Later, in similar situations, the researcher remembers the frustration and refuses to play the game again.

Consider the literary researcher who hoped to retrace the steps of Mark Twain in Hawaii. Twain had been sent there by the *Sacramento Union* in 1865 to write "lively sketches." In one of his "Letters from the Sandwich Islands" (as Hawaii was then known) Twain mentions a wonderful party at "Sam Brannon's bungalow." The question: Where was Brannon's bungalow? A hundred years had passed, Honolulu had changed, and everyone living in Brannon's time was dead. The odds were against turning up an aged resident who might remember having heard a grandparent say that Sam Brannon had lived here or there. The researcher gave up.

What he failed to do was put the question in its simplest form, state it in general terms. If he had been looking for a living resident of Honolulu, he would have needed only a city directory and a map. He needed no more than that to fix the location of Sam Brannon's bungalow. The City Directory of Honolulu for 1865 lists Brannon and his address, and a map shows the precise location—the bungalow once stood on the site of the present Federal Building in downtown Honolulu.

This example illustrates some central points in library research. First, the question *must* be well defined. In this case, it was; the researcher wanted to know the exact location of the bungalow. Usually, though, librarians are frustrated by vagueness. One points out: "Often, people don't know *exactly* what they want to know because they are vague and hazy about the problem to be solved. Until they can fairly well define what they are after, the professional question-answerer is nearly helpless. Also, people don't want to appear stupid. Most of them don't really mind *being* stupid, they just don't want to appear stupid. So we must somehow elicit exactly what they are after without making them appear stupid."

Reference librarians also stress that researchers should make proper use of what they already know. The Mark Twain researcher failed because he made a problem of history difficult by thinking of it only historically. Had he put it in his own time and used his knowledge and experience, the question would have answered itself.

The following questions suggest that there are clear avenues through the maze of reference sources—and that there are usually several options.

Biographical

Where can one find a brief biographical sketch of John Steinbeck?

This answer is easy to find (the *New York Times Obituaries Index* is one clue) because Steinbeck is so widely known. In other cases of biographical and bio-bibliographical research, however, it is especially important to be specific about who the subject is. Knowing the nationality, occupation, and approximate period during which the subject lived often lightens the task considerably. The researcher can go to the general encyclopedias and biographical dictionaries for bibliographies that lead to more specific and detailed sources.

When did Walter Reed live?

1851—1902

If one does not know that Reed is dead and an American, the first source to check is Hyamson's *Dictionary of Universal Biography* (London: Routledge and Kegan Paul, 1951). The information is also in the *Dictionary of American Biography*. The researcher who knows that Reed is dead and an American might want to use *Who Was Who in America 1897—1960* (Chicago: Marquis, 1942—1960, 5 volumes).

Geographic

Where is Riobamba?

This example illustrates that a general reference is often the quickest source. The *Encyclopedia Americana* will give the answer. So will more specialized sources, such as a detailed index to an atlas.

Literary

What is the origin and significance of the title of Aldous Huxley's book *After Many a Summer Dies the Swan?*

This involves three research problems, the first of which is identifying the line of poetry from which the title was taken. Many literary encyclopedias and handbooks list the line and give its source, but it is usually wise when tracing literary allusions to start with standard works like *Bartlett's Familiar Quotations*. In *Bartlett's* this turns up under the key words "swan," "summer," and "dies." To understand the significance, it is necessary to use *Bartlett's* to find the poem among Tennyson's works (thus solving the second research problem). Then one can consult a classical dictionary of mythology such as *Oxford Companion to Classical Literature* or *New Century Classical Handbook*—and solve the third problem.

The answer: Huxley's protagonist is like the mythical person in Tennyson's poem "Tithonus" (from which the title came), who received immortality from the gods, but not eternal youth, so he became a decrepit old man longing for the sweet release of death.

What was the leading American fiction best-seller in 1959?
Exodus by Leon Uris.

Any question involving a particular year can often be answered through the general yearbooks. The *World Almanac, Information Please,* and the British *Whitaker's Almanack*. Trade journals in the various fields also publish leading statistics (in this case, *Publishers' Weekly*). Much more detail is available in the general encyclopedia yearbooks—the annual volumes that try to summarize notable events in all areas of human endeavor. The *Britannica Book of the Year* for 1960 (the 1959 statistics on publishing are not compiled until after the turn of the year, of course) carries an index item under "Best Sellers." This leads the researcher to an article on "Book Publishing and Sales," which places the answer in a meaningful context.

Where can one find a list of books by David Riesman, author of The Lonely Crowd?

Building bibliographies is hazardous. Few are complete because periodical literature can turn up almost anywhere, and translations into other languages are sometimes unrecorded. (Several of Riesman's books have already been translated into German, French, and Italian.) Thus, the researcher should define exactly what is needed. Supposing that the aim is a list of books in English alone, the printed card catalog of the Library of Congress is a good beginning. Most books by American publishers turn up there. The next step is a methodical search of *Cumulative Book Index*, which is a world listing of books in English. Other steps—searches in the British Museum catalogue, for example—may ensure reasonable completeness.

What is the title and who is the author of the poem in which appears the line, "I am the master of my fate"?
"Invictus" by William Ernest Henley.

Although the floods of poetry written during the last two thousand years make it difficult to find isolated lines in undistinguished poetry, finding memorable lines is usually easy. *Bartlett's Familiar Quotations* and *Granger's Index to Poetry* are the most often used of the hundreds of research tools. *Bartlett's* has an alphabetical *key word* index which places the quoted passage in the main body of the work. Thus, to identify the line, one looks under "master" or "fate" and is guided to the poem. *Granger's*, on the other hand, is a *title and first line* index. "I am the master of my fate" would be listed under "I" if it were the first line of "Invictus." But it is not.

Since many memorable quotations are from great authors or from the Bible, literary researchers should become acquainted with the concordances, which list every occurrence of selected words in a given body of works, along with the location of each occurrence. Thus, identifying a line from Shakespeare, the Bible, or James Joyce requires only referring to a Shakespeare Concordance, a Bible Concordance, or a Joyce Concordance. One should always use the general references first, however. A quick glance through *Bartlett's* or *Granger's* requires little work; finding specific sources through a card catalog ("Milton, John—concordances") takes more time.

Where can one find a review of Margaret Mitchell's Gone with the Wind? New York Times Book Review, July 5, 1936, page 1.

As in the preceding case, one asks simple questions: Where are general-interest books reviewed? Answer: In general magazines and newspapers. Where are these indexed? Answer: In *Book Review Digest, Book Review Index, or Index to Book Reviews in the Humanities.*

Again, one faces the problem of looking through many volumes of *Book Review Digest* to find the appropriate year. The shortcut is the card catalog in a large library (or the printed catalog in a small one), which will carry the date of publication of the book. With the 1936 publishing date, the researcher can go directly to the 1936 volume of *Book Review Digest*, find Mitchell in the alphabetical list, and read the synopsis of reviews for all the leading media.

Law and Government

Where can one find legal comment on the last appeal made by Caryl Chessman?
Notre Dame Lawyer, Volume 32, May 1957, page 522
American Bar Association Journal, Volume 43, August, 1957, page 735.

For the layman, legal research is a jungle, and it is usually necessary to appeal to a reference librarian. The problem is that to find the text of a court's decision and all subsequent references to it, one must go to a reference that reports all appellate cases (those taken to a higher court) to read the case, then "Shepardize" it—search for further developments through a reference series known as *Shepard's*.

Where would you find a biographical sketch of the senior senator from Colorado if you don't know his name?

This could be found with the use of one reference work—*Official Congressional Directory*, issued for each Congress—which includes biographical sketches of the members of Congress. If the researcher seeks information on a specific former Congressmen, *Biographical Directory of the American Congress 1774—1961* is useful.

Where can one find congressional committee hearings?

Recognizing the widespread and deep interest in government publications, officials long ago designated many large libraries as depositories for U.S. documents. In a sense, each depository library is a little Library of Congress which receives the majority of congressional or legislative publications (bills and resolutions, hearings, committee reports, Senate and House documents, journals, debates, laws, and codes) and executive publications which deal with the organization, structure, and administration of the executive branch. These arrive in such volume that government documents librarians have become proud specialists. They can guide researchers quickly to the relevant documents, but only if they know precisely what the researchers want. What hearing of which committee in what year?

Music

What was Johannes Brahms's education and musical training?

The first problem in doing research about composers and musicians is to determine in which branch of music the subject is or was active. This can usually be done easily with the help of a dictionary such as Grove's *Dictionary of Music and Musicians*. For jazz composers and musicians, the best source is Leonard Feather's *Encyclopedia of Jazz*, the greater part of which consists of biographies of jazz celebrities. There are many other sources as well.

Communications

How can I find Nielsen ratings for television programs?

Nielsen is one of the many audience research companies that sell their rating services. Available at first only to clients, Nielsen ratings later are printed, especially in broadcasting trade journals. The broadest research approach is to consult the *Business Periodicals Index* under "Television broadcasting—Program rating."

Where can one find a review of the movie It Happened One Night, starring Clark Gable?
New Republic, Volume 78, May 9, 1934, page 364.
Literary Digest, Volume 117, March 10, 1934, page 38.

To find reviews, one asks first: Where are general movie reviews published? Answer: In general magazines that appeal to the general public. Where are general magazines (*Time, New Republic*, and the like) indexed? Answer: *Readers' Guide to Periodical Literature*, which extends farther into the past then the newer (and more convenient) *Magazine Index*. Now the researcher *could* start back through *Readers' Guide* looking under "Moving Picture Plays—Criticism, plots—single Works" and eventually arrive at 1934 and be able to trace down the reviews. But he or she could save hours by posing another question: When was the movie released? Two books that give such information are *Halliwell's Film Guide* and *Halliwell's Filmgoer's Companion*. There, in alphabetical listings, the researcher would find the date along with the film title. He or she could also use The New York Times Film Reviews.

Science

Where and how does one find the difference between the atomic bomb and the hydrogen bomb?

Such timely and general questions are easy to answer with a standard encyclopedia, and *Collier's Encyclopedia* is especially useful to the layman looking into science. The complete answer—sometimes in specialist's language—will be found in a specialist's tool, a general *science* encyclopedia like *McGraw-Hill Encyclopedia of Science and Technology*.

What scientist headed up the development of the atomic bomb at the Los Alamos Scientific Laboratory (also called "The Manhattan Project")?
J. Robert Oppenheimer.

Since this is a fairly well-defined question on a general subject, the first search should be made in the index volume of a large encyclopedia. There, Oppenheimer is listed as a subentry for both "Manhattan Project" and "Los Alamos." Both articles also give the information that Oppenheimer was director. More complete information on Oppenheimer can then be found under his name.

Business

> *Who was the president of the Bates Shoe Company of Webster, Massachusetts, in 1964, and how many employees worked for the company?*
> Edgar A. Craven; 475 employees.

Virtually every profession and industry is served by a directory that is easy to locate in a library catalog under the appropriate entry followed by "—Directories" (for example, "Physicians—Directories"). *Standard & Poor's Register of Corporations, Directors and Executives* is cataloged under several subject entries, among them "Directors of Corporations—U.S.—Directories" and "Capitalists and financiers—U.S.—Directories."

> *What was the net income of the New York Times for 1963?*
> $1,069,127.

Every company holding stock must make public its financial situation and usually does so in an annual report. Any large business library files many annual reports. More important, since the financial condition of all large companies is newsworthy, salient excerpts from annual reports are published in such papers as the *Wall Street Journal* and the *New York Times*, and many business journals analyze annual reports. Thus, the *Wall Street Journal Index* (which began in 1958) and the *New York Times Index* are prime sources, and so is the *Business Periodicals Index*.

Although these examples barely touch the range of possible questions, they suggest the basic method. They also emphasize the importance of being aware of central sources, many of which are described in Chapters 6 and 7 of this book.

EXERCISES

1. Describe the cataloging system and the card catalog at your library. Does the library use the Dewey Decimal or the Library of Congress system? Is the card catalog divided into subject and author/title catalogs? Is the alphabetizing word-by-word or letter-by-letter? Is there a separate card catalog for the reference room? Does the library use a combination of cataloging systems?

2. Find out why James Thurber and Seán O'Faoláin enjoyed reference books: Try browsing through two or three of the "books of miscellany" listed in Chapter 6, and list an interesting fact or two from each.

3. See how many different ways you can look up the following topics in a library card catalog. For two of the following subjects, look up at least six different citations from different headings in the card catalog, then go to the Library of Congress listings and

find three more headings as well. Look for reference sources under each of the headings from the Library of Congress.

a. Ernest Hemingway's years in France.

b. The history of the advertising industry in the United States.

c. The history of the insurance industry in the United States.

d. The struggle for social justice reflected in Latin American literature.

e. The state of storytelling in the United States.

f. The characteristics of American humor.

g. Toxic chemicals used in the semiconductor industry.

h. Blacklisting in the McCarthy era.

i. Education on U.S. Indian reservations.

4. The section for government documents and archives in various libraries can be an invaluable source for your research on local or federal governments' functions and activities. Consult the government documents for these:

a. What document should you check to know Congress's decision on tax reform?

b. What is the law in your state concerning abortion?

c. How is the city mayor elected?

d. How was the Watergate scandal exposed?

FIGURE 1.   Author Card

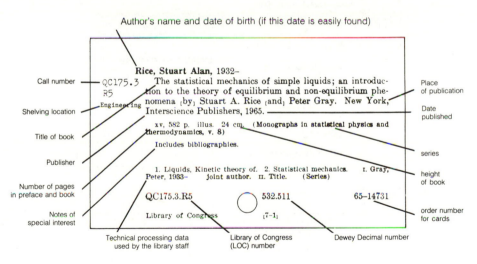

FIGURE 2.   Title Card

The statistical mechanics of simple liquids.

Rice, Stuart Alan, 1932–

QC175.3   The statistical mechanics of simple liquids; an introduc-
R5   tion to the theory of equilibrium and non-equilibrium phe-
Engineering nomena ₍by₎ Stuart A. Rice ₍and₎ Peter Gray. New York,
          Interscience Publishers, 1965.

  xv, 582 p.   illus.   24 cm.   (Monographs in statistical physics and
  thermodynamics, v. 8)

  Includes bibliographies.

  1. Liquids, Kinetic theory of.   2. Statistical mechanics.   I. Gray,
  Peter, 1933–   joint author.   II. Title.   (Series)

  QC175.3.R5   532.511   65–14731

  Library of Congress   ₍7–1₎

FIGURE 3.   Subject Card

LIQUIDS, KINETIC THEORY OF.

Rice, Stuart Alan, 1932–

QC175.3   The statistical mechanics of simple liquids; an introduc-
R5   tion to the theory of equilibrium and non-equilibrium phe-
Engineering nomena ₍by₎ Stuart A. Rice ₍and₎ Peter Gray. New York,
          Interscience Publishers, 1965.

  xv, 582 p.   illus.   24 cm.   (Monographs in statistical physics and
  thermodynamics, v. 8)

  Includes bibliographies.

  1. Liquids, Kinetic theory of.   2. Statistical mechanics.   I. Gray,
  Peter, 1933–   joint author.   II. Title.   (Series)

  QC175.3.R5   532.511   65–14731

  Library of Congress   ₍7–1₎

FIGURE 4.   Series Card

Monographs in statistical physics and
   thermodynamics, v.8.

Rice, Stuart Alan, 1932–

QC175.3   The statistical mechanics of simple liquids; an introduc-
R5   tion to the theory of equilibrium and non-equilibrium phe-
Engineering nomena ₍by₎ Stuart A. Rice ₍and₎ Peter Gray. New York,
          Interscience Publishers, 1965.

  xv, 582 p.   illus.   24 cm.   (Monographs in statistical physics and
  thermodynamics, v. 8)

  Includes bibliographies.

  1. Liquids, Kinetic theory of.   2. Statistical mechanics.   I. Gray,
  Peter, 1933–   joint author.   II. Title.   (Series)

  QC175.3.R5   532.511   65–14731

  Library of Congress   ₍7–1₎

5

Using
Databases

The typical student starting a term paper tackles it like a hiker climbing up a trailless hill without map or compass. Instead of determining the best way to reach the top, the hiker does the first thing that comes to mind—walks straight up, through the brambles and over the rocks, until he or she is tired out. Then perhaps the hiker will think again and find an easier way.

Similarly, students beginning a term paper usually take the course that is most familiar. They usually go straight to the *Reader's Guide to Periodical Literature*. There they will make wild guesses about what topics to look under. Suppose they are interested in literary hoaxes. They might look under "forgeries" and "handwriting analysis," where they will be referred to "graphology," "hoax," and others. Perhaps they will remember, say, Clifford Irving's forgery of Howard Hughes's autobiography and look under "Irving" and "Hughes." Perhaps they will remember the alleged Hitler diaries and look up "Hitler" and "*Stern.*" They will check five or six recent monthly volumes and four or five years of cumulated volumes. Then they will look up the same topics in the card catalog. In short, they will do just what the inexperienced hiker does: head straight for the brambles and try to hack their way through.

As far as it goes, *Reader's Guide* is not a bad starting place for research, though it indexes only general interest periodicals. The researcher who wants to do good research with a minimum of pain, however, is better off becoming acquainted with the great variety of tools available. One of them is the marvelous new tool called database reference services.

LIBRARIES ONLINE

It's always easy to do the next step, and it's always impossible to do two steps at a time.

—Seymour Cray

Online databases—references supplied via telephone line to computer terminals—can save researchers much legwork and grief. Database services are available, often for a fee, in most university libraries in the United States, and they are ever more common in the business community. Even companies not yet plugged into commercial database networks have in-house, private databases. In short, few students can get through both college and their careers without encountering database services.

Commercial database networks usually provide four kinds of databases: bibliographic, like online *Reader's Guides*; directory, which lists names, addresses, telephone numbers, and so on; numeric, providing statistical and other numerical data; and full-text, like online newspapers and encyclopedias. Libraries use bibliographic databases most, but full-text databases are gaining ground.

The first database users were chemists, engineers, and physicians. Dialog, the first database network broad enough in scope to serve the general public, began in 1964, as a service for engineers at Lockheed Missiles and Space Company in California. Dialog "went commercial" in 1972, the same year that Mead Data Central started its LEXIS database for lawyers. Now database networks extend, like long nerve systems, across the country.

Even students who never use database services in college or in their careers will probably meet close cousins of databases in their local libraries. Not only the massive Library of Congress but local public libraries have computerized card catalogs, some developed from already computerized circulation records systems. To call them "computerized card catalogs," however, understates their capacities. Many offer the same kinds of search strategies that database network use, including Boolean logic. The result is a whole new kind of reference tool. Library patrons will find it easier to learn new systems if they know the concepts that computerized card catalogs and database networks share.

Databases offer unparalleled convenience and speed. One librarian estimates that using a bibliographic database can cut academic research time in half. In one test manual and online searches were compared, and of the entire list of relevant articles, the online search identified almost 87 percent of titles while the manual search pinpointed only 37 percent.[1] Furthermore, an electronic search may take less than an hour, whereas a manual search could take days. Outside academia, database users find that pulling two or three newspaper articles or stock quotes or an address off the wire—even printing them "offline" after the database has been disconnected—is much quicker and cheaper than chasing the information down by telephone or driving to the local library. Database networks are also a boon to small libraries that cannot afford to stock little-used specialized references.

Furthermore, the contents of databases are sometimes more extensive or are organized differently than their print counterparts. One version of Dun and Bradstreet's *Million Dollar Directory*, for example, offers—like the print version— annual sales, the number of employees,and primary and secondary SIC Standard Industry Classification) codes, which identify major product areas. But the database also offers the Securities and Exchange Commission disclosure information, which provides a wealth of financial information that is less easy to find.

Databases also tend to be more up-to-date than printed references. True, most databases are updated only as often as their print sources, but such databases as Psych Briefs, PsychAlert, Magazine ASAP, LEXIS, NEXIS, and Newsearch, none of which have direct print counterparts, make abstracts and articles accessible just a few days after periodicals are published.

Not all is rosy. One practical drawback of database is that graphs, charts, and photos are not generally available. Some chemical structures can be depicted online, but so far, graphics are not integrated into most database services. Technology advances with furious speed, however. Optical disk technology, for one, may soon bring database graphics into wider use.

It has long been the pride of libraries to be not just storehouses, but sources, of information. The older goal may have been epitomized by the strong protests of Columbia University librarians when Columbia trustees voted in 1858 to keep the library open for ten hours a week intead of nine. At about the same time John Langdon Sibley, head librarian at Harvard, was hurrying across campus one day when he was stopped by a friend who asked why Sibley looked so happy. He replied, "All the books are in excepting two. Professor Agassiz has those, and I am going after them."

The advent of databases is at least a small step in the opposite direction. The effect of public and academic libraries is to *lower* the cost of reading and to make more books accessible for more people. Database networks, in contrast, are neither free nor cheap. The researcher pays into four pockets: the telephone company's, the telecommunication company's, the database service's, and the database publisher's. Most librarians can only stand by and wring their hands as the searching costs are passed on to the user. And since the libraries usually absorb the cost of staff time, they may offer database services only when librarians consider it necessary which is rarely.

The issue cuts to the heart of public library ideals—that information is "forever free." If a library cannot afford to stock some references and library patrons cannot afford databases, they will have to travel to a larger library or arrange an interlibrary loan. The search will require much more time, and some patrons will have to settle for a lesser source. If the patrons can pay database fees, however, they will cut research busywork.

The impact could be especially pronounced if individual databases supplant printed references. A number of references have been developed to be available only online. Other databases have enhancements that their print counterparts do not. It takes little imagination to picture a lessening in the number of print sources—a small dark cloud, at least, for library users.

Further, database networks hobble any self-reliant researcher. In 1985 training sessions for a typical database network took a full day, with advanced half-day and full-day sessions optional. Once a searcher is trained, it may take two days a month just to keep searching skills in trim. It is cheaper and easier for a researcher to pay for a trained searcher's time, and the result is that the reference librarian is information provider as well as an intermediary.

Moreover, there is a certain educational inertia involved. At one university the undergraduate library is organized so that a student can hardly avoid entering the computer age: It has no conventional card catalog, but only the online card catalog system, called "Socrates." Socrates not only is simple to use but provides such features as a "browse" mode and Boolean commands for searching. One recent afternoon a new student meandered up the library stairs and asked where he could find the card catalog. "We have only Socrates system here," the librarian told him.

"No card catalog" the student asked.

"Not here," the librarian said. "The main library has a card catalog, though."

The student brightened. "Really?" He pointed. The library over there?"

The librarian nodded, and the student wandered happily down the stairs again.

Searches for Students

Barring a noncurious student or two, almost any researcher will find databases tempting. But are they necessary for undergraduate research? To the univeristy administrator stretching this year's budget to cover next year's research equipment, the answer is often no.

In fact, databases are usually *not* necessary for undergraduates. A good-sized library provides all the encyclopedias, books, newspapers, indexes, and magazines that most students will need. In addition, if students need yesterday's news, they can always skim the newspapers and journals. Even political science and journalism students rarely need news so new that it demands online services. Further, a four-page paper does not require 60 references. Finally, even if databases were to become so widespread and popular that they are used often, students would still need to be able to fall back on traditional research techniques—and their professors would want them to be able to do so.

Still, databases are gaining ground in undergraduate research, especially in the sciences. "There's a greater need for currency," one library says. "You're often interested in currently ongoing research." Experimental data also lend themselves to being recorded in machine-readable form, and the vocabulary is more standardized—at least, more manageable—than in the humanities.

Nonetheless, the humanities are catching up. For example, ERIC, the U. S. government's educational database, is an excellent history resource, according to one commentator, who says that "it covers virtually every aspect of the field of education and includes, as well, valuable material on psychology, counseling, testing, and statistics."[2] Further, access to a news wire service is valuable for seeking out news stories that did not reach print, as well as for getting articles that an online index has pinpointed in a newspaper the library does not stock.

Beyond their advantages in research, databases are increasingly becoming part of college curricula because students need to be prepared to use them in the professional world. Take, for example, journalists.

Databases for Journalists Stephen Hess, author of *The Washington Reporters*, once said that the journalists he interviewed for his book used *no* documents in three-fourths of their stories.[3] An occasional hurried telephone call to a reference library may be all a reporter can manage in the face of deadlines. But databases can help reporters prepare for interviews, double-check sources' statements, and add background to news stories despite time pressure.

There are drawbacks, of course: If all reporters use the same databases, their articles will share the same background—and, with "dirty data," the same mistakes. Further, the reporter must rely on the editorial judgment of publishers of such databases as LEGI-SLATE, which takes information from the Congressional Quarterly and the Federal Register. Finally, there is inevitably, the drawback of the cost. Still, database lines are creeping into newspaper offices: The 1985 Directory issue of the *Washington Journalism Review*, for example, devotes several pages to an article that lists ten helpful databases ranging from LEGI-SLATE to the PR NEWSWIRE.

Databases for Businesspeople In businesses, databases take on an almost limitless number of tasks. A consultant says he once used database reference services for an oil company. He compared the patterns of dry holes and wildcat wells and calculated the success rate for individual oil fields; he also compared the surface area of successful oil fields with the amount of oil the fields produced. "Looking at that, you could make an estimate of how much oil was in the basin," he said. "It used to be that the only way to find how much oil was in the field was to ask a geologist." He noted, "You can extrapolate from historical data—looking at what you find probabilistically." That is, one can make an educated guess.

An econometrician does economic analysis based on his own data supplemented with database figures. "An econometrician would want more of what they call time series data—that is, general historical information," the same consultant said. "Say they want to find out what the demand for silk is. The econometrician would take gross national product, some demographics, and so on, and look at the total economy along with more specialized data. A lot of things are correlated with the GNP." The researcher would then compare the figures with a generalized economic model and anticipate demand based on the model.

A more homely example in a single business might be projections of Christmas sales for electric razors, home computers, and toys, based on previous years' sales figures compared with the gross national product, local sales characteristics, and the year's sales.

Training and Costs

Students benefit from knowing how to search databases, but the training and practice costs are prohibitive. In libraries where students have taken classes and training programs to learn to do their own searching, library staff time has skyrocketed as librarians answer the inevitable questions of new users. Having students search even simple databases may seem impractical.

The biggest question, though, is the unavoidable one of who will pay. Some universities subsidize database searches, but the cost is too high to make the trend widespread—yet. As for students, undergraduates in particular may be unable or unwilling to pay even $5 for a library-subsidized search.

Nonetheless, there is hope for student users. Some systems are menu-driven. Some software can simplify log-on procedures, and some can translate commands for one system to suit another system so that the user can get by with learning fewer commands. Some companies put data on hard disks or optical disks that can be updated and shipped to libraries every few weeks, so that patrons can search off line (not through the telephone line) at leisure.

Students can profit from the fact that database services seem prepared to tackle the problems of reaching the potentially large home market. There are several reduced-rate services, such as Dialog's Knowledge Index and Bibliographic Reference Services' BRS After Dark, both of which operate only outside business hours. Such services are being used in universities to encourage students to do their own searches. Both offer fewer databases, of a more general nature, than their full-fledged counterparts. However, both are easier to use than the full-scale, full-rate services: Knowledge Index is menu-driven, and menus are optional on BRS After Dark. There are also a few freebies. Some database networks offer low-cost classroom instruction time; Mead Data Central's Westlaw is actually free to users, although its range is specialized.

DATABASE SEARCHING

No matter what your present condition, there's something a little better right within your reach.

—Irving R. Allen

As one database company spokesman puts it, "Just having the information on a computer doesn't mean it's the answer to all your prayers." Databases provide a far more limited range of options for asking questions than a reference librarian. That is, the computer requires the questioner to adapt to its way of "thinking," while a human being can adapt to the questioner. A student can't simply meander to a computer screen and ask whether a snake has lungs. A reference librarian could probably suggest six different ways to answer such a questions, but a computer would fail.

It makes sense for students to learn about searching and to get hands-on practice. Of primary importance is learning what to expect from a database, including what kinds of questions it can answer and the way a question must be framed. Second, just as knowing French helps when a student wants to learn Spanish, and using an Apple helps one who wants to use an IBM, learning about even a simplified database system helps show how all databases work. In this section we will present a conceptual framework, a model, through which the reader can understand the systems.

One note: In actual database searches, the commands and abbreviations are specific to both the database systems and the databases themselves. The commands for "logging on" vary from one system to another; so do the procedures for moving from one searching step to another.

Fields

Let's start at the beginning. In a database, every item of information tucked in a *file* is stored in a special slot called a *field*. In a directory, some fields might be "name," "street address," "zip code," "telephone number," and "primary SIC code." In a full-text database, fields might be "date," "author," "title," "abstract," and "subject."

The user finds what he or she is looking for by naming any one of the fields. In *American Men and Women of Science*, the user might specify "name," and ask for "Pauling, Linus." The computer would retrieve the file for Linus Pauling, and the user could then look into all the other fields in the Linus Pauling file (such as universities attended, awards won, address, and so on) to get more information. A telephone book works the same way: the searcher looks up a name to find the address and telephone number of the person. Simple, yes?

The main difference between a telephone book and a database is that in a telephone book the name is the only field that can be used to look up information— the only "access field." The yellow pages provide a different strategy: In looking up, say, Automotive Repair to find a mechanic, the searcher is using a subject field to look up names, addresses, and numbers. Similarly, "reverse directories" or city directories, also called "Polk directories" and "Cole directories" after their publishers, are organized by fields other than names. One Polk directory lists addresses along with the names and telephone numbers of residents; another is a numerical list of telephone numbers with names and addresses. One of the Cole directories, for example, lists office buildings with telephone numbers of tenants. All of these are simply reference books organized according to fields other than names.

In a database, though, the user is the one who chooses which field to search. Suppose the user has forgotten Linus Pauling's name but wants information on the scientist who came up with a controversial theory about Vitamin C. The user could look up "Vitamin C" by summoning up the subject field. Print sources cannot provide that convenience.

Boolean Logic and Logical Operators

The next step in learning to search is to understand Boolean logic, that branch of mathematics tagged with the rather intriguing name of its creator, George Boole.

Boolean logic is not difficult to learn. It revolves around three terms—And, Or, and Not. When a searcher uses these terms, called "logical operators," he can request information from several different fields at once, making the search more precise. A search that uses logical operators is sometimes called a multiple-level search.

AND

Suppose a searcher wanted to find how many Lost Lake University graduates are Nobel laureates. He or she would look through a database such as *Who's Who* or *American Men and Women of Science* and would link two fields, "degrees" and "awards," something like this.

Find degrees: Lost Lake University AND awards: Nobel

Suppose the searcher wanted articles on "ping-pong diplomacy" for a paper on how it affected the opening of trade between the United States and China. In looking through a printed index, the searcher would probably look under "U. S. Foreign Relations," then search for the subheading "China." In a database search, that request narrows down to:

Find U. S. Foreign Relations AND China

In a Venn diagram, the request would look like this:

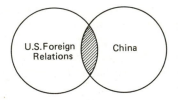

The articles in the overlapping area cover *both* U. S. Foreign Relations and China. On a computer screen, the response might look like this:

14506   U. S. Foreign Relations
 1278   China
   94   U. S. Foreign Relations AND China

The computer has 14,506 articles in the files that list U. S. Foreign Relations, 1,278 articles that list China as a subject, and 94 that list both as a subject. (Notice that articles can be listed as having more than one subject.)

The results from such a request would range from statements by Chairman Mao to articles on Coca-Cola, just as they would in a print index like the *Reader's Guide*. However, in a database search, the request can be made even more specific with an additional level of AND.

Find U. S. Foreign Relations AND China AND Sports

The Venn diagram version is this:

The articles in the shaded area encompass all three subjects.

OR

The command OR adds another level of precision to the database search. For example, a request for "sports" narrows down the number of articles, but it still pulls in articles on the Olympics and many other topics. Yet the searcher would request "sports" because a more specific term, "ping-pong," would bypass articles that used, say, "table tennis" to refer to the same game. The command OR would allow the following request:

Find U. S. Foreign Relations AND China AND Ping-Pong OR Table tennis

A particluarly observant reader might notice the ambiguity in this statement: Does it mean U. S. Foreign Relations AND China AND ping-pong, plus an additional, totally separate subject, table tennis? That search would produce the following results:

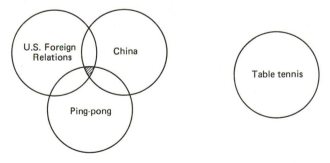

The search has just dragged in the entire gamut of articles on table tennis— tournaments in Florida, paddle-holding techniques, and all—in addition to articles on ping-pong diplomacy.

To solve that problem, the searcher adds parentheses, just as an algebra student would add them to "a × (b + c)," to make the statement clear.

Find
U. S. Foreign Relations AND China (Ping-pong OR Table tennis)

The request produces something like this:

14506   U. S. Foreign Relations
 1278   China
   65   Ping-pong
  271   Table tennis
   21   U. S. Foreign Relations AND China AND Ping-pong AND Table tennis

In short, using OR has both made the search more precise. The search has been expanded to include "table tennis" as well as "ping-pong," yet the search terms have been narrowed from the broader term "sports."

NOT

Another useful command, NOT (or AND NOT), can help strain out extraneous information. For example, when ping-pong diplomacy was at its heights, there was some doubt about whether the United States was going to recognize the government of Red China or that of Taiwan as the official government of mainland China. To strain out any random articles on ping-pong in Taiwan, the searcher could write a request as follows:

Find U. S. Foreign Relations AND (China NOT Taiwan) AND (Ping-pong OR Table tennis)

You might get the following results:

14506   U. S. Foreign Relations
  806   China
  472   Taiwan
   65   Ping-pong
  271   Table tennis
   20   U. S. Foreign Relations AND (China NOT Taiwan) AND (Ping-pong OR Table tennis)

Index Fields

The search for ping-pong diplomacy here is more complex than most database searches, largely because the search involves the subject of the articles, rather than the more predictable fields, like author, title, publisher, company name, address, number of employees, and so on. The ping-pong example, however, does illustrate some aspects of using databases. First, the access field used in the search is one that *describes* article subjects. The field is something like a table of contents for the article, and something like an index. In fact, such a field is often called an "index field."

Think for a moment of the purposes that a book's table of contents serves. First, it lists the topics the book covers. Second, it tells the order in which the chapters are arranged. If the table of contents is detailed, the reader has clues about how the author thinks about the topics, how they are organized, the emphasis that the author gives to different aspects of the book, and so on. The index, though, tells the reader where to find names, specific topics, and minor points that occur in the article. In a database, the purpose of the index field is to list the many different subjects the article touches on—something like a table of contents, but one that does not give clues about the organization of the article.

We have already seen that articles can have more than one topic listed as subject. Take, for example, the following excerpt from a paper on videotex:

> Advertising on videotex could help reduce the cost of the service. PRESTEL pages have two to three lines per page of cross-referencing ("routing") information, and Ceefax, a British teletext system, uses two lines per page for advertisements. Similarly, two or three lines could be dedicated to advertisements on American videotex systems. Classified advertising and a version of "home shoppers," organized to be accessed on demand by the consumer like teletext advertising systems, could also take down subscription costs.

This article clearly gives information on more than just videotex. The subject listing, then, might include not only "videotex," but subsidiary topics, such as:

Advertising
Teletext
Databases
British computer systems

Notice that two of these terms, "databases" and "British computer systems," are not used in the article itself. They are subjects that are discussed within the article—ideas that might prove to be of value to someone doing research on databases or computer use in Britain, or, for that matter, the spread of technology in old-world countries.

Just as an index lists items that may be merely mentioned in articles and books—and lists them because a reader may want to look up a reference to that item—so an index field lists items that may not necessarily be the main topic of the article. True, the searcher may retrieve a few articles that are only peripheral to his or her main topic. The purpose, though, is to make as much relevant information as possible available to the database user.

Controlled-Vocabulary Searching and Thesauri

A second aspect of the ping-pong example is that the searcher must strain out imprecise terms and second-guess what terms will be used to describe the subjects of articles.

The problems may be as minor as differences in spelling. "Ping pong," "ping-pong," and "pingpong" are all potential candidates for indexing terms. By the same token, the paper on videotex might well have been indexed under "videotext." A single letter's variation could keep the article from being retrieved. More likely, though, the problem will arise when entirely different words are used to describe the same topic, like "ping-pong" and "table tennis." One searcher might look for "test-tube babies" when "in-vitro fertilization" is called for, for "foreign relations" when "foreign policy" is the proper term, and so on. The possibilities for confusion are endless.

To counter the problem, database publishers have developed controlled-vocabulary searching. The publishers simply determine what terms will be used for a specific topic, then issue a thesaurus, in which database users can look up which term to use in a computer search. In effect, it is similar to the Library of Congress subject listings; the thesaurus specifies terms under which the topic is filed. The ERIC (Educational Resources Information Center) database, for example, has a very extensive thesaurus, which is based on the Sears subject headings, an offshoot of the Library of Congress subject listings that was designed for smaller libraries.

Free-Text Searching

Controlled-vocabulary searches, since they do involve a limited vocabulary, are effective primarily for index fields. They cannot be used effectively for full-text databases, for abstract text, or for any other fields that use "natural language." The searching technique for such fields that is called "free-text" or "natural language" searching. Free-text searching allows the user to request literally any words, names, and numbers that he or she deems worth looking for.

For example, a searcher may be interested in looking for articles on Humphrey the Wrong-Way Whale, who took a four-week, 40-mile detour into the San Francisco Bay during his northern migration in 1985. No thesaurus would list a subject called "Humphrey the Whale." In that case, the searcher would use an abstract or text as an access field, rather than using the subject. The request could be worded something like this:

Find Humphrey AND Whale

These commands would retrieve articles that have both the word "Humphrey" and the word "whale" somewhere within the text. Using both words along with AND screens out most extraneous articles—articles on, say "Hubert Humphrey" and "Places to Go Whale Watching in the San Francisco Bay Area."

Truncation   In searching for "Humphrey AND Whale," though, the same problem crops up as in the ping-pong diplomacy example: By specifying "Humphrey," articles that referred to, say, "A humpback whale," "A wrong-way whale," or a "confused cetacean" would be left behind.

The same problem often occurs when a single word takes on different gram-matical endings. For example, take the word "taxation." Articles could conceivably be written with "tax," "taxing," "taxable," and so on, and if the searcher used the wrong word in a free text search, he or she would miss worthwhile articles.

Database vendors tackle this problem by *truncation*. To "truncate" means "to shorten," and truncation in database searching is a way to use the root of any word rather than all the possible grammatical versions of it. You can search for any variation of the word by truncating it, thus:

Find: Tax-

The character used to indicate truncation, of course, will vary depending upon the database publisher or vendor. Dialog databases use a question mark; BRS databases, a dollar sign.

Expansion   A second way to check for articles on a given subject is by using the *expansion* feature. Expansion effectively taps into an "instant thesaurus" of indexing terms that database publishers have used in putting the database on line. For the Humphrey the Whale story, for example, an expansion command might display the following list:

Whale
Whales
Whaling
Whale migration routes

Expansion, though, is more limited than a thesaurus: The command usually displays only the alphabetical listings that surround the term requested in the expansion command.

Proximity Searching   The ping-pong example was hypothetical in more ways than one: search items can usually be only one word long. "Table tennis" is two words long, and "U. S. Foreign Relations" is three. Free-text searching however, often involves terms of more than one word. "Tax rate" is one example; so is "fire station," not to mention "Presidential candidate" and a host of others. Multiple-word search items are possible when the searcher uses proximity searching. Words can be linked by a number of commands, depending on the database and the database vendor. Some typical terms might be the following:

Tax ( ) rate
Fire ( ) station
Presidential ( ) candidate

or even

Ping ( ) pong ( ) diplomacy

Free-Text Versus Controlled-Vocabulary Searches

Free-text searching, then allows the searcher to use virtually any database field, and controlled-vocabulary searching focuses on index fields. Which search strategy is "better" depends upon the purpose of the search. According to one librarian's report, free-text searching tends to retrieve articles that mention a specific facet of a topic. Those articles tend to be broader in scope than the search topic. Free-text searching also retrieves articles in which one facet of a topic is assumed but not explicitly mentioned in article abstracts. "Both methods retrieved some unique relevant documents," the librarian wrote. "[Free-text] searches retrieved detail, index code searches [subject searches] retrieved concepts and broad subjects."[4]

In short, the difference between the two searching techniques harks back to the old difference between looking through a table of contents and an index. The table of contents provides an overview of the ideas and concepts the book covers, while an index pinpoints specific terms, names, and topics. Whether the reader looks into the table of contents (controlled vocabulary) or the index (free-text) to find information depends entirely on what kind of information he or she wants. In planning a search strategy for a database, the difference is worth remembering.

Precision Versus Recall

When the search is over and all the relevant articles, abstracts, names, and numbers have been printed off line, a brand-new searcher may find a few surprises.

If the search is bibliographic, the sheer number of articles may be a shock. Not all the articles will be relevant to the searcher's topic. On the other hand, there may be a distressingly small number of references.

The differences between the two results has to do with how precise your search has been. There is a direct relationship between how general the search question was and how wide the search results are. If the search was precise, like the search for articles on ping-pong diplomacy, there will be just a few, probably highly specific articles on just that topic. That is a high-precision, low-recall search. If, on the other hand, the search was for articles on U. S. Foreign Relations with China during a certain five-year span, the number of articles would probably be immense, and only a few of them would discuss ping-pong diplomacy—a high-recall, low-precision search.

A search strategy can be tailored for high-recall or high-precision searcher's (but not both!). The search should be tailored to the searcher's needs. If the searcher wants a fairly small detail to buttress a point, the goal is a high-precision search; if the searcher is starting a lengthy term paper, he or she will need a high-recall search.

In addition, even if a search is quite precise, it is still likely to retrieve a number of irrelevant articles. A researcher who uses a print index automatically screens out irrelevant articles, something the computer cannot do.

On the other hand, no search will retrieve every single relevant article and book. Any search strategy—high or low precision, high or low recall—is likely to bypass perfectly relevant—even excellent—articles, no matter how well planned the search. For example, a controlled-vocabulary search will bypass an excellent relevant paragraph that happens to be peripheral to an article as a whole. A free-text search may pick up that paragraph but miss articles with excellent discussions on the concepts and issues surrounding the subject if the terminology in the article is different from the terms used in the search. (Remember the example on videotex: If an author used the term "videotext," a full-text search for "videotex" would leave that article behind.)

In either case, remember that, on the whole, electronic searching tends to bring up at least as many relevant articles as a manual search.

Print Reference or Database Services?

Clearly, database services provide some vast advantages over printed references. Primary among them, perhaps, is the flexibility that a choice of access fields allows; other advantages include speed, the benefits of searching with Boolean logic, and a greater number of reference services available.

There are also limitations in using databases, however. The questions must be framed so the computer can answer. The money must be paid. And the researcher loses a certain potential for serendipity—fortunate discoveries—when he or she cannot browse. Searching through a book, mulling over its table of contents, and reading selectively, becoming familiar with its organization, convey a great deal of information to a researcher. So does leafing through journals and indexes.

The important thing to remember is that there are many different ways to approach research, many ways to ask questions, and many ways to answer them. Database services are merely another, highly useful reference tool.

EXERCISES

1. Find out what database services are available in your college library.
    a. Does the library subscribe to a database reference service? Does it share a database service subscription with another library? Does the library use any kind of computer/system, even for checking out books? If your library does not offer any database reference service, find the nearest one that does.
    b. Who can use the database services? Can undergraduates do searches themselves? Can they have librarians do searches for them? How often? Who pays? How much does it cost?
    c. Are there plans for increasing the database services available to students?
2. Get a database reference service catalog, such as that of Bibliographic References Services (BRS) or Dialog. Spend twenty minutes or so reading it. Write down the names of some of the databases that you might want to use for a research paper you are currently working on (or did last term), and also write down what you would want to find out from each database.
3. Using Boolean logical operators, write commands for the following bibliographic searches. Assume that you are searching index files. Pretend that you do not need a thesaurus.
    a. Articles on the correlation of the poverty rate and the crime rate in urban areas.

b. Articles on the popularity of bonsai in the United States.

c. Articles on the growth of the database industry.

4. Using Boolean logical operators, write commands for a bibliographic search for a topic that you are currently researching (or a topic you researched last term).

5. Using Boolean logical operators, write commands for the questions in Exercises 3 and 4 but assume that you are using free-text searching.

6. Draw Venn diagrams for each of the searches for which you wrote commands in Exercises 3 and 4.

7. Become familiar with the computer system at the library. Use the computer to locate these:

a. Determine the birth date and birthplace of the Chinese sage Confucius.

b. Who is the author of the American national anthem *The Star-Spangled Banner?*

c. Determine why President Johnson decided to escalate the Vietnam War.

d. Find out the origin of silk making.

e. What does "New Frontier" mean, as John F. Kennedy referred to it during his election campaign in the 1960's.

6

Ready
References _____

In a light article on his research experiences, Tracy Early told of finding in one reference book that Martin Luther King, Jr., earned his Ph.D. at Boston University, in another, at Harvard. For another article, Early said

> I needed to know how many member churches the World Council of Churches had at its founding in 1948. For such information you are not dependent just on the *New Catholic Encyclopedia*, which says 145. Or on the authoritative *History of the Ecumenical Movement*, edited by Rouse and Neill, which says 147. Fortunately, the Council published the official report of the Founding Assembly. So you can get the number from the general secretary's report to the Assembly—150. Or, if you don't mind taking the time, you can turn to the back of the book, where the churches represented are listed, and count them—133.

Wandering into a reference collecion for the first time is enough to strike almost anyone with awe. The sheer amount of information, the bewildering variety of the references, and the scholarship they represent, may shock a fledgling researcher into a calf-like belief that the books, somehow, can be *trusted*.

That is not the case. As vast and imposing as the number of reference books may be, the researcher should also consider the limitations of even the most painstaking compiler of reference sources.

For example, the researcher should be aware that the editors of the august *Encyclopaedia Britannica* sometimes assign the writing of *Britannica* biographical articles to friends of the subjects. Similarly, the *Britannica* editors sometimes assign articles about business firms to those who control them. Frederick R. Kappel was Chairman of the Board of American Telephone and Telegraph Company when he wrote an article on AT&T. Also the article on the Federal Bureau of Investigation was once written by "J.E.H." The late J. Edgar Hoover certainly knew the organization he directed, but one could wish for an authority with a more detached perspective.

The *Who's Who* volumes suffer the same kind of problem: the biographical sketches therein are dependent on information supplied by the biographees.

The researcher who remembers that all those who write, compile, and edit reference books are subject to certain influences and errors is a researcher who understands sources. At the same time, he or she must be also realize that most reference sources are produced by specialists whose ambitions and goals may push them as close to an objective state as humans are likely to reach.

What is the proper attitude toward reference collections? Certainly not to regard them suspiciously, although estimates are sometimes wrong, practices questionable, limitations insurmountable, and sources in disagreement. Just as the awe of the beginner is inappropriate and injurious, so is cynicism. A researcher working with reference sources should simply remember that all books, including reference books, are made by people.

THE "INFORMATION EXPLOSION"

> I find that a great part of the information I have was acquired by looking up something and finding something else on the way.
>
> —Franklin P. Adams

Beyond the fact that research books are made by human beings, there is also the fact that, as with humans, there seem to be a lot more of them around than there used to be.

Even ten years ago Constance Winchell's *Guide to Reference Books* listed a bewildering 7,500 references, and estimates of scholarly journals ranged from 200,000 to 600,000. Now, the number of reference works is burgeoning, thanks to technology that, among other things, allows publishers to store and update reference materials on databases, then typeset them without having to re-keyboard the information. The "information explosion," a term coined not many years ago, applies well to reference libraries.

The result is that the researcher is likely to be able to find information much faster, and find much more of it, with much less effort—as long as he or she learns just a bit about *how* to do so. The listings of reference books that follow in this chapter and the next contain some of the reference standards and some of the most promising of the many sources available. There's no need to stop with this list, however; you should use it to find further directions for your research.

The following terms are used often in reference research and appear throughout this and the next chapter.

Abstract   A summary, usually quite brief, that sketches the essential points of a book, pamphlet, article, thesis, or other writing. Unlike a digest, it does not pretend to convey all, or even most, of the points of a work—just the major conclusions.

Almanac   This word has two meanings. (1) An annual publication containing a calendar, frequently accompanied by astronomical data and other information. (2) An annual book of statistics and other information, sometimes limited to a particular field.

Annotation   A note that describes, explains, or evaluates, or all three.

Archives   This term has two meanings. (1) An organized body of records. (2) An institution that preserves particular records.

Atlas   A book of maps, engravings, and tables, with or without descriptive text.

Digest   A condensation, sometimes quite brief, of a written work, sometimes in words other than those of the original. In law, a *digest* is a systematic summary of laws, cases, and decisions.

Gazetteer   A geographical dictionary.

In press   Anything that is in the process of being printed.

In print   Publications available from the publisher (as distinguished from those out of print, which may be available from another source but are no longer sold by the publisher).

Monograph   A scholarly book, usually comparatively short, written on a limited area of research. It may or may not be part of a series.

Periodical   A publication with a distinctive title intended to appear in successive numbers at scheduled or regular intervals. Most periodicals contain articles by several contributors. Librarians do not consider newspapers as periodicals and do not catalog them as such. Nor are periodic memoirs, proceedings, and journals of societies cataloged among periodicals.

Serials   Any publications (including periodicals, newspapers, proceedings, reports, and numbered monographs) published indefinitely.

Standard   A work recognized as having permanent value.

In the following lists, the notes reading *1942–*, *1956–*, and so on indicate that the sources so identified are not single or irregular publications but have been issued continually since that date.

WORDS

The difference between the right word and almost the right word is the difference between a lightning bug and lightning.

—Mark Twain

Unabridged Dictionaries

Oxford English Dictionary on Historical Principles
   Sir James A. Murray. Oxford: Claredon Press, 1888-1933. Reprinted, 1961, in 14 vols. plus supplement. Supplement vols. I, II, III issued in 1972, 1976, 1982, and 1986.

The O.E.D., as it is known to professors, graduate students, and those faking erudition, represents the most compelling feat in dictionary making. (Confusingly, it is also know as N.E.D., for "New English Dictionary.") It shows when, how, and in what form each word has come into the language and the changes in spelling, meaning, and usage. The history of each word is illustrated by a series of quotations ranging from its first known occurrence in the written language to its latest usage. In short, the O.E.D. tells more about the English language than many of us would care to know.

In 1986 Oxford issued the fourth of a four-volume supplement to the massive 1933 main dictionary. In the meantime, technology has caught up with the O.E.D.: its editors plan to put the entire 14-volume work—and the four-volume supplement—online. With luck, the supplement and main dictionary can be integrated.

The dictionary makers of Oxford have also started a telephone service called Oxford Word and Language Service (OWLS) to answer the queries of puzzled Britons. OWLS has been a fruitful idea, judging from the wide response it has received. One billboard painter, for example, set down his brush in midstroke to confirm that "accommodation" has two m's before returning to his work.

A *Dictionary of American English on Historical Principles*
> Edited by William A. Craigie and James R. Hulbert. Chicago: University of Chicago Press, 1936-1944. 4 vols.

William Craigie's great *Dictionary of American English*, which is known as the D.A.E. might be described as the colonial equivalent of the *Oxford English Dictionary*. The O.E.D. must be consulted for the full history of any word that originated in the British Isles, but for the many words of American origin (which are marked with a plus sign), this dictionary is excellent, if a bit dated. It shows when, how, and in what form each word has come into the American version of the English language, and gives all changes in spelling, meaning, and usage. Compiling it took 40 years.

Webster's Third New International Dictionary of the English Language
> Springfield, MA.: Merriam-Webster, 1981.

Until *Webster's Third* appeared in 1961, "controversial" was a word one looked for in, rather than associated with, a dictionary. The editors of "the Third" took a risky new direction: They decided to *describe* each word as it was currently used, rather than *prescribe* the way that experts said the word should be used. The *Third* appalled traditionalists.

The oldest and most famous American dictionary, *Webster's* had found its way to editors' desk throughout the publishing business. However, many a newspaper editor jumped off the bandwagon when the third edition appeared, switching to Simon and Schuster's *New World Dictionary*, or sticking with Webster's second edition.

By other measures, though, Merriam-Webster's gamble paid off. The *Third* is the dictionary most often used in book publishing—it is recommended in the *Chicago Manual of Style*, the premier book publishing stylebook—and the concept of keeping up with language as it changes, rather than prescribing its use, is reflected in numerous other dictionaries.

Shorter Dictionaries

Webster's Ninth New Collegiate Dictionary

Frederick C. Mish, Editor-in-Chief. Springfield, MA: G. & C. Merriam Company, 1984.

The *New Collegiate* is the desk-size version of the controversial *Webster Third*. The editors of the *Ninth New Collegiate* have added extensive usage notes for selected words, and entries now include the date a word first appeared in print, a feature unique among American dictionaries. Even so, some grammarians may be less than pleased. Here, for example, is how *Webster's Ninth New Collegiate* describes the usage of "comprise" (as opposed to "compose"):

> *usage*   Although it has been in use since the late 18th century, sense 3 [compose, constitute] in still attacked as wrong. Why it has been singled out is not clear, but until comparatively recent times it was found chiefly in scientific and technical writing rather than belles lettres. Our current evidence shows a slight shift in usage: sense 3 is somewhat more frequent in recent literary use than the earlier senses. You should be aware, however, that if you use sense 3 you may be subject to criticism for doing so, and you may want to choose a safer synonym such as *compose* or *make up*.

Webster's New World Dictionary of the American Language
> David B. Guralnik, Editor-in-Chief. Cleveland: Simon and Schuster, 1984. Second College Edition.

Newspapers flocked to the *New World*, which is published by Simon & Schuster, after Merriam-Webster brought out the controversial third edition of Webster's in 1961. According to Simon & Schuster, the *New World* is used by the *New York Times*, the *Los Angeles Times*, *The Wall Street Journal*, and the Associated Press wire service. It is recommended in the 1984 edition of the *Associated Press Stylebook*, a journalistic standard.

The *New World* is strong on Americanisms. It was the first dictionary to list origins and explanations of American place names. All the entries, including names of people and places, and placed within the main body of the dictionary, so the reader need not search through appendices to find, say, "Corpus Christi."

American Heritage Dictionary
> Boston: Houghton Mifflin, 1982. Second College Edition.

A prestigious array of contributors and consultants helped produce this 1568-page volume. The entries give contemporary meanings of the word first, "with the other shades of meaning following logically from this current central concept." Those who applaud the *American Heritage Dictionary* for its readability will be even happier with this edition's many well-written usuage notes.

Specialized Dictionaries

New-Word and Slang Dictionaries

Dictionary of American Slang
> Compiled and edited by Harold Wentworth and Stuart Berg Flexner. New York: Thomas Y. Crowell Company, 1975. Second supplemented edition.

The more conventional dictionaries, once chiefly concerned with the language spoken by taste-makers, long left a wide field to the collectors of informal English. The field is narrowing because these days fewer lexicographers sniffily dismiss slang in a few offhand words. There is still room, though, for scholars like

Wentworth and Flexner. As they write, "Slang is best defined by a dictionary that points out who uses slang and what 'flavor' it conveys." In other words, look to the lexicographer who really cares.

Wentworth and Flexner cast a wide net, terming all slang used in the United States as "American," regardless of its country of origin or use in other countries. They define it: "American slang is the body of words and expressions frequently used by or intelligible to a rather large portion of the general American public, but not accepted as good, formal usage by the majority."

> *The Second Barnhart Dictionary of New English*
> New York: Barnhart/Harper & Row, Publishers, 1980.

Published three years ahead of schedule because of the proliferation of new words, this book is an update of *The Barnhart Dictionary of New English Since 1963.* Entries give the year of earliest ascertainable use, along with quotations and notes on word origin. British words are also included.

> *Dictionary of Slang and Unconventional English*
> Eric Partridge. Edited by Paul Beale. London: Routledge & Kegan Paul, 1985. Eighth edition.

The late Eric Partridge was the Noah Webster of flavorful English. He published the first volume of this controversial collection in 1937, afterwards publishing dictionaries of the underworld, of catch phrases, and of clichés, as well as such tomes as *A Chamber of Horrors: Officialese, British and American.* For British slang, Partridge's *Dictionary of Slang and Unconventional English* is unrivaled. American slang, though, is limited to words transplanted to the British Isles.

> *The Jonathan David Dictionary of Popular Slang*
> Anita Pearl. Middle Village, NY: Jonathan David Publishers, 1980.

Words are listed and defined, unfortunately without notes on origin and usage. This is more up-to-date than Wentworth by five years, though far less extensive.

Abbreviation and Acronym Dictionaries

> *Abbreviations Dictionary*
> Ralph de Sola. New York: Elsevier Science Publishing Co., 1981. Expanded international sixth edition.

The publishers thought well enough of this book to bring out six editions. It is the reference to use when an article leaves the researcher awash on a sea of capitals.

> *Acronyms, Initialisms, & Abbreviations Dictionary*
> Ellen T. Crowley and Helen Sheppard, editors. Detroit: Gale Research Co., 1984-1985. Ninth edition. 3 vols.

To keep the set up-to-date, the editors produce these volumes in a bewildering variety of editions and parts that are published in subsequent years. Volume 3 is a valuable reference dedicated to *reverse* acronyms. If a researcher needs to find the proper abbreviation for some long-handled term like the Office of the Assistant

Administrator for Research and Development for the United States Department of Health, Education, and Welfare, he or she will find it here—OAARD for the HEW. There is also an international version of the same reference.

Thesauri

A thesaurus is what writers use when they have a word that almost fits but can't think of the exact word they want. Before 1852, when Peter Mark Roget (row-*jay*, with a soft *j*) brought out his first book of synonyms and antonyms, thesauri were rudimentary lists or words, hard to use and small in scope. But Roget, a British doctor of wide interests and talents, gave new life to the idea by developing a usable system that categorized the words according to their meaning.

Using today's thesaurus is easier than using Roget's original version, but it still involves looking up "the word that almost fits" in an index in the back of the book, finding the number of the category in which "the word that fits" is likely to be, then turning to that section in the main thesaurus. Traditional thesauri provide cross-references as well, which users, by most reports, find exasperating.

Roget's International Thesaurus
    Robert L. Chapman. New York: Harper & Row, 1984. Fourth edition.
    Proclaiming their book "The Classic, Standard, Definitive" Roget's thesaurus, the publishers of this book say that it "remains faithful to the original system . . . put forward by Dr. Peter Mark Roget in the nineteenth century." The thesaurus catalogs 256,000 words and phrases, making it more comprehensive by some 100,000 words and phrases than any other traditional thesaurus.

Webster's Collegiate Thesaurus
    New York: G. & C. Merriam, 1976.
    Fearful that readers will find Roget's system hard to use, several publishers have produced thesauri arranged like dictionaries. *Webster's Collegiate Thesaurus* is one of them. A dictionary-style thesaurus works much like the index of a Roget-style thesaurus: You look up the word that's almost right and search for synonyms. Like dictionaries of synonyms and standard thesauri, Webster's lists antonyms and opposing words. It also lists slang. The synonyms for "razz," for example, include "raspberry," "bazoo," "bird," "boo," "Bronx cheer," "catcall," "hiss," "hoot," "pooh," and "pooh-pooh."

Webster's New Dictionary of Synonyms
    Springfield, MA: Merriam, 1978. Second edition.
    A thesaurus jogs the writer's memory; a dictionary of synonyms feeds the writer's vocabulary. Compare "dodge" in *Webster's New Dictionary of Synonyms* with "dodge" in *Webster's Collegiate Thesaurus*: In the dictionary, the entry describes the meanings of dodge, parry, sidestep, duck, shirk, fence, and malinger, with examples of usage, in 54 lines; in the thesaurus, the six synonyms appear, along with eight other related words, in less than three lines.

FACTS

To treat your facts with imagination is one thing, but to imagine your facts is another.

—John Burroughs

Encyclopedias

The makers of encyclopedias are futility's traveling companions. Like Bacon, they try to make all knowledge their province. They fail. It is nonetheless true that anyone who can read is in their debt. Even though a researcher must go far beyond an encyclopedia for a detailed examination of almost any subject, the encyclopedia is still the place to go for first principles. Most encyclopedias rely on authorities, and most of those authorities are well chosen. The clue to using an encyclopedia is this: It is a good place to start, but a bad place to end.

Encyclopedias, of course, are inevitably behind the times. Unlike databases, they cannot be updated quickly. The major companies—Britannica, Americana, Collier's and others—publish yearbooks to fill in the lag between new editions. Such yearbooks carry obituaries for the year and chronological indexes of the year's events. The *New International Yearbook* features an excellent list of leading national and international "Societies and Organizations," giving the founding date, president, and current address for each.

Although at least two encyclopedias are available online, the *Academic American Encyclopedia* and the *Encyclopaedia Britannica*, library users can expect to continue to use the print counterparts. *Academic American Encyclopedia's* entries are short, averaging only about 300 words—perfect for, say, a small business that may need quick access to a reference source, but not extensive enough for many student papers. The *Britannica*, (printed version) by special arrangement, is not available to libraries.

Encyclopedia Americana
New York: Americana Corp. (a division of Grolier, Inc.), 1985. International edition. 30 vols.

The *Americana* is not the American counterpart of the *Britannica*. Both are published in the United States; both try to cover the world of knowledge. Nevertheless, the *Americana* may be considered appropriately titled because of its attention to American places—some of them quite small—organizations, and institutions. This focus and an unusual collection of articles on the histories of the centuries of mankind make the *Americana* distinctive and valuable. Like the *Britannica*, the *Americana* issues an extraordinary useful index volume that enables a researcher to winnow subjects and find the right volume rapidly. It also publishes a yearbook, *The Americana Annual*.

Encyclopaedia Britannica
Encyclopaedia Britannica, Inc. Chicago: Benton, 1979. Fifteenth edition. 30 vols.

Today's *Britannica*, the fifteenth edition, is markedly different from previous versions because of its new three-part structure. A two-part *Propaedia* provides an "outline of knowledge," the *Micropaedia* gives a brief overview of selected topics, and the *Macropaedia* provides more extensive treatment of other topics. The three-part structure has had decidedly mixed reviews.

Chamber's Encyclopaedia
   London: International Learning Systems, 1973. New Revised edition. 15 vols.
   Although the British perspective is obvious in many passages, this 15-volume set ranks with the best of our encyclopedias in its usefulness to Americans. Comprehensive, international, accurate, it has grace and clarity that sometimes make the writing in American volumes seem limp.

Collier's Encyclopedia
   New York: Collier-Macmillan, 1983. 24 vols.
   Collier's Encyclopedia is resolutely modern. It is so bright with large print and many illustrations and so attentive to today (sometimes scanting yesterday and the day before) that many scholars refuse to rank it with the *Britannica* and the *Americana*. Putting the bibliographies in the index volume instead of attaching them to the appropriate articles is tidy, but inconvenient for the reader. Nevertheless, *Collier's Encyclopedia*, which is supplemented by *Collier's Encyclopedia Year Book*, is useful and authoritative—often used by reference librarians, one said, because it is so "fact-conscious."
   Jerome K. Miller compared *Collier's Encyclopedia Americana, Encyclopaedia Britannica* (third edition), *World Book Encyclopedia*, and *Academic American Encyclopedia*. On the basis of copyright entries, he found *Collier's* the best for "nitty-gritty" information, with the *Encyclopaedia Britannica* best for historical information.

Desk Encyclopedias

The New Columbia Encyclopedia
   New York: Columbia University Press, 1975. Fourth edition.
The Concise Columbia Encyclopedia
   New York: Columbia University Press, 1983.
   Designed for high school students, adult laymen, and most of those between the two groups, the *Columbia Encyclopedia* is the handiest quick-reference book available. Nonetheless, the volume is about the size and heft of an unabridged dictionary, so in 1983 the Columbia University Press produced a streamlined version called *The Concise Columbia Encyclopedia*. Though the entries are shorter and less numerous than in the full-fledged version, they are up-to-date as of January 1, 1983.

Lincoln Library of Essential Information
   Buffalo, N Y: Frontier Press, 1982. Forty-second edition. 2 vols.
   Little-known except to librarians and others who specialize in general research, this collection was organized for self-education, but it is also an excellent research tool. A bit superficial for anyone who wants information in depth, it is

nonetheless a useful source in literature, fine arts, music, education, and biography.

Yearbooks and Almanacs

Information Please Almanac
   Boston: Houghton Mifflin, 1947–. Annual.
This is the book to consult for the curious fact, the odd detail. Some of the information presented in other almanacs is also here, but the editors have been so imaginative in selecting areas to cover that *Information Please Almanac* can be used as a supplement to almost any book of facts. It features broad, useful coverage of statistics in geography, U. S. government, and general biography.

The World Almanac and Book of Facts
   New York: Newspaper Enterprise Association, 1868–. Annual.
Perhaps the most often-used reference in the United States, this is a deservedly famous mine of miscellany. It is not, of course, "complete"—no reference book deserves that adjective—and research specialists can name more comprehensive sources in almost any field. As a general rapid-reference tool, however, *World Almanac* is invaluable.

Foreign Yearbooks and Almanacs

The Europa Year Book
   London: Europa Publications, 1959–. Annual.
Once a loose-leaf compilation, this source is now issued annually in two compact volumes. Information on the UN, its agencies, and other international organizations is followed by detailed information about each country of the world arranged alphabetically in each volume, giving an introductory survey, a statistical survey, the government, constitution, religion, press, publishers, radio and TV, finance, trade and industry, transportation and tourism, atomic energy, and a brief list of universities.

Whitaker's Almanack
   London: Whitaker, 1869–. Annual.
This British counterpart of the American *World Almanac* covers the world but its British origin shows, especially in its detailed focus on orders of knighthood, Members of Parliament, tables of British rulers, and the like. The statistics on Great Britain and the Commonwealth are excellent.

Canadian Almanac & Directory
   Toronto: Copp Clark Pitman Ltd. 1847–. Annual.
Unlike the almanacs of infinite scope, this one is resolutely Canadian. Within these limits, it is satisfyingly comprehensive. Little of the wide range of Canadiana has escaped this net—from "abbreviations" to "zoological gardens."

Atlases

The Times Atlas of the World
   New York: Times Books, 1980. Comprehensive edition.

There is no shortage of atlases to provide detailed maps and statistics on the countries of the world. *The Times Atlas* is merely one of the best known of them. The comprehensive edition has 123 beautiful and clear maps and a 227-page glossary; the same publisher produces more specialized atlases, such as *The Times Atlas of the Oceans, The Times Atlas of World History,* and others.

National Geographic Atlas of the World
    Washington, DC: National Geographic Society, 1981.
This is another good general atlas which provides coverage of major cities, political boundaries, and geographic characteristics of nations, and gives such additional information as the temperature and rainfall for selected areas and thumbnail descriptions of countries.

Books of Miscellany

The Guinness Book of Records
    Compiled by Norris and Ross McWhirter. London: Guinness, 1985. Thirty-first edition.
What is the longest place name? That of a hill in New Zealand called Taumatawhakatangihangakouauotamatea (turipukakapikimaungahoronuku) pokai-whenuakitanatahu, of course. What woman holds the record for the most spouses in a monogamous society? Mrs. Beverly Nina Avery, a Los Angeles barmaid, who was married to fourteen different men, five of whom, she alleged, broke her nose. These are the kinds of facts that fill *The Guinness Book.* First published in England in 1955 to serve as a Guinness promotion piece in pubs (where drinkers are forever betting on mosts, leasts, longests, shortests, etc.), it has become the best-selling reference book in England and one of the best-sellers in the United States (where it is titled *The Guinness Book of World Records*).

Famous First Facts
    Joseph Nathan Kane. New York: Wilson, 1981. Fourth edition.
A surprisingly popular reference work when it was first published, *Famous First Facts* went into a supplementary edition when the author learned of other firsts; then the original and the supplement were tied together in one volume. The first occurrence of almost anything can be found here: athletic feats, discoveries, inventions, and bizarre incidents.

The American Book of Days
    Compiled and edited by Jane N. Hatch. New York: Wilson, 1978. Third edition.
This is a book-calendar of celebration and commemoration, including religious and historical holidays, birthdays of famous Americans, local festivals, and unexpected information on such anniversaries as the first balloon ascent. The researcher can get at entries in two ways: by topic through the index, or by day of celebration through the day-by-day arrangement. Originally compiled by George William Douglas, published in 1937, this edition has been revised, updated, and expanded. It includes the birthdays of presidents as recent as Jimmy Carter.

Book of Days: A Miscellany of Popular Antiquities

Edited by Robert Chambers. Detroit: Gale Research Co., 1967. Reprint of 1862 edition. 2 vols.

A view of customs and holidays, primarily in Britain, this volume is arranged according to the calendar (with a helpful index). It is excellent for finding out-of-the-way information, and for browsing.

The Book of Festivals
   Dorothy Gladys Spicer. Detroit: Gale Research Co., 1937. Republished 1969.

The title is a bit misleading. Dorothy Spicer is concerned here primarily with religious feasts and folk festivals that spring from church holidays. There are enough church-oriented holidays and feasts described, though, to cause one to wonder how Europeans get anything done. An abridged edition, *Festivals of Western Europe*, was published in 1958 (New York: Wilson).

A Guide to World Fairs and Festivals
   Frances Shemanski. Westport, CT: Greenwood Press, 1985.

Not exhaustive, but useful, this book includes musical, artistic, religious, folkloric, and cultural as well as religious festivals.

PEOPLE

If you want to understand democracy, spend less time in the library with Plato, and more time on the buses with people.

—Simeon Strunsky

Biographical Dictionaries and Indexes

Dictionary of American Biography
   Edited by the American Council of Learned Societies. New York: Scribner's 1928-1981. 20 vols., index, and supplements 1-7.

Widely known as the greatest of all American biographical dictionaries, the D.A.B. has been called "an assessment of what the American people have thus far accomplished in all fields of endeavor." Scholars, divines, politicians, authors—every American is sketched who satisfies two requirements: the person must have made a significant contribution, and the person must be dead. J .G. E. Hopkins abridged this giant set in 1964, producing the *Concise Dictionary of American Biography*. Its third edition, which includes a supplement covering 1951–1960, was published in 1980.

Biography and Genealogy Master Index
   Detroit: Gale Research Co., 1980. Second edition. 8 vols.

What looks like page after dreary page of single-spaced names in tiny type—it *is* page after dreary page of single-spaced names in tiny type—is in fact a valuable guide to further information. The eight volumes of the second edition list 3,200,000 citations of famous people both alive and dead in over 350 biographical references that range from *Who's Who in America* to the *Oxford Companion to the*

Theatre. The 1984 supplement alone added 370,000 citations to the number. Also available: *Performing Arts Biography Master Index, Historical Biographical Dictionaries Master Index,* and *Author Biographies Master Index.*

Biography Index
New York: Wilson, 1946–. Quarterly.
The researcher who has always leaned heavily on *Reader's Guide* should take a good look at *Biography Index.* It will provide a wealth of information that *Reader's Guide* simply does not offer. Though it is limited to information on persons, it has an overwhelming scope, indexing biographical material and articles in current books and in 2,600 periodicals.

Current Biography
New York: Wilson, 1940–. Monthly.
Anyone who is prominent in the news of the day may be sketched in the informal word portraits that make up *Current Biography.* (Many of the biographical articles provide pictures as well.) The monthly issues are cumulated in annual volumes called the *Current Biography Yearbook.*

A Dictionary of Universal Biography: Of All Ages and of All Peoples
Albert M. Hyamson. New York: E. P. Dutton, 1951. Second edition Reprinted, 1981. Detroit: Gale Research Co.
Albert Hyamson measured out his life in the three-by-five index cards that pulled together this excellent source. He wrote upon completing the first edition: "The largest biographical work in existence has not a tithe of the entries which this volume contains." Hyamson had reason for pride, but this is not a biographical dictionary in the conventional sense. Unlike the long articles in *Chamber's Biographical Dictionary* (New York: St. Martin's Press, revised edition, 1974), which cover the great of all nations and all times, most of Hyamson's "biographies" are single-line entries made up of name, birth and death dates, nationality, profession, and the reference source that gives full information. Without detracting from the value of Hyamson's work, it is fair to say to that he provides a thumbnail of fact and a guide to more comprehensive biographies.

National Cyclopedia of American Biography
New York: White, 1982-1980.
This series, the most comprehensive American reference source, indexes not only biographical articles, but also names, institutions, events, and other items mentioned in the biographies. Its 1980 volume was the final volume under the current publisher and was a compilation of all the data remaining in the editorial files.

Dictionary of American Negro Biography
Edited by Rayford W. Logan and Michael R. Winston. New York: Norton, 1982.
To be one of the elite 600 people listed in this reference, one must have died before 1970. Nonetheless, the book is extremely well written and filled with detail, and reference sources for each of the signed articles are given with each entry.

International Dictionary of Women's Biography
    Compiled and edited by Jennifer S. Uglow. New York: Continuum, 1982.
Once published as the *Macmillan Dictionary of Women's Biography*, this reference contains brief biographies of over 1,500 prominent women, both alive and dead. The focus is on women of the Western world.

Index to Women of the World from Ancient to Modern Times: Biographies and Portraits
    Norma Olin Ireland. Westwood, MA: F. W. Faxon, 1970.
Women sometimes get short shrift in biographical sources, and this book is one step toward rectifying the matter. It indexes almost a thousand biographies of women who lived throughout recorded history.

New York Times Obituaries Index
    New York Times, 1970 and 1980. 2 vols.
This is an important tool—two cumulated indexes to the obituaries that have appeared on the obituary pages of the *Times*. The first volume covers 1858-1968; the second, 1969-1978.

Books of Quotations

Bartlett's Familiar Quotations
    John Bartlett. Boston: Little, Brown, 1980. Fifteenth edition.
Commonly known as *Bartlett's*, this famous source lists sayings and writings of ancient and modern speakers and authors from 2000 B.C. to the present. Its arrangement—chronological by author—is irritating and mystifying, but the comprehensive index is helpful. Those not familiar with this work may think that using it is like solving a puzzle, but the phrase they want may be *somewhere* within those 1,540 pages.

Home Book of Quotations: Classical and Modern
    Compiled by Burton E. Stevenson. New York: Dodd, Mead, 1984. Tenth edition.
A comprehensive collection of more than 50,000 quotations, arranged alphabetically by subject. The author index gives the full name of the person quoted, birth, and death dates, and references to all quotations cited. *Stevenson*, as it is known among librarians, is more comprehensive than *Bartlett's*.

PUBLICATIONS

Book Publishers

Literary Market Place: The Directory of American Book Publishing
    New York R. R. Bowker. 1940–. Annual.
This business directory of American book publishing is so much more than such an identification suggests that it cannot be described concisely. It lists publishers, their addresses, and chief publishing house officers and editors, and it identifies publishers by specialty. *Literary Market Place* also lists literary agents,

literary awards and prizes, book clubs, data processing services, clipping bureaus, and almost any other agency or service useful in placing, promoting, and advertising literary property.

There is also an *International Literary Market Place*, also annual, that includes the publishers, book trade organizations, major booksellers and libraries, and so on, of some 160 countries, along with such useful information as banking and shopping hours, language, currency, and religion.

Books Lists

Books in Print
New York: R. R. Bowker. Annual. 10 vols.

Books in Print is a standard, often-used reference on books currently available from their publishers. Books are listed by author (3 vols.), title (3 vols.), and subject (4 vols.). There is also a *Forthcoming Books*.

United States Catalog and *Cumulative Book Index* New York: Wilson, 1928, and 1928–.

United States Catalog lists all U. S. Books in print as of 1928. *Cumulative Book Index* takes up the same task at that point and lists books in print up to the present. Both are useful in locating titles, publishers, prices, and publication dates.

American Book Publishing Record
New York: R. R. Bowker.
    Cumulative 1876-1949. 1980. 15 vols.
    Cumulative 1950-1977. 1978. 15 vols.
    1979–, annual.

This is a comprehensive guide to books published from 1876 to last week, compiled from the Library of Congress listings that Bowker has published since 1876. If there is a fact you need about any book ever published in America, this is the place to find it. It lists, in over 30 volumes, the titles, facts of publication, and occasionally a brief description, of almost all American books. The most recent entries start with the *Weekly Record* of Library of Congress listings, which are cumulated into monthly and then yearly volumes.

Paperbound Books in Print
New York: R. R. Bowker, 1955–. Biennial. 3 vols.

PBIP, as it is known to librarians and publishers, indexes currently available paperbacks ranging from classics to those hastily written tales designed for travelers who need something to do while airborne so they won't have to think. With author and title entries plus a selective subject index, this source has everything but a sexy cover.

Publishers Weekly
New York: R. R. Bowker, 1955–. Weekly.

This is a basic source for locating books published too recently to be listed in sources published at longer intervals. The weekly issues also announce the forthcoming publication dates of important books. In addition to alphabetical listings of books (with title, publisher, date of publication, edition, and price), *PW* contains general information about book publishing.

Guides to Book Reviews

Book Review Digest
New York: Wilson, 1905–.

This book review guide provides both condensations of reviews and suggestions for further reading. It focuses on almost 90 English and American general periodicals, all but ignoring *avante garde* magazines and the literary quarterlies. Within these limitations, *Book Review Digest* does first-rate work, skillfully condensing critical opinion and guiding the researcher to many reviews of books. *Book Review Digest* is one of the best places to go when you are writing a paper on literature, from it, you can find what other, professional critics thought of a work and, from that, sharpen your own comments.

Book Review Index
Detroit: Gales Research Co., 1965–. Annual.

This is more comprehensive than *Book Review Digest* because it indexes reviews from some 450 publications. It does not digest or quote reviews. *Book Review Index* started as a monthly, then became a bimonthly, and began annual publication in 1969. The citations are indexed by the name of the authors whose works are reviewed.

An Index to Book Reviews in the Humanities
Williamston, MI: Phillip Thompson, 1960–. Annual.

Like *Book Review Index*, this volume cites reviews under the name of the author of the book, but it indexes many more reviews, covering some 700 popular and scholarly journals.

Newspaper, Magazine, and TV News Indexes and Lists

Editor & Publisher International Yearbook
New York: Editor & Publisher, 1920–.

The international sections are slender, but this annual does offer some data on newspapers over the world. What it does extraordinarily well is to list daily newspapers of the United States and Canada and to provide basic information about them: circulation, advertising rates and regulations, key personnel, and line upon line of other information.

The same company issues the handiest key to information about syndicates, *Editor & Publisher Syndicate Directory*, and annual supplement to *Editor & Publisher* magazine. Syndicates are listed with the features they sell, features are categorized by subject with the name of the author and the syndicate for each, and authors are listed with their features and syndicates.

IMS/Ayer Directory of Newspapers and Periodicals
Fort Washington, PA: IMS Press, 1864–.

Known throughout the world of journalism as *Ayer's*, this volume is unique. Some of the material is duplicated elsewhere, but no other reference carries this much data. It covers the United States, Canada, Puerto Rico, Bermuda, the Virgin Islands, and the Philippines, trying—and failing by only a little—to list geographically all the daily and weekly newspapers and magazines and to provide the skeletal framework of fact and figure that will enable the researcher to see the publication in its local context.

Facts on File
New York: Facts on File, Inc. Weekly, with annual bound volumes.

This current encyclopedia of events, which is combined in a loose-leaf file, culls the news of the day from many metropolitan daily newspapers. The researchers who compile and compress the record of events work day by day, issue reports weekly, and manage to retain their sanity and perspective throughout. The indexes cumulative, making it unnecessary to consult more than two in any year.

Magazine Index
Belmont, CA: Information Access Corporation.

This index is one of the most useful references available to the general researcher. It is available in many libraries in microfilm form, and through Dialog as a database, and despite the awkwardness of the microfilm format, it is well worth using because of its comprehensiveness. It indexes about 400 different general readership magazines and cumulates five years of references. That means that, instead of searching through five successive cumulations of a print index like the *Reader's Guide* for each topic (in addition to the latest monthly issues), you need search only once per subject topic. The index is ordinarily issued twice a month. The same company produces a *Trade and Industry Index*, and both the indexes have database counterparts called, respectively, *Magazine* ASAP and *Trade and Industry* ASAP, which provide the full text of many periodicals online 24 hours after their publication.

National Newpaper Index
Belmont, CA: Information Access Corporation.

One of the drawbacks to printed newspaper indexes is that they are devoted to a single newspaper. They also take months to appear in print. The *Newspaper Index*, which is available online as well as on microfilm, indexes The *New York Times*, *The Wall Street Journal*, the *Christian Science Monitor*, the *Washington Post*, and the *Los Angeles Times*. The index is updated about once a month, and in the meantime, *Newsearch*, another online index, provides a daily update. *Newsearch* covers not only the *National Newspaper Index*, but *Magazine Index*, the *Trade & Industry Index*, and *Legal Resource Index*.

New York Times Index
New York. New York Times, 1851.

This is a semi-monthly subject index to the issues of the *Times*. Finding an item in the index is occasionally an adventure, but this is a valuable guide to the

Times. It helps date events and thus often helps researchers locate reports on the same events in other newspapers that are not indexed. The *London Times Index, The Christian Science Monitor Index,* and the *Wall Street Journal Index* are all excellent guides to reports that have appeared in those papers.

> *Poole's Index to Periodical Literature, 1802–1906*
>   Boston: Houghton Mifflin, 1891. Revised edition. 2 vols. 5 supplements,
>   1887-1908.

W. F. Poole, a student at Yale, deplored the fact that the information in American magazines was inaccessible because there was so much of it. Judged by current standards, this pioneer index, which is limited to subject entries, is weak. But it indexes periodicals dating from 1802 and is virtually the only research tool of its kind for the nineteenth century.

> *Public Affairs Information Service Bulletin*
>   New York: PAIS, Inc., 1915–. Annual

Somewhat similar to the better-known *Readers' Guide,* PAIS has a loftier standard. It indexes selectively by subject (from about 1,400 periodicals, selected books, pamphlets, federal, state, and city publications, and reports of public and private agencies) materials concerning what is broadly defined as "public affairs."

> *Reader's Guide to Periodical Literature*
>   New York: Wilson, 1900–.

Reader's Guide, as it is widely known, indexes the contents of almost 200 general magazines. Most student researchers make a beeline for this source when they enter a library. This is a pity: The *Reader's Guide* is valuable, but it does not include some high-quality magazines. Published eighteen times a year, it is issued also in other paperback cumulations and finally in annual bound volumes. *Nineteenth Century Readers' Guide to Periodical Literature* (New York: Wilson, 1944) indexes 51 periodicals of the last century, primarily in the 1890s.

> *Willing's Press Guide*
>   East Grinstead, West Sussex: Thomas Skinner Directories, 1874–.

For a careful overview of the British press, this annual is recommended. It provides much the same kind of detailed information on the British press that *Editor & Publisher International Yearbook* provides on the American press.

A service somewhat similar to that provided by *Willing's* is *Benn's Press Directory* (London: Benn Bros., 1946–), which is also an annual.

> *Television News Index and Abstracts*
>   Nashville, TN: Vanderbilt Television News Archives, Vanderbilt University,
>   1972–. Monthly.

Since August 1968 Vanderbilt has collected on videotape the evening news broadcasts of the three major television networks. The collection, which is available at $15 per hour, is known as the Vanderbilt Television News Archive. It also includes related programs, primarily documentaries on major news events. In January 1972 the Archive began issuing *Television News Index and Abstracts* as a guide to the videotape collection. This is an indispensable source for research in network television news broadcasts. Except in unusual instances, neither videotapes nor scripts are available from the networks.

Guides to Government Publications

The U. S. government is such a prolific publisher—the largest in the world—that many government workers are frustrated by sheer volume and have trouble locating the more obscure books and pamphlets that carry the proud imprimatur: Washington, D. C., Government Printing Office. The Bureau of National Affairs, a private concern, takes advantage of the confusion by selling to government agencies publications that index and summarize government publications.

It is nonetheless true that there are several handy keys to the masses of government publications. They are needed, because most government-published books and pamphlets cannot be found in lists of books in print, and not all of them are listed in library card catalogs.

(General references on government and political science—some of them issued by the government—will be found in the next chapter.)

Monthly Catalog of United States Government Publications
    Washington, DC: Government Printing Office, 1895–.
This catalog, the most comprehensive list of current publications, was started in 1895, though it has had several title changes since then. The *Catalog* is indexed annually, and there are cumulations every five years.

Subject Guide to Major United States Publications
    Ellen P. Jackson. Chicago: American Library Association, 1968.
This 175-page volume lists hundreds of the government publications that researchers have found most useful.

Government Reports Index
    Springfield, VA: National Technical Information Service.
This semimonthly index covers reports produced by government agencies, government-funded consultants, and research projects funded by grants. It is supplemented by *Government Reports Announcements*, which abstracts the reports.

A *Descriptive Catalog of the Government Publications of the United States*
    Compiled by Benjamin Perley Poore. Washington, DC: Government Printing Office, 1885. 2 vols.
This source, commonly called *Poore's* after its editor, covers government publications from September 5, 1774, through March 4, 1881. It almost catches up with the *Monthy Catalog*. The years between the two publications are bridged by John Griffith Ames's *Comprehensive Index to the Publications of the United States Government*, which is known simply as *Ames*.

Statistical Abstract of the United States
    Washington, DC: U. S. Department of Commerce. Government Printing Office, 1878–. Annual.

This is a digest of data collected by all the statistical agencies of the U. S. government and some private agencies. Another Government Printing Office publication, *Historical Statistics of the United States, Colonial Times to 1970* (Washington, DC: Government Printing Office, 1975), is helpful for early records.

In 1967 the U. S. Bureau of the Census began issuing biennially a handier supplement titled *Pocket Data Book*, 300 to 400 pages of the central information on this country.

EXERCISES

1. If you are a typical human being, you will probably not want to use references unless you are already familiar with them. This exercise will familiarize you with where they are located. Look up one of the references listed in each of the sections of this chapter: unabridged dictionaries, shorter dictionaries, specialized dictionaries, thesauri, encyclopedias, desk encyclopedias, yearbooks and almanacs, foreign yearbooks and almanacs, atlases, books of miscellany, biographical dictionaries, books of quotations, book publishers, book lists, guides to book reviews, media indexes, and guides to government publications. Describe the location of each—for example, *"The Times Atlas* is in the far corner behind the globe on the second floor in the oversized book bookshelf, third from the top." Humdrum as this exercise may seem, it will make you much more inclined to use a broader scope of references as you continue in your college studies.

2. Find as many different sources as you can for the following bits of information. Stop when you reach twelve or one half hour, whichever comes first. Try not to badger the reference librarian.
   a. The number of books Ernest Hemingway wrote.
   b. The U. S. Gross National Product for 1985.
   c. The year nylon was invented.
   d. The total population of Rhode Island.
   e. The number of square miles (*or* square kilometers) of land in Sudan.
   f. The number of gallons (*or* liters) of water that flow from the Amazon each year.
   g. The birthplace of singer Sarah Vaughn.
   h. The broadcast frequencies used for television (remember, you do not have to report what the frequencies are—just tell where to find them).
   i. The wingspread of the world's largest moth.

3. Compare a U. S. yearbook or almanac with one of the concise encyclopedias listed in this volume—*Lincoln Library of Essential Information* or *Concise Columbia Encyclopedia*. What are the major differences between the two sources? Is the yearbook significantly more up-to-date than the encyclopedia? What different kinds of information do they cover? For example, which provides the better coverage of population statistics for the United States? Which has more information on national monuments? Finally, write down what kind of information you might generally expect to find in a yearbook compared with the concise encyclopedia.

4. Find the Magazine Index in your library. Look up articles on two of the following topics and count the number of citations you find. If there are more than 40, write down the subheading(s) you checked and make an estimate of the total number of citations.

a. The tobacco industry
b. Tariffs on cars imported into the United States
c. Tourism (any specific area)
d. Semiconductor industry
e. Learjets
f. Nobel prize winners.

Next look up the same two topics in the *Reader's Guide to Periodical Literature*. You need consult only the two latest bound volumes. List the subheadings you checked. Which of the two indexes will you use for your next research paper?

If your library does not subscribe to *Magazine Index*, substitute the *New York Times* index or another newspaper index for *Magazine Index*. Answer this question: What kind of information am I likely to find in a newspaper article that I would not find in one of the magazine articles listed in *Reader's Guide*? What would a magazine article tell me that a newspaper article probably would not?

5. Each member of the class must turn in the name of his or her favorite dictionary. Choose three dictionaries from the compiled list and examine all three. Write a one-page report on the one you prefer.

6. Find a book of quotation collections, and look for:
   a. Thomas Jefferson on "freedom of the press."
   b. Mark Twain's maxim on "human nature."
   c. "A minute's success pays the failure of years."
   d. "Literature is printed nonsense," by August Strindberg.
   e. Aristotle's saying: "A good style must have an air of novelty, at the same time concealing its art."

7

Sources for Specialized Fields

Modern librarians are there to help, but a librarian finds it difficult to help those who are not certain what they want to know. Sally Drew, former chief reference librarian of the Redwood City (California) Public Library, said that library patrons sometimes ask for material on impossibly broad subjects. Once, she was asked by a patron:

"Where are all your books on houses?"

"What would you like to know about houses? How to build them? How to decorate them? The history of houses?"

"Ah, gee, I don't know. I'll have to think about that." The patron walked away, looking distracted.

The library provides an almost unlimited number of answers for those who can ask specific, or at least appropriate, questions. Yet the process of developing specific questions is one that takes practice and thought. A research question is by nature fairly broad. As Chapter 3 describes, the writer seeks information on a topic for the purpose of focusing more and more closely into a thesis. The question, "Why would anyone want to use videotex?" is typical of research questions—it is broad and thus would be difficult to answer directly in a library.

The skill that makes a curious student into an expert researcher is that of framing specific questions with which to answer the broader research question.

To take another example, suppose the student wants to compare the history of the Amazon with the development of the American west, hoping, perhaps, to draw from it some predictions for the future of the Amazon. The research question, "How does the development of the Amazon parallel the development of the American west?" is much too broad to tackle in a library. Instead, the student must ferret out specific facts that will give the answer to the broader question—such questions as "How good is Amazon land for farming?" "How easy is it to get land in the area?" "How rich or educated or influential are the people who do get the land?" Then the student can track down answers to these more specific questions and use the kaleidoscope of data to better understand the situation in the Amazon.

Once the researcher begins to zero in on specific questions, he or she can take advantage of the rich variety of sources available in any library. Even small libraries may be bigger than they seem if the researcher approaches the question creatively.

For example, city directories and telephone directories are mines of unused information, much of it valuable. The typical city directory lists address, telephone number, head of household, occupation, employer, and spouse (or whether either spouse is deceased) and indicates ownership or co-ownership of business firms. Preceding the main body of information are facts and figures on the city, such as area, bank debits, bonded debt, automobile registrations, and the like. Following the main body, typically, are listings by address, alphabetically by street, then a "numerical telephone directory" listing all the numbers of an area and giving the name of the party to whom each number belongs. Thus, having only an address, or only a telephone number, one can learn much more.

A Central Intelligence Agency official once admitted just how helpful a telephone directory can be to a researcher who knows how to use it creatively. The official commented that telephone directories were hot items on both sides of the Iron Curtain. Studying directories of military camps and nearby cities reveals much to a perceptive analyst, including dispositions of units and classifications of forces. Sociologists have traced immigration and emigration by analyzing the names that appear over a period of years.

Even those who seek precise information may be unaware of how many different kinds of specific questions libraries can answer. Local libraries in particular carry copies of local ordinances, laws, community studies, and agendas of local board meetings. A library may have lists of special book collections in its area, descriptions of local public service organizations, clubs, recreational opportunities, and information on local residents who have special talents. The range and volume usually depend on the degree to which reference librarians clip and file newspaper items, but most public libraries try to serve as headquarters for community information.

This chapter provides references for a long list of topics—references that, if they are not in a specific library, can at least point to some directions a researcher might take to track down an elusive fact. With a bit of practice and a bit of imagination, the researcher can find answers to virtually any research question.

REFERENCES FOR THE HUMANITIES

In every child who is born, under no matter what circumstances, and of no matter what parents, the potentiality of the human race is born again.

—James Agee

Art and Architecture

Some Leading Journals

Apollo. London: Apollo Magazine Ltd. Monthly.
The Art Bulletin. College Art Association of America. Quarterly.
ARTnews. New York: ARTnews Associates. Monthly, September-May; quarterly, June-August.
The Burlington Magazine. London: The Burlington Magazine Publications, Ltd. Monthly.
Progressive Architecture. Cleveland: Reinhold Publishing. Monthly.

Encyclopedia of World Art
    New York: McGraw-Hill, 1959-1968. Revised printing, 1972. 15 vols, with 1983 supplement.
The publisher devoted ten years to bringing out these volumes, for good reason. This is not so much a set of books as it is a museum containing 7,000 full-page plates and hundreds of essays that embrace all of humanity's greatest achievements in the visual arts through the centuries. This is the leading historical synthesis in the world of art.

Oxford Companion to Art
    Edited by Harold Osborne. New York: Oxford University Press, 1970.
Like the other Oxford companions, this volume aims to cover a broad field in relatively few pages. Like the others, too, it is authoritative and readable.

Index to Reproductions of American Paintings
    Lyn Wall Smith and Nancy Dustin Wall Moure. Metuchen, NJ: Scarecrow, 1977.
What can a researcher do when articles on art compare works and comment upon them? Without reproductions, the articles are next to useless. Smith and Moure's excellent reference source makes it possible to find works of U.S. artists reproduced in books and catalogs of annual exhibitions in art museums. The book also covers pictures in permanent collections.

Dictionary of Architecture and Building
    Russell Sturgis. New York: Macmillan, 1901. Reprinted, 1966, by Gale Research Co.
This three-volume classic describes famous buildings, sketches the architecture of many countries, and carries biographies of architects. Although its 1901 publication makes it seem far out of date, specialists say the historical value is high, especially because these volumes may be nicely supplemented by Banister

Fletcher's *History of Architecture,* which has proved its worth by surviving through eighteen editions (New York: Scribner's, 1975).

For more recent architecture, try *Highlights of Recent American Architecture* by Sylvia Hart Wright (Metuchen, NJ: Scarecrow, 1982). Finally, for such modern topics as fire protection and facilities for the handicapped, a good choice is *Encyclopedia of American Architecture* by William Dudley Hunt, Jr., F.A.I.A. (New York: McGraw-Hill, 1980).

Dance and Theater Arts

Some Leading Journals

Dance Magazine. New York: Dance Magazine, Inc. Monthly.
Drama: The Quarterly Theatre Review. London: British Theatre Association. Quarterly.
The Encyclopedia of Dance and Ballet
  Mary Clarke and David Vaughan. New York: G.P. Putnam's Sons, 1977.
This reference is ten years newer than *The Dance Encyclopedia* (New York: Schirmer, 1967) and *The Complete Guide to Modern Dance* (Garden City, NY: Doubleday & Co., 1967), and it is an excellent source of information on choreographers and individual dancers of the modern dance style.

Art Index
  New York: Wilson, 1929—. Quarterly, with annual cumulations.
This series indexes over 200 international publications on the following topics: archaeology, architecture, art history, city planning, crafts, films, graphic arts, industrial design, and on and on. You never knew the word "art" could mean so much.

American Art Directory
  Edited and compiled by Jaques Cattell Press. Federation of American Artists. New York: R.R. Bowker, 1984. Fiftieth edition. Biennial.
First published in 1898, this leading directory carries information on museums, associations, art schools, publications, scholarships, and fellowships. It covers both American and Canadian art.

The New-York Historical Society's Directory of Artists in America 1564-1860
  George C. Groce and David H. Wallace. New Haven: Yale, 1957.
This comprehensive volume provides a long look into the artistic past, with information on 11,000 artists of all descriptions.

Annals of the New York Stage
  George C.D. Odell, New York: AMS Press, Inc. 1927-49. Reprint of 1927 edition.
  15 vols.
Despite the growth everywhere of Little Theatres, drama guilds, and theater workshops, New York has always been the American drama capital. Odell's painstaking labors are thus valuable, at least for antiquarians. From playbills, pamphlets, autobiographies, from yellowing letters, diaries, and account books, he has

recreated the rich history of American drama from the beginning to 1894.

The Best Plays Of . . .
New York: Dodd, 1899—. Annual.
This annual reference appears shortly after the close of each theater season and, in addition to abridging the texts of "the ten best," lists statistics, awards, long runs, and other facts that excite the passions of drama buffs.

The Oxford Companion to the American Theatre
Edited by Gerald Bordman. Oxford: Oxford University Press, 1984.
Actors, issues, theater groups, theater personalities, and a great many of the significant plays of American theater history are among the topics treated in *The Oxford Companion to the American Theatre*. Not to be confused with *The Oxford Companion to the Theatre* (Oxford, 1983, fourth edition), another one of Oxford's mammoth one-volume references. *The Oxford Companion to the American Theatre* takes an original, entirely different approach to the theater of Britain's biggest cousin.

The Entertainment Media

Banned Films: Movies, Censors, and the First Amendment
Edward de Grazia and Roger K. Newman. New York: R.R. Bowker, 1982.
A law professor who successfully defended *I Am Curious Yellow* and an historian who writes biographies of civil libertarians could hardly be more qualified to write a book on first amendment rights. This narrative discusses the many issues associated with censorship and the film industry. A second section details 122 of the many films that have been banned or threatened with banning in the United States.

Catalog of Copyright Entries, Cumulative Series: Motion Pictures, 1894-1912, 1912-1939, 1940-1949, 1950-1959
Washington, DC: Government Printing Office, 1951-60. 4 vols.
These lists enable the researcher to determine when particular movies were released and to find the source of a movie based on a book. Other information on thousands of motion pictures is available here.

Library of Congress National Union Catalog: Motion Pictures and Filmstrips
Washington, DC: Government Printing Office, 1953-1972.
Library of Congress National Union Catalog: Film
Washington, DC: Government Printing Office, 1973—.
These series pick up where *Catalog of Copyright Entries* leaves off.

Halliwell's Film Guide
Leslie Halliwell. New York: Charles Scribner's Sons, 1983. Fourth edition.
This is the successor to *Halliwell's Filmgoer's Companion*, which went through six editions. It is an alphabetical list of American film titles with such basic information as the country and year of origin, film company, director, stars, and film size in millimeters. There is also a pithy, usually nasty, synopsis and review. A typical entry, for *National Velvet*, reads:

Children train a horse to win the Grand National. A big bestseller from another era; its flaws of conception and production quickly became apparent.

International Motion Picture Almanac
  Edited by Richard Gertner. New York: Quigley Publications, 1929—.
The saving quality of this diverse service is that it carries information on movies and the movie industry that is not available elsewhere. One can mine from these pages data on an aspect of motion pictures that is usually hidden: the corporate structure, including organization and personnel, distributing services, circuits, and organizations.

Movies Made for Television
  Alvin H. Marill. New York: New York Zoetrope, 1984. Revised edition.
Calling made-for-TV movies the successors of the "beloved" Grade-B movies, the author has compiled basic information like credits, date and network of airing, run time, and synopsis, and has organized them in chronological order according to the dates of their first showings.

New York Times Film Reviews
  New York: Times Books, 1970, 1971—. Biennial.
Some of the best film reviews in the nation are reprinted here, complete with photos, from the *New York Times* files. The 1970, six-volume version of this work included reviews from 1913 to 1968. From 1971 on, the works have been published every other year, and the publishers promise continued supplements.

History

Some Leading Journals

American Historical Review.
  Washington, DC: American Historical Association. Five times per year.
  Journal of American History. Bloomington, IN: Organization of American Historians. Quarterly.
  Journal of Modern History. Chicago: University of Chicago Press. Quarterly.

Dictionary of Events
  Compiled by George Palmer Putnam. New York: Grosset & Dunlap, 1936.
Putnam's work—a bare-bones guide to the past—begins at 5,000 B.C. and works its way forward to 1936. Only a certified antiquarian would want to *read* this; many others will find it useful. For another 37 years' worth of the same kind of information, try the *Dictionary of World History* (London: Nelson, 1973).

Documents of American History
  Edited by Henry Steele Commager. New York: Appleton-Century-Crofts, 1973. Ninth edition.
"Properly speaking," Commager writes, "almost everything of an original character is a document: letters, memoirs, ballads, folklore, poetry, fiction, newspaper reports and editorials, sermons, and speeches, to say nothing of inscriptions, stamps, coins, buildings, painting and sculpture, and all the innumerable memori-

als which man has left in his effort to understand and organize the world." Commager offers this list to indicate the impossibility of including all the important documents. But he need not have been apologetic. If this book is incomplete, it is nonetheless the best available guide to primary sources in American history.

> *Encyclopedia of American History*
> Edited by Richard B. Morris. New York: Harper & Row, 1982. Sixth edition.

Although there have been many challengers over the years, this remains the handiest single work endeavoring to summarize and revitalize the facts of the American experience.

> *Guide to Historical Literature*
> Edited by G.F. Howe and others. New York: Macmillan, 1961.

For three decades it was necessary to get along with the 1931 edition of this guide. The 962-page 1961 edition is a careful survey of the entire range of historical writing. Compiled by many experts, the *Guide* points up the best books for scholars, students, and laymen.

> *The New Illustrated Encyclopedia of World History*
> Edited by William Leonard Langer. New York: Abrams, 1975.

The latest edition of this work, which went through five editions before it became the present, illustrated version, is basically a series of outlines running from prehistoric eras to the middle of the twentieth century. It is so neatly compiled that a researcher can find any important historical event that occurred at any time in any part of the world.

> *The Times Atlas of World History*
> Edited by Geoffrey Barraclough. Maplewood, NJ: Hammond, 1978.

The complexities of world history are presented in clear, colorful maps and charts, accompanied by running text. Shepherd's *Historical Atlas* (William R. Shepherd. New York: Barnes and Noble, 1964, ninth edition) is similarly useful. Long the most-used historical atlas, it reaches back to 2,000 B.C. and forward to 1964.

Literature

Some Leading Journals

> *College English.*
> National Council of Teachers of English. Urbana, IL. Monthly (September-April).
> *ELH (English Literary History).* Johns Hopkins University. Quarterly.
> *Modern Fiction Studies.* Lafayette, IN: Purdue University, Department of English. Quarterly.
> *Philological Quarterly.* Iowa City: University of Iowa. Quarterly.
> *PMLA: Publications of the Modern Language Association of America.* New York: Modern Language Association of America. Six times a year.

More than one English student has slipped through college by writing opinion alone. But when a literature student interprets a work, nothing succeeds like background information and additional critical opinion. The following references will provide the former, and the references listed in Chapter 6 under "Guides to Book Reviews" will provide the latter. All these references are well worth looking up, mulling over, and incorporating into literature papers.

The Cambridge History of English Literature
Cambridge: University Press, 1907-33. 15 vols.

These fourteen volumes (the fifteenth is an index) sketch English authors and their work and defines literary allusions and fictional names from the time of *Beowulf.* A third edition of a companion, *Concise Cambridge History of English Literature* (1970), extends the reach by assessing recent literature, including that written in the United States and the Commonwealth countries. Written by George Sampson, the almost 1,000 pages of this volume make it seem concise only by comparison with the basic set. Its sparkle is indicated by Sampson's assessment of Henry James: "painfully explaining the farthest reaches of the obvious."

The Oxford History of English Literature
Oxford: Clarendon Press, 1979.

These thirteen volumes give a concise picture of English literature dating back to the Norman Conquest up to the modern period. They intend to satisfy the immediate curiosity of the common reader quickly, easily, and clearly. They also direct the reader to find the further sources of information about English literature. These volumes contain "a comprehensive list of English authors, literary works, and literary societies which have historical or present importance."

The Oxford Companion to American Literature
James D. Hart. New York: Oxford University Press, 1983. Fifth edition.

This is the Western hemisphere version of *The Oxford Companion to English Literature,* beloved by college students everywhere. The faint flavor of condescension apparent in many British surveys of American literature is absent here. The definitions and descriptions of American literary schools and movements are especially acute. The aim throughout has been to treat the tides of literature concisely, but it is difficult to find anything properly describable as scant.

The Oxford Companion to English Literature
Compiled and edited by Margaret Drabble. Oxford: Oxford University Press, 1985. Fifth edition.

Primarily a compendium of brief articles on English authors and their writings, the fifth edition of this one-volume reference suffers from inevitable overexpansion: its readers are now referred to *Brewer's Dictionary of Phrase and Fable* (Harper & Row, 1981) for the identification and explanation of allusions and fictitious names. Still, the book is useful for both specialists and laymen.

Contemporary Authors
Detroit: Gale Research Co., 1962—. Semiannual.

This series provides information about many authors whose biographies are not published in other sources—over 75,000 authors in all. Beginning in 1982 *Contemporary Authors* has been available in the original form and in a New Revised Edition, which includes only entries that have been updated since the previous volume was published. Entries for both editions are indexed. Also available since 1984: *Contemporary Autobiography Series*.

> *Index to Black American Writers in Collective Biographies*
> Dorothy W. Campbell. Littleton, CO: Libraries Unlimited, 1983.

The trek through *Contemporary Authors* will be much easier with the aid of this slim volume, which lists nearly 2,000 black American writers. The book gives not only bare-bones information, but references to many information sources.

> *A Bibliography of Criticism of Contemporary Chicano Literature*
> Compiled by Ernestina N. Eger. Berkeley, CA: Chicano Studies Library Publications, University of California, 1982.
> *A Decade of Chicano Literature (1970-1979): Critical Essays and Bibliography*
> Edited by Luis Leal and others. Santa Barbara, CA: Editorial La Causa. Dist. by Presidio Books, Goleta, CA, 1982.

One of the trickier problems that researchers of minority literature face is how to find the names and works of, and criticism for, the newer and less prominent of the authors. These references will help immeasurably. The *Bibliography of Criticism* is a comprehensive, though not exhaustive compilation of unannotated references—over 2,000 entries. A *Decade of Chicano Literature* lists almost every creative work published in the last decade by Chicanos and includes some of the more noteworthy critical literature as well.

> *The New Century Handbook of English Literature*
> New York: Meredith Publishing Company, 1967.

This handbook seeks to answer those questions about English writers, works of literature, characters from works of literature, and various related (but not necessary English) items which are most likely to be raised by modern American readers of English literature. It is intended to add to the enjoyment of the vast number of people who read primarily for pleasure and whose reading tastes have been influenced by college literature courses. Students, teachers, editors, writers, librarians, lawyers, and clergymen who want to check a literary allusion or confirm a reference will find it a rewarding source of information.

> *The Reader's Adviser: A Layman's Guide to Literature*
> New York: R.R. Bowker, 1974-1977. Twelfth edition. 3 vols.

This was once limited to investigation by specialists, but each succeeding edition has tended to make these volumes a wide-ranging guide for anyone who cares about books. It is not quite true that it covers "absolutely everything," as one admiring librarian holds, but it ranges across fiction, poetry, essays, foreign literature, travel and adventure, Bible, and reference books. The concise annotations make it much more than a listing. *The Reader's Adviser*, as it is usually known also suggests which translations of foreign works are preferred.

The Reader's Encyclopedia
>William Rose Benet. New York: Thomas Y. Crowell, 1965. Second edition.

Issued again in 1965 after long languishing as a well-remembered but outdated reference, this 1,118-page edition is a triumph of literary memorabilia: characters, themes, authors, artistic and literary movements, names of famous swords, and the reason for Mona Lisa's enigmatic smile (it was a convention of the time). This is a small part of an imposing array.

Short Story Index
>Compiled by Dorothy Cook and Isabel S. Monro. New York: Wilson, 1953. Supplements annual, with five-year cumulations.

The first volume of this series indexed 60,000 short stories in 4,320 collections, and each of seven supplements has added 6,000 to 16,000 more. The stories are indexed by author and title (and in some cases by subject). The latest bound supplement, 1979-1983, added 16,633 stories to the total.

The Library of Literary Criticism of English and American Authors
>Charles Wells Moulton. Magnolia, MA: Peter Smith, 1959. Reprint of 1901-1905 edition. 8 vols.

Moulton, as this series is known to many critics, was *the* compilation of critical reviews for more than five decades. The tracing of criticism begins with *Beowulf* and ends in 1904, but it has more than antiquarian value. The editor was a shrewd judge of standards, and some authorities hold that his selections set the tone for English and American criticism until the coming of the New Critics. A *Library of Literary Criticism: Modern American Literature* (New York: Ungar, 1969, fourth edition) can be considered an extension of *Moulton* for Americans. It includes excerpts from the major criticisms of 300 authors. The New Criticism is represented, in remarkable balance with the more traditional approaches to literary judgment.

Dictionary of Classical Mythology
>Robert E. Bell. Santa Barbara, CA: ABC-Clio, 1982.

There's no reason to let a mere myth intimidate you. This book is organized so that the reader can find the source of allusions to mythology by looking up the concept that is associated with them. What god brought fire to human beings? Look under "fire." Also included are numerous cross-references and a section on alternate names. Another excellent source, despite its age, is the comprehensive, illustrated *Mythology of All Races* (Boston: Marshall-Jones, 1916-32, 13 vols.)

Masterplots
>Edited by Frank N. Magill. Englewood Cliffs, NJ: Salem, 1976. Revised edition. 12 vols.

Suppose a student wants to compare the plot of a novel with the plot of one or two other well-known novels, or look up a few facts on the publication of some book not originally written in English, or double-check a forgotten detail from a book read long ago. *Masterplots* can simplify the task. It gives a detailed synopsis of 2,010

literary masterpieces along with some facts of publication. It gives critical evaluations of 1,300 of the works.

Granger's Index to Poetry
    Edited by William J. Smith and William F. Bernhardt. New York: Columbia
    University Press, 1982. Seventh edition.

The seventh edition of *Granger's* indexes 248 volumes of poetry anthologies
published since 1970, giving (1) a title and first-line index, (2) an author index, and
(3) a subject index. For poems in anthologies issued before 1970, the editors refer
the reader back to the sixth edition.

Music

Some Leading Journals

High Fidelity. A.B.C. Leisure Magazines. Monthly.
Music and Letters. Oxford: Oxford University Press. Quarterly.

The New Oxford Companion to Music
    Denis Arnold. Oxford: Oxford University Press, 1982. Eleventh edition. 2 vols.

This reference has been a standard since 1938, but, as the editor points out in
the preface, white Anglo-Saxon music could no longer be the sole province of a
comprehensive musical dictionary. The current version is vastly updated and
expanded.

The New Grove Dictionary of Music and Musicians
    Edited by Stanley Sadie. New York: Macmillan, 1980. 20 vols.

A new version of a music reference standard. Once only five volumes, the
current twenty-volume *Grove's* includes articles written by almost 2,500 experts. It
covers terms, history, theory and practice, instruments, musicians, songs, and so
on.

The Music Index
    Detroit: Information Service, 1949.

This is a monthly subject index to about 400 periodicals, some of them
foreign. It cumulates annually and includes author entries.

Baker's Biographical Dictionary of Musicians
    Edited by Nicolas Slonimsky. New York: G. Schirmer, 1978. Sixth edition.

Although the definitive work does not exist, *Baker's* tries comprehensively to
sketch musicians of all periods and countries in one huge volume. It is excellent.
"Musicians" is interpreted broadly; composers, musicologists, performers, and out-
standing music teachers are sketched here.

The Best of Country Music
    John Morthland, New York: Dolphin Books (Doubleday), 1984.

This is an annotated directory to country music albums, written by a critic
and editor. Morthland discusses 100 of the albums and describes 650 others briefly.

Other references for specialized music genre of this century are the excellent *Rock Record* (Facts on File, 1982), *The Harmony Illustrated Encyclopedia of Rock*, (New York: Harmony, 1984, fourth edition), and *The International Encyclopedia of Hard Rock and Heavy Metal* (London: Sidgwick & Jackson, 1983).

Black Music in the United States
    Samuel A. Floyd, Jr., and Marsha J. Reisser. Millwood, NY: Kraus, 1983.

This is a list of some 300 references on black American musicians, each reference fully annotated. Also included are annotated lists of special collections, useful for hunting down specific songs and recordings.

An excellent dictionary for blacks in music is *Biographical Dictionary of Afro-American and African Musicians* (Westport, CT: Greenwood, 1982).

Blues Who's Who
    Sheldon Harris. New Rochelle, NY: Arlington House, 1979. Paperback edition, Da Capo Press, 1981.

The author, an advertising executive with a keen interest in blues, took a frantic four years to put together the notes of a lifetime. Illustrated and informative, the book is more of an encyclopedia than the title implies.

The Encyclopedia of Jazz
    Leonard Feather. New York: Horizon Press, 1960.

Leonard Feather is known as the Boswell of Basin Street. There is almost nothing about jazz—from instruments to foot-tapping with an appropriate beat—that he does not consider worthy of lengthy treatment. Fortunately for those who are not as dedicated but who are interested in jazz, Feather writes informatively and readably about his love. He has also published two continuations, *The Encyclopedia of Jazz in the Sixties* (Horizon, 1961) and *The Encyclopedia of Jazz in the Seventies* (Horizon, 1967).

Religion and Philosophy

Some Leading Journals

Journal of Philosophy. The Journal of Philosophy, Inc., Columbia University. Monthly.
Journal of Religion. University of Chicago. Quarterly.
Philosophical Review. Sage School of Philosophy, Cornell University. Quarterly.
Religion in Life. Abingdon Press. Quarterly.

Abingdon Dictionary of Living Religions
    Edited by Keith Crim. Nashville, TN: Abingdon, 1981.

This book doesn't cover ancient heresies unless they are reflected in current religions, but it is readable and informative.

A Dictionary of Comparative Religion
    Edited by S.G.F. Brandon. London: Weidenfeld & Nicolson, 1970; and New York: Scribner, 1970.

A good, solid, quick reference to religious terms and symbols, including those of Buddhism, Hinduism, Islam, the far eastern religions, and Greek and Roman mythology, as well as Christianity.

Theological and Religious Reference Materials: General Resources and Biblical Studies
   G.E. Gorman and Lyn Gorman with Donald N. Matthews. Westport, CT: Greenwood, 1984.

This first in a four-volume series represents to religious reference books what Sheehy's *Guide to Reference Books* represents to reference books in general. It is an enormous annotated bibliography of reference materials for studying various aspects of religion ranging from biblical studies to comparative religions.

Catholic Periodical and Literature Index
   Haverford, PA: Catholic Library Association, 1930—. Bimonthly with biennial cumulations.

Well over a hundred Catholic periodicals, newspapers, and bulletins are indexed here. The range is broad, serving as a guide to Catholic interests and concerns besides religion. A detailed book review index is included.

Encyclopedia Judaica
   Edited by Cecil Roth. Jerusalem: Macmillan, 1972. 16 vols.

This excellent encyclopedia provides a detailed and comprehensive picture of all aspects of Jewish life and knowledge from ancient times to the present. It updates the *Jewish Encyclopedia* and is the best English-language guide to the world community of Judaism.

A more up-to-date alternative is the *American Jewish Yearbook* (Philadelphia: Jewish Publication Society of America).

Masterpieces of Christian Literature in Summary Form
   Edited by Frank N. Magill. Englewood Cliffs, NJ: Salem, 1963. 2 vols.

Sometimes a book you run across in your reading, or a second or third work by an author you are studying, can provide a valuable perspective on your thinking and research. However, if the book is, say, Martin Luther's *The Bondage of the Will* or Erasmus's *Manual of the Christian Soldier,* you're not likely to find the time to read and study them. A collection of summaries like this one can fill the gap.

The Interpreter's Dictionary of the Bible
   Keith Crim, general editor. Nashville: Abingdon, 1967. 5 vols.

This is so ambitious that most -ologies—phil–, the–, arche–, and the like—are woven into the text. Considered by specialists to be one of the great biblical reference works of all time, these five volumes present all the major findings of recent scholarship.

New Catholic Encyclopedia
   Catholic University of America. Reprint of 1967 edition by McGraw-Hill. 17 vols.

These volumes are so broad in scope and concern that one hesitates to include them among religious references. The volumes that make up the set answer questions on medieval history, literature, philosophy, and art, although there is an emphasis on Catholic doctrine and history.

Handbook of Denominations in the United States
Frank S. Mead. Revised by Samuel S. Hill. Nashville: Abingdon, 1985. Eighth edition.

This is the quickest guide to various church histories and doctrines. It sketches in brief and impartial accounts the histories and current beliefs of over 200 denominations.

Atlas of the Islamic World Since 1500
Francis Robinson. New York: Facts on File, 1982.

Students who need an introduction to Islam will do well to look at this book. This history and culture of Islamic civilization are beautifully illustrated. There is a chronological table that shows the impact of Islam on the continents it has touched.

A Concordance of the Qur'an
Hanna E. Kassis. Berkeley: University of California Press, 1983.

A concordance helps the researcher pinpoint passages that tell about specific topics and issues. This 1,400-page volume is the first English-language concordance of the Koran, or Qur'an, and it provides special indexes, a table of transliterations, and other aids as well.

Handbook of World Philosophy: Contemporary Developments Since 1945
Edited by John R. Burr. Westport, CT: Greenwood Press, 1980.

"Exploratory, not definitive," the editor says in the preface. This is nonetheless an excellent resource for students who wish to research the ideas that have influenced various geographical areas. Different sections cover Western Europe, North and South America, Israel, Australia, and so on.

Research Guide to Philosophy
Terrence N. Tice and Thomas P. Slavens. Chicago: American Library Association, 1983.

In its 30 essays and its bibliographies, the *Research Guide to Philosophy* discusses the history and the areas of philosophy. There is also an annotated list of reference sources.

Masterpieces of World Philosophy in Summary Form
Edited by Frank N. Magill. New York: Harper & Row, 1961.
World Philosophy: Essay-Reviews of 255 Major Works
Edited by Frank N. Magill. Englewood Cliffs, NJ: Salem, 1982. 5 vols.

What *Masterpieces of Christian Literature* does for Christian writings, these books do for historically important works in philosophy. *World Philosophy* is an expansion of *Masterpieces of World Philosophy*. A library may have one or the other or both of these works: both are excellent.

The Writer's Craft

The Elements of Style
  William Strunk and E.B. White. New York: Macmillan, 1979. Third edition.
If this book were any longer, it would be the complete guide to writing well. As it is, it is a famous informal style manual, and one that virtually every college student runs across sooner or later.

On Writing Well: An Informal Guide to Writing Nonfiction
  William K. Zinsser. New York: Harper & Row, 1985. Third edition.
This, appropriately enough, is not a textbook but a highly readable guide. Zinsser discusses such matters as simplicity, clutter, writing about places, and humor. It is an excellent reminder, and perhaps will be an inspiration as well, to the student struggling with the craft of writing.

The Writer's Survival Manual
  Carol Meyer. New York: Crown, 1982.
Whether the writer is ready to publish a book or not, he or she will find in this volume essential information on the book publishing trade, written from the writer's angle. Book contracts and copyright law are explained in plain English—the book is meant to be used.

The Craft of Interviewing
  John Brady. Cincinnati: Writer's Digest Books, 1975.
A painless guide to interviewing.

On Becoming a Novelist
  John Gardner. New York: Harper & Row, 1983.
Gardner, himself a novelist, directed this book toward uncompromising artists—those who desire "not publication at any cost, but publication one can be proud of." The rhythm of words, the sound of a sentence, as well as the perils of the more crass aspects of the publishing trade, are covered here.

Writer's Market
  Cincinnati: Writer's Digest, 1930. Annual.
The purpose of *Writer's Market* is to tell prospective magazine writers what they need to know to get articles published in specific magazines. It tells the aspiring writer what kind of article a magazine will publish—length, topic, style—the editor's name, the cost of a sample copy of the magazine, how long it takes to reply, and, perhaps most important, how much it pays. The source for works of fiction is *Fiction Writer's Market*, (Cincinnati: Writer's Digest, 1984-85, third edition).

Words Into Type
  Marjorie E. Skillin and R. Gay. Englewood Cliffs, NJ: Prentice-Hall, 1974. Third edition.
There are many style manuals that give definitive answers about the details of punctuation and grammar. *Words into Type* focuses a bit more on grammar than some and is comparatively easy to use.

The Chicago Manual of Style
   Chicago: University of Chicago Press, 1982.
This book is the heavyweight champion of publishing style manuals. If a point of style isn't mentioned here, it isn't worth knowing about.

The MLA Style Manual
   New York: The Modern Language Association of America, 1985.
The recent changes in MLA style, after years of study and deliberation by various MLA committees as well as by the association's Executive Council, not only compelled a second edition of the Handbook (1984) but also occasioned this new manual for the scholar and graduate student. The revised handbook focuses more sharply on its primary audience, the undergraduate student. The *MLA Style Manual* attempts to meet the scholar's need for a comprehensive guide to publishing and to address the problems scholars encounter in their writing.

REFERENCES FOR THE PHYSICAL AND APPLIED SCIENCES

Science is a flickering light in our darkness, but it is the only one we have and woe to him who would put it out.

—Morris Cohen

General References

Applied Science and Technology Index
   New York: Wilson, 1958. Monthly, with annual cumulations.
Liberal arts students will find this index particularly helpful because its format is the same one used in *Reader's Guide* and other indexes produced by H.W. Wilson. Besides the monster journals of science, it also indexes many popular scientific periodicals that liberal arts students will find helpful.

Another helpful index is *Science Citation Index*. It is a favorite tool of scientists, but nonscientists might use it, say, to demonstrate how influential an individual article or author has been. It lists each mention of a given article in publications produced after that article first appeared.

Dictionary of the History of Science
   W.F. Byrum, E.J. Browne, and Roy Porter. Princeton, NJ: Princeton University Press, 1981.
"Dictionary" is a little too modest: Entries in this nearly 500-page volume range from a few hundred words up to a few pages. It is clearly written, a valuable quick reference for the nonscientist researcher.

Handbook of Chemistry and Physics
   Edited by Robert C. Weast. Boca Raton, FL: CRC, 1982. Sixty-third edition.
This book is rumored to be on the shelf of every upper-division student at MIT. It is a definitive reference for the "hard facts" that so delight the chemists and physicists of this world. Not for the fainthearted.

Research Centers Directory
    Mary Michelle Watkins, editor, Detroit: Gale Research Co., 1985. Tenth edition.
A listing of 8,354 permanent nonprofit research organizations that study topics ranging from agriculture to religion. There is also an *International Research Centers Directory* (Detroit: Gale, 1983). For information on laboratories that are not nonprofit, check *Industrial Research Laboratories of the United States*, (Jaques Cattell Press. New York: R.R. Bowker Co., 1985, nineteenth edition). It is an alphabetical listing of the research laboratories of 5,996 parent organizations and 4,981 subsidiaries.

Scientific, Technical, and Related Societies of the United States
    Washington, DC: National Academy of Sciences, 1927.
Keeping up with the world of science is like trying to catch a waterfall in a tin cup, but one can measure growth roughly by marking the increases in scientific societies. This volume provides more than conventional directories—details of history, aims, memberships, medals and awards, and so on.

Van Nostrand's Scientific Encyclopedia
    Douglas M. Considine. Princeton, NJ: Van Nostrand Reinhold, 1982. Sixth edition.
Long one of the leading publishers of handy science references, Van Nostrand issues references that are not beyond the reach of the layman. This enormous volume contains more than 7,300 diverse entries. At almost 4,000 pages, the book should be a favorite of both scientists and weightlifters.

McGraw-Hill Dictionary of Scientific and Technical Terms
    New York: McGraw-Hill, 1984. Third edition.
This is a good choice for a quick answer on scientific words. It provides 1,800 pages of illustrated definitions culled from some fifteen different specialized technical dictionaries.

Biological Sciences

Biological and Agricultural Index
    New York: Wilson, 1916–.
Some 200 periodicals in agriculture and associated fields are covered here in a subject index.

Biological Abstracts
    Philadelphia: Geological Abstracts, Inc. 1926. Semimonthly with semiannual cumulations.
The researcher who hopes to pick his or her way through the masses of biology literature must begin with a large view. The semimonthly *Biological Abstracts* provides that scope, guiding the researcher to works in a host of subjects.

The Encyclopedia of the Biological Sciences
    Edited by Peter Gray. New York: Van Nostrand Reinhold, 1970. Second edition.
This encyclopedia, which is designed for laymen, is authoritative in its cover-

age of a wide range of areas: developmental, ecological, functional, genetic, structural, and taxonomic.

Larousse Encyclopedia of Animal Life
New York: McGraw-Hill, 1967.

This 649-page volume covers the world of animals from protozoans to mammals and includes a classification table, a glossary, and a bibliography. Another informative, well-rounded, and well-recommended work is *The Encyclopedia of Mammals* (New York: Facts on File, 1984).

North American Horticulture
Compiled by the American Horticultural Society. Barbara W. Ellis, editor. New York: Scribner's (Macmillan), 1982.

This book is an expanded version of the American Horticultural Society's 1977 *Directory of American Horticulture*. The first was useful; the second is said to be invaluable. Organized in directory format, it contains information on a vast number of issues, organizations, and programs in horticultural and related fields.

The Complete Book of Garden Plants
Michael Wright. New York: Facts on File, 1984.

It covers over 9,000 different garden plants that grow in temperate climates. Wild plants can be identified in various field guides, including the Peterson series listed below.

The Peterson Field Guide Series
New York: Houghton Mifflin, Inc., 1982.

Among the many field guide series available, the Peterson series is one of the best for amateur naturalists. The list includes guides to animal tracks, birds' nests, Pacific coast shells, Rocky Mountain wildflowers, stars and planets, and reptiles and amphibians. For birders, the *Audubon Society Encyclopedia of North American Birds* (New York: Knopf, 1981) and the *Audubon Society Handbook for Birders* (New York: Scribner, 1981) also come highly recommended.

Chemistry

Some Leading Journals

Accounts of Chemical Research. Washington, DC: American Chemical Society. Monthly.
American Chemical Society Journal. Washington, DC: American Chemical Society. Fortnightly.

Chemical Abstracts
Columbus, OH: Chemical Abstracts Service of the American Chemical Society, 1907–. Weekly, cumulated every five years.

Chemists eat this reference for breakfast. It is *the* basic, comprehensive reference for periodical literature in chemistry. Though a nonchemist might find most of the articles cited to be far too technical to be helpful, this is still the place to go for information on chemistry periodicals. There is also an online version.

Chemical Formulary
New York: Chemical Publishing Co., 1933–.
This is a handy guide to formulas used in making thousands of things, from complex industrial chemicals to perfumes and cosmetics.

Glossary of Chemical Terms
Clifford A. Hampel and Gessner G. Hawley. New York: Van Nostrand Reinhold Co., 1976.
This specialized dictionary makes sense of such terms as "naphtha," nano-," and "carnauba wax," as well as the more arcane terms, such as "acidulant," "Stokes' Law" and "clathrate."

Computer Science and Engineering

Engineering Index
New York: Engineering Information, Inc., 1920–. Monthly, with annual cumulations.
This index is for engineers who eat their Wheaties. It is extensive and strongly keyed to engineering; it provides abstracts organized by subject and cross-referenced. There is an online version, Compendex, as well.

Encyclopedia of Computer Science and Engineering
Anthony Ralston, editor. Edwin D. Reilly, Jr., Associate Editor. New York: Van Nostrand Reinhold Co., 1983. Second edition.
If a student thinks "cycle-stealing" is something that only the police can handle, this book will clarify the matter. Though not for the rank beginner, this desk-sized encyclopedia can fill in some technological gaps for the interested non-engineer.

McGraw-Hill Dictionary of Science and Engineering
Sybil P. Parker, editor in chief. New York: McGraw-Hill Book Co., 1984.
An abbreviated, specialized version of *McGraw-Hill's Dictionary of Scientific and Technical Terms*. Yet another, still more specialized option is *Data Communications Dictionary* by Charles J. Sippl (New York: Van Nostrand Reinhold, 1984). It defines terms in language that is understandable but not overly simple.

The Way Things Work
New York: Simon & Schuster, 1967 and 1971. 2 vols.
The most understandable part of this reference may be its title, but it does give good, reasonably clear explanations of such marvels as cameras, pumps, and mirrors.

Earth and Space Sciences

Some Leading Journals

Aerospace Historian. Air Force Historical Foundation, Kansas State University. Quarterly.

AIAA Journal. American Institute of Aeronautics and Astronautics. Monthly.
Earth Science. Alexandria, VA: American Geological Institute. Quarterly.
Journal of Astronautical Sciences. Alexandria, VA: American Astronautical Society. Bimonthly.

Bibliography and Index of Geology
    Alexandria, VA: American Geological Institute. 1969–. Monthly.
The virtue of this reference is its scope. It is worldwide and, according to one authority, "includes more geologic references than any other existing work."

The Cambridge Atlas of Astronomy
    Cambridge: Cambridge University Press, 1985.
An up-to-date, colorful atlas that covers the sun, the solar system, the stars, the galaxy, the extragalactic domain—and some more prosaic topics, such as the history of astronomy. Another option is *The New Atlas of the Universe* by Patrick Moore (New York: Crown Publishers, Inc., 1984).

The Climates of the Continents
    Wilfred G. Kendrew. Oxford: Clarendon Press, 1961. Fifth edition.
This 608-page volume provides a worldwide view of climates, including information on altitude, temperature, and monthly precipitation for all of the great cities of the world and for many other cities as well.

A Dictionary of Geology
    John Challinor. Cardiff: University of Wales Press, 1978. Fifth edition.
The editor is careful to flesh out many of the terms he defines here with apt quotations from the literature of geology.

Minerals Year Book
    U.S. Department of the Interior, Bureau of Mines. Washington, DC: Government Printing Office, 1932–. Annual. 3 vols.
This volume will give the researcher information about various individual commodities: production, consumption, stocks, prices, and other data. It is not so much a field guide as a businessman's handbook.

The Times Atlas of the Oceans
    Edited by Alastair Couper. New York: Van Nostrand Reinhold Co., 1983.
This colorful atlas is full of statistical maps and texts as well as standard maps of the ocean's bottom and is a good comprehensive reference for matters from geography to shipping, ports, and pollution.

Jane's Spaceflight Directory
    London: Jane's Publishing Co., Ltd, 1984.
Really a short but specialized encyclopedia, *Jane's Spaceflight Directory* can set the researcher straight on a number of aeronautic matters. Jane's publishes so many definitive yearly works of aeronautical equipment, in fact, that the researcher's first step for finding data about specific craft should be to consult such Jane's publications as *All the World's Aircraft, Airport Equipment,* and *Surface*

Skimmers. For periodical articles, check the *Air University Library Index to Military Periodicals* (U.S. Air Force, Alabama, 1949–). It indexes "significant articles" in 76 English-language military and aeronautical periodicals.

> *Dictionary of Space Technology*
> Joseph A. Angelo, Jr. New York: Facts on File, 1982.

"Ancient Astronaut Theory" and "Positive G" (also known as "eyeballs down") are among the terms defined here.

Mathematics and Physics

Some Leading Journals

American Journal of Mathematics. Baltimore: Johns Hopkins University Press. Bimonthly.
American Mathematical Monthly. Washington, DC: Mathematical Association of America. Monthly.

> *Prentice-Hall Encyclopedia of Mathematics*
> Beverly Henderson West and others. Englewood Cliffs, NJ: Prentice-Hall, 1982.

This encyclopedia is for the weak and tottering liberal arts student. Most of the 90 or so articles are at least a page long, but they are clearly written and discuss such matters as scientific notation and statistics with examples taken from everyday life. Another good source is *The Facts on File Dictionary of Mathematics*, which, at a slender 200 pages, is a highly useful volume.

> *The Encyclopedia of Physics*
> Edited by Robert M. Besancon. New York: Van Nostrand Reinhold Co., 1985.

This source is fat, comprehensive, and informative. If the nonscientist is attempting to find a way through a semitechnical or technical article, this may be the only thing that keeps him or her afloat.

Note: See also the indexes listed under Computer Science and Engineering and General References.

REFERENCES FOR CURRENT EVENTS AND THE SOCIAL SCIENCES

We live in a Newtonian world of Einsteinian physics ruled by Frankenstein logic.

—David Russell

General References

> A *Dictionary of the Social Sciences*
> Edited by Julius Gould and W.F. Kolb. New York: Free Press (Macmillan), 1964.

This UNESCO-sponsored dictionary emphasizes terms used in political science and sociology, but its scope is general for the most part and it is more than a dictionary of terms. It provides definitions, history of usage, and usage in various fields of social science.

Census of Population, 1980
    U.S. Bureau of the Census. Washington, DC: Government Printing Office.

Of the many census publications, this is the most widely known and used. The Bureau of the Census also publishes many special reports and special censuses of agriculture, housing, business, and other fields.

Atlas of Demographics: U.S. by County, from the 1980 Census
    Boulder, CO: Infomap, 1982

The editors have taken a pictorial approach to presenting statistics in this well-illustrated atlas. Population data are presented in colorful maps, supplemented by statistics presented both on the maps and in tables. Many of the statistics are presented in percentages and in medians, making the results of the 1980 census very easy to understand.

Datamap: Index of Published Tables of Statistical Data
    Jarol B. Manheim and Allison Ondrasik. New York: Longman, 1984. Second edition.

This book indexes 29 different standard sources for statistical data, making the detective process much easier for the researcher.

Encyclopedia of Associations
    Detroit: Gale Research Co., 1959–. Annual. 4 vols.

Another massive disgorgement of data from the computer files. Over 19,100 trade associations, labor unions, fraternal and patriotic organizations, and the like are listed in the 1986 edition. Somewhere in there is the one the researcher wants.

The Foundation Directory
    The Foundation Center. New York: The Foundation Center, 1983. Ninth edition.

More than 4,000 nonprofit foundations are listed in this volume. Here the researcher will find address, date of establishment, donor, purpose and activities, financial data, and so on. For information on grants, go to *The Foundation Grants Directory* by the same publisher. The thirteenth edition (1984) lists sources and sums for 32,165 grants of $5,000 or more.

Yearbook of International Organizations
    Edited by the Union of International Organizations. Philadelphia: International Publications Service (Taylor & Francis). Biennial.

This much-used source is an encyclopedic dictionary of currently active international organizations and associations. It covers their aims, functions, finances, activities, publications, and leading officials.

Business and Economics

Some Leading Journals
The American Economic Review. American Economic Association. Quarterly.

Econometrics. Evanston, IL: Econometric Society of Northwestern University. Published in Bristol, England. Quarterly.

Harvard Business Review. Harvard University. Bimonthly.

Management Review. New York: American Management Association. Monthly.

Business Periodicals Index
    New York: Wilson, 1958–.

Known from 1913 to 1957 as the *Industrial Arts Index*, this book indexes over 330 periodicals of various business fields. There is also an *Accountants' Index* (New York: American Institute of Accountants, 1921–).

Best's Insurance Reports
    New York: Best Company. Life–Health, 1906–. Property–Casualty, 1899–.

Best's Insurance Reports cover two major fields: Life–Health and Property–Casualty. They are published annually and supplemented in part by the monthly *Best's Review*, which has both Life/Health and Property/Casualty editions.

Commodity Year Book
    New York: Commodity Research Bureau, 1939–. Annual.

This is a compilation of data on objects from cotton and coal to lard and honey. It covers production, prices, imports, exports, and the like.

Custom House Guide
    Philadelphia: North American Publishing Co., 1986.

Heavy with data on the leading customs ports in the United States—such as steamship lines, banks, warehouses, foreign consuls—and lists of commodities with import duties, this annual publication is supplemented monthly by *American Import and Export Bulletin*. Similar information about foreign ports is carried in *Exporters' Encyclopaedia* (New York: Dun & Bradstreet International. Annual).

Directory of Corporate Affiliations
    Lafayette, IL: National Register (Macmillan), 1967–. Annual.

"Who Owns Whom" is the subtitle of this reference. It includes boards of directors and lists of subsidiaries of over 4,000 parent companies, and there are several indexes, including a geographical index and an SIC index (listing a company's primary product or service). It is a good place to find data on the corporate labyrinth.

Encyclopedia of Banking and Finance
    Glenn C. Munn. Edited by F.L. Garcia. Boston: Bankers Publishing, 1983. Eighth edition.

When F.L. Garcia took over in the 1950s as editor of this old standard, he set out to provide a comprehensive exposition of the financial system. This authoritative volume is the result.

For an explanation of economic terms and theories, try *Encyclopedia of Economics* (New York: McGraw-Hill, 1982). If a straightforward definition will serve, there is *The McGraw-Hill Dictionary of Modern Economics,* (New York:

McGraw-Hill, third edition 1983). It combines a dictionary of terms and a directory of organizations.

Moody's Manual of Investments, American and Foreign
    New York: Analyses Publishing, 1904–1914, Moody's Investors Service, 1915–. Annual.

One of the most important business research tools, *Moody's*, as it is widely known, is a leader in compiling current data. Seven annual volumes—transportation, public utilities, municipal and government, bank and finance, industrial, OTC industrial, and international—are updated by weekly and semiweekly supplement sheets.

Standard & Poor's Register of Corporations, Directors and Executives
    New York: Standard and Poor's, 1928–. Annual.

This widely used annual (which is supplemented three times a year) is in three volumes: (1) a list of about 45,000 corporations and their officers and directors, (2) an alphabetical list of about 72,000 directors and executives, with brief biographical data, and (3) indexes of industrial products and the companies selling them.

A similar service is provided by *Who's Who in Finance and Industry* (Chicago: Marquis, 1936–).

Thomas' Register of American Manufacturers
    New York: Thomas Publishing Co., 1905–.

Issued annually since 1905, this is one of the most useful buyers' guides in the world of business. Though the first look at product listings may suggest that this is a generalized maze, it provides a wealth of information for the researcher on the track of specific game.

Kelly's Manufacturers and Merchants Directory (East Grinstead, England: Kelly's Directories, Ltd., 1887–) has a slightly different cast, but it supplements *Thomas' Register* by putting a focus on Great Britain.

Communication/Journalism

Some Leading Journals

Mass Communication Review. Philadelphia: Association for Education in Journalism and Mass Communication, Temple University. Three times per year.
Communication Research. Beverly Hills: Sage Publications, Inc. Quarterly.
The Newspaper Research Journal. Columbia: University of South Carolina, Association for Education in Journalism and Mass Communication. Quarterly.
Editor & Publisher. New York: Editor & Publisher Co. Weekly.
Presstime. Reston, VA: American Newspaper Publisher's Association. Monthly.
ASNE Bulletin. Washington, DC: American Society of Newspaper Editors. Nine times per year.
P.R. Journal. New York: Public Relations Society of America, Inc. Monthly.

Journalism Abstracts
    Muncie, IN: Ball State University, Association for Education in Journalism, 1963–. Annual

This service provides abstracts of Master's theses and Doctoral dissertations for U.S. and Canadian schools.

Basic Books in the Mass Media
Eleanor Blum. Urbana, IL: University of Illinois Press, 1980. Second edition.
This book is an immense annotated bibliography of references in communication. It is an excellent starting point for research on communication topics.

Handbook of Free Speech and Free Press
Jerome A. Barron and C. Thomas Dienes. Boston: Little, Brown, 1979.
At over 750 pages, this book scarcely qualifies as a "handbook," but it provides thoughtful syntheses of the major judicial decisions on censorship, prior restraint, speech in the local forum, newsgathering, and the like. For simpler explanations, try *Say It Safely* by Paul P. Ashley (Seattle: University of Washington Press, 1976, fifth edition).

Newsroom Guide to Polls and Surveys
G. Cleveland Wilhoit and David H. Weaver. Washington, DC: American Newspaper Publishers Association, 1980.
This slim volume summarizes the information any poll-watcher needs to evaluate the validity of polls and surveys reported in the news media. It covers such topics as bias in survey questionnaires, kinds of random sampling, margin of error, the definitions of mean, median, and mode, and how to report results accurately. For a chattier explanation of the subject, try Philip Meyer's *Precision Journalism*, (Bloomington, IN: Indiana University Press, 1979 second edition).

The Reporter's Handbook
Investigative Reporters & Editors, Inc. John Ullmann and Steve Honeyman, editors. New York: St. Martin's Press, 1983.
This book is for working reporters, and it tells how to do serious legwork in documents that range from birth certificates to hospital accreditation reports. A college student may not need the kind of information that requires, say, wheedling a case file out of a friendly prosecuting attorney; nonetheless, some of the leads on documents can be invaluable for in-depth papers.

How to Use the Federal FOI Act
Washington, DC: FOI Service Center, 1984.
While it is hardly a complete guide, this pamphlet is a practical one. It gives information ranging from a general description of the Freedom of Information Act down to sample letters.

Media Controversies
Edited by Lester A. Sobel. New York: Facts on File, 1981.
At just under 100 pages, this book is a good bare-bones introduction to the many controversies that buffeted the media during the hectic decade of the 1970s: the media versus the Nixon administration, media performance, ownership and control of the media, and so forth.

Guide to Non-English-Language Broadcasting
   Joshua A. Fishman and others. Rosslyn, VA: National Clearinghouse for Bilingual Education, 1982.
This is a good place to pin down details on specific non-English-language stations. More than 1,400 radio and television stations are listed. There is also a *Guide to Non-English Language Print Media* (Rosslyn, VA: National Clearinghouse for Bilingual Education, 1981).

Education

Some Leading Journals

Educational Record. American Council on Education. Quarterly.
Harvard Educational Review. Harvard University. Quarterly.
Journal of Higher Education. Ohio State University. Monthly
Teachers College Record. Columbia University. Eight issues annually.

ERIC: Educational Resources Information Center
   Phoenix: Oryx, 1964–.
Out of the labyrinth of government publications has risen a series of extremely useful—by now, indispensable—indexes to both published and unpublished educational documents. The *Educational Resources Information Center,* which produces the indexes, was begun in 1964 and since 1966 has been operated by the National Institute of Education of the U.S. Department of Education.
   ERIC consists of:

- the ERIC database, from which the printed index is created monthly (the information is also accessible online)
- the corresponding printed index and list of abstracts called *RIE: Resources in Education* (monthly, with bound annual cumulations)
- a corresponding microfiche with complete articles (printed copies of most articles are also available)
- the *ERIC Thesaurus* of descriptors, which are keyed to Library of Congress catalog descriptions, and cross-references to facilitate searches in the indexes
- an alphabetical *Title Index*

To use the series, the researcher must:

- go to the thesaurus and look up the subject to find the appropriate abbreviation (and find related subjects)
- then go to the RIE index and find the numbers of the abstracts of articles that might be helpful
- next go to the numerical listing of abstracts to find out which articles are going to tell the researcher what he or she wants to know
- finally, go to the microfiche or journal to read the entire article

One alternative to ERIC is the following:

CIJE: Current Index to Journals in Education
    Phoenix: Oryx, 1969–. Monthly.
The single most comprehensive educational index, CIJE covers about 660 different periodicals. Unlike ERIC, though, the articles have to have been published to be included here.

Finally, there is the *Education Index* (Bronx, NY: Wilson, 1929–). If ERIC is a little more than the researcher needs, this more traditional index is a good reference choice.

Comparative Guide to American Colleges
    James Cass and Max Birnbaum. New York: Harper & Row, 1983. Eleventh edition.
When a *Time* article cited the percentage of students who actually chose to go to Harvard after being accepted there, the reporter probably got the statistic here. This often-used reference rates American colleges in terms of selectivity, academic prestige, annual costs, and so on.

Two other good reference sources are the following:

American Universities and Colleges
    American Council on Education. Hawthorne, NY: Walter de Gruyter, 1983. Twelfth edition.
The College Blue Book
New York: Macmillan, 1983. Nineteenth edition. 5 vols.
These volumes sketch thousands of colleges in tables and prose descriptions, and cover most of the central features of college life, including scholarships, fellowships, and grants. The last volume provides information on junior and senior high schools in the United States. Macmillan also publishes the *College Blue Book of Occupational Education*.

Digest of Educational Statistics
    United States Department of Education, National Center for Educational Statistics, 1962–. Annual.
A well-chosen statistic can buttress a point like nothing else, and some of the most important educational statistics are presented here in just over 200 pages.

Encyclopedia of Educational Research
    Edited by Harold E. Mitzel. Sponsored by the American Educational Research Association, Washington, DC: Free Press (Macmillan), 1982. Fifth edition. 4 vols.
This source will help the researcher who wants to take the pulse of educational research. It synthesizes and interprets recent studies on grades and grading systems, child guidance clinics, and the like. Yet more recent articles can be found in the quarterly *Review of Educational Research* (American Educational Research Association, 1931–). For research with an international scope, the writer may wish to consult the *International Yearbook of Education* (Geneva: International Bureau of Education; Paris: UNESCO, 1948–). Once annual, this handbook now alternates every two years between descriptions of educational systems and educational trends. The 1983 edition had a hefty statistical appendix of 107 countries.

Health Sciences

Some Leading Journals

American Journal of Medicine. New York: Yorke Medical Group. Monthly.
Journal of the American Medical Association. Chicago: American Medical Association. Monthly.
Journal of Clinical Investigation. American Society for Clinical Investigation. New York: Rockefeller University Press. Monthly.
New England Journal of Medicine. Waltham, MA: Massachusetts Medical Society. Weekly.
Index Medicus
Washington, DC: National Library of Medicine, 1960–. Monthly, with annual cumulated issues.

The monthly issues of *Index Medicus* cover articles in almost 3,000 different journals (2,695 journals in January 1984). They are cumulated annually in *Cumulated Index Medicus*, which is the most comprehensive guide to advances in the health sciences.

PDR: Physicians' Desk References
    Oradell, NJ: Medical Economics Co., 1984. Thirty-eighth edition. Annual.
Here is a reference that explains the whats and whys of prescription drugs. It is as essential a piece of medical equipment as a stethoscope, listing trade names, manufacturers, side effects, generic and chemical names, and even photographs of the pills. Also available: *PDR for Nonprescription Drugs*.

Essential Guide to Nonprescription Drugs
    David R. Zimmerman. New York: Harper, 1983.
This is another reference for nonprescription drugs. It gives additional information on ingredients: the claims of manufacturers, the FDA reviews of the drugs, and a chart comparing the drugs in the 70 categories of drugs covered in the book.

Stedman's Medical Dictionary
    Baltimore: Williams & Wilkins, 1982. Twenty-fourth edition.
An average medical article is a jungle of multisyllabic words. This book is the student's compass and machete.

American Medical Directory
    Chicago: American Medical Association, 1906–. Twenty-ninth edition, 1985. Irregular.
This book is the place to find the primary and secondary specialties, type of practice, and related information on physicians listed in the AMA's Physician Masterfile database.
For nursing associations, look in the *National Nursing Directory* (Rockville, MD: Aspen Systems, 1982). The range is diverse. from professional associations to credentialing agencies, state boards to outreach groups.

The Complete Guide to Women's Health
    Bruce D. Shephard and Carroll A. Shephard. Tampa, FL: Mariner, 1982.
This is an excellent guide to women's health, less overtly political in tone
than the more famous *Our Bodies, Our Selves* (Boston Women's Health Collective,
1976. Second edition).

The Encyclopedia of Alcoholism
    Robert O'Brien and Morris Chafetz. New York: Facts on File, 1983.
The definitions in this resource range from just a sentence or two to several
pages, and tables and graphs supplement them. The student can find a wide range
of useful data on this pernicious and widespread affliction.

Psychiatric Dictionary
    Robert Jean Campbell. New York: Oxford University Press, 1981. Fifth edition.
Brevity is the rule here. The framework is psychiatric terms, with allied fields
well represented.

Minorities and Women

Harvard Encyclopedia of American Ethnic Groups
    Edited by Stephan Thernstrom et al. Cambridge, MA: Harvard University Press,
    1980.
This 1,102-page book defines ethnic groups that range from Alaskan tribes to
Zoroastrians, as well as various issues, such as immigration. It is a good modern
companion to the *Handbook of American Indians North of Mexico* (U.S. Bureau of
American Ethnology. Washington, DC: U.S. Government Printing Office,
1907-1910. Reissued 1919; reprinted, 1969. New York: Pageant Books. 2 vols.).
This reference lists tribes and settlements and describes them. Finally, a highly
detailed bibliography of sources is available in *A Guide to Research on North
American Indians* by Arlene B. Hirschfelder, Mary Gloyne, and Michael A. Dorris
(Chicago: American Library Association, 1983).

Negro Almanac
    Harry A. Ploski and James Williams. New York: Wiley, 1983. Fourth edition.
This comprehensive guide covers a diverse spread of topics, and it should be
one of the first steps to researching blacks in America. For a look into the past, try
Black Chronology from 4000 B.C. to the Abolition of the Slave Trade by Ellen I.
Diggs (Boston: G.K. Hall, 1983). It puts historical events in a framework that
facilitates comparison.

Sourcebook of Hispanic Culture in the United States
    Edited by David William Foster. Chicago: American Library Association, 1982.
This reference is an extended bibliography of Hispanic culture in the United
States. Most references are for 1975 and earlier, but it is a valuable starting point
nonetheless. Another excellent source is *Dictionary of Mexican American History*
by Matt S. Meyer and Feliciano Rivera (Westport, CT: Greenwood Press, 1981).

Women Helping Women
    New York: Women's Action Alliance, 1981.

Organized state by state, this is a directory of counseling and shelter services of all kinds. There are entries for employment services as well, but a better resource on careers for women is *The Directory of Special Opportunities for Women* (Martha Merrill Doss, New York: Garrett Park Press, 1981).

Psychology and Sociology

Some Leading Journals

The American Journal of Psychology. University of Illinois Press. Quarterly.
Journal of Abnormal Psychology. American Psychological Association. Quarterly.
Journal of Applied Psychology. American Psychological Association. Quarterly.
Journal of Social Psychology. Washington, DC: Heldreth Publications. Bimonthly.

Social Sciences Index
    New York: Wilson, 1974–. Quarterly, with annual cumulations.
A general-interest periodical index cannot compete with an index like this one for covering the specialized field of the social sciences. Some 250 journals are covered. For references other than periodicals, check *Sources of Information in the Social Sciences* (Carl M. White and Associates. Chicago: American Library Association, 1985, third edition). It gives bibliographic reviews of basic works and annotated reviews of reference sources, so the researcher can simply consult one volume to avoid a wild goose chase around the social sciences wing of the library.

A Dictionary of Social Science Methods
    Compiled by P.M. Miller and M.J. Wilson. New York: Wiley, 1983.
Once the researcher has tracked down the best reference source, this book will enable him or her to understand it. Setting aside theories and philosophy of the social sciences, the editors of this book have concentrated on *techniques* used in the field, including statistics. Various issues are also treated. For fuller explanations of social science topics, consult *International Encyclopedia of the Social Sciences* (New York: Macmillan, 1968. 17 vols.) It emphasizes analytical and comparative aspects of the field and their theory and methodology. Its predecessor, *Encyclopedia of the Social Sciences*, (New York: Macmillan, 1930-1935. 15 vols. Reissued in 1937 in 8 vols.) provides what the *International Encyclopedia* does not: information on the historical, descriptive, and practical aspects of the field.

Psychological Abstracts
    Washington, DC: American Psychological Association, 1927–.
Psych Abstracts, as it is generally known, abstracts U.S. and foreign books, journals, dissertations, monographs, and reports. It is classified by subject, with separate author and subject indexes in each issue.

Encyclopedic Dictionary of Psychology
    Edited by Rom Harre and Roger Lamb. Cambridge, MA: MIT Press, 1983.
This wide-ranging source has won acclaim from librarians and is somewhat more manageable in size than the excellent *Encyclopedia of Psychology* (New York:

Wiley-Interscience, 1984). Either one will explain the mysteries behind psychological terms.

U.S. Foreign Relations and International Politics

Some Leading Journals

American Journal of International Law. American Society of International Law. Quarterly.
Foreign Affairs. Council on Foreign Relations. Quarterly.

American Foreign Relations: A Documentary Record
    New York: New York University Press, 1971–.
Council on Foreign Relations.
Documents on Foreign Relations.
    New York: Simon & Schuster, 1938-1970.
The United States in World Affairs
    New York: Harper & Row, 1931–1970 (suspended 1941-44).

These three series on foreign relations are not indexes but are compilations of documents, including presidential messages and speeches, official statements and comments and so forth. *The United States in World Affairs* provides a comprehensive narrative account. It was superseded in 1971 by *American Foreign Relations.* The first two series listed will provide the researcher with primary sources; the second, a means to help interpret them.

For history, look into *Guide to American Foreign Relations Since 1700* by Richard Dean Burns and the Society for American Foreign Relations (Santa Barbara, CA: ABC-Clio, 1982). It carries enough annotated references, maps, and charts to satisfy the needs of virtually any undergraduate researcher. The book is organized chronologically and by region, and its range extends to 1981.

Worldmark Encyclopedia of the Nations
    New York: Harper & Row, 1976. Fifth edition. 5 vols.

The mammoth subtitle describes these volumes for the curious researcher: "A Practical Guide to the Geographic, Historical, Political, Social & Economic Status of All Nations, Their International Relationships, and the United Nations System." It may be supplemented nicely by *Encyclopedia of the Third World* by George Kurian (New York: Facts on File, 1978, revised edition. 3 vols.), which offers statistics and other data on the Third World. A perceptive synthesis of such data is available in *The Current Historical Encyclopedia of Developing Nations* (New York: McGraw-Hill, 1982).

International Yearbook and Statemen's Who's Who
    London: Burke's Peerage, 1953–.

A good first source for short profiles of countries and the name of officers in power, this annual is in three parts: International Organizations, States of the World, and Biographical Section. The last is a world's who's who.

The Statesman's Yearbook
> New York: St. Martin's Press, 1864–. Annual.
> This yearbook is one of the most famous reference sources for foreign relations. It carries concise, readable information on diverse aspects of the governments of the world.

U.S. Government

Some Leading Journals

American Political Science Review. Washington, DC: American Political Science Association. Quarterly.
Gallup Report. Princeton, NJ: Gallup Poll. (Formerly the *Gallup Opinion Index.*)
Harvard Political Review. Harvard University. Quarterly.
Journal of Politics. University of Florida, Gainesville; Southern Political Science Association. Quarterly.
Political Science Quarterly. New York: Academy of Political Science. Quarterly.

Congressional Record
> U.S. Congress. Washington, DC: Government Printing Office, 1873–. Daily.

It is not quite true that this is the record of every word spoken on the floor of the House and the Senate. At least once, the *Record* published a speech that was never delivered; and in cooler moments, members of Congress sometimes have second thoughts about what they have said and edit the *Record*. But almost every word of Senate and House debate and many other congressional actions are recorded, and so the *Record* is indispensable for tracing the full development of legislation—and for providing the gaseous sentences the *New Yorker* once memorialized under the general heading "Wind on Capitol Hill."

Congressional Quarterly Weekly Report
> Washington, DC: Congressional Quarterly, 1945–. Weekly.

CQ, as it is widely known, is the best continuing record of congressional activities. The weekly reports are indexed quarterly and annually, and the *Congressional Quarterly Almanac* summarizes and cross-indexes the year's congressional actions. In 1971 the publisher produced a huge and valuable volume entitled *Congressional Quarterly's Guide to the Congress of the United States: Origins, History, and Procedures.*

Official Congressional Directory
> U.S. Congress. Washington, DC: Government Printing Office, 1809–. Annual.

Congressional Staff Directory
> Compiled by Charles B. Brownson. Washington, DC: Congressional Staff Directory, 1959–. Annual.

The *Congressional Directory* is one of the most widely used government publications. It is the best source for biographical information on the members of Congress and their committee assignments. Charles Brownson, who was a congressman from 1951 to 1958 and knew the pivotal roles of congressional staffers, began publishing his *Congressional Staff Directory* in 1959. It includes reports on the staffs of the officers and members of the House and Senate, the Joint Committees, state delegations, the General Accounting Office, and on down to the congressional districts of major cities and more.

The United States Organization Manual
Office of the Federal Register, National Archives and Records Service, General Services Administration. Washington, DC: Government Printing Office, 1935–.

This indispensable reference is to the executive what the *Congressional Directory* is to the legislative—an anatomy in print. Nearly half the manual is given over to the boards, commissions, and committees that are not part of departmental structures, among them the Interstate Commerce Commission, the National Aeronautics and Space Administration, and the Veterans Administration.

U.S. Code
Washington, DC: Government Printing Office, 1982.

The Code, as it is known to legal researchers, is the basic set of documents in a pyramid of publications that seek to bring order to research in law. Revised fairly frequently, it includes all laws passed by Congress and still in force. Supplements are cumulated annually to enable researchers to find up-to-date information between editions. An annotated version of the Code is titled *United States Code Annotated.* It offers additional information, such as judicial interpretations, opinions of attorneys general, and historical and critical essays.

Politics in America
Edited by Alan Ehrenhardt. Washington, DC: The Congressional Quarterly, 1979. Fifth edition.

This book is a rundown on the lowdown on members of Congress. Some of the topics covered are their politicking style, their political interests, and a bit about how they got elected; also provided are personality profiles.

Another similar source that is said to be well used by newspaper reporters is *The Almanac of American Politics* (Michael Barone and Grant Ujifusa. Washington, DC: The National Journal), 1986.

The Book of the States
Lexington, KY: Council of State Governments, 1935–. Biennial.

This volume provides an overview of each state ranging from newly elected officials (kept up-to-date with supplements) to the state's official song.

Moving down the size scale for geographically organized information, there is the following:

Municipal Year Book
(Washington, DC: International City Managers Association, 1934–. Annual.

The definition of "municipality" is so broad here that only hamlets seem to be omitted. There is a directory of chief officers for cities of 2,500 or more and information on federal and state actions affecting cities, officials' salaries, fringe benefits, and on and on. It is an excellent resource for any papers that touch upon local politics.

Legal Resource Index
   Belmont, CA: Information Access Co., Inc.
   The American Association of Law Libraries oversees this index, which covers more than 750 legal periodicals. Like IAC's other microfiche/online indexes, the *Legal Resource Index* is updated monthly and cumulates five years' worth of articles. A more traditional index is H.W. Wilson's *Index to Legal Periodicals* (New York: Wilson, 1908–. Monthly, with quarterly and annual cumulations). Information Access Company also produces the highly useful *Government Publications Index*.

Martindale-Hubbel Law Directory
   New York: Martindale-Hubbel, 1931–. 4 vols. Annual.
   Primarily a directory of U.S. and Canadian attorneys, this noted source is valuable for the student researcher because of its digest of state, Canadian, Puerto Rican, and Virgin Island laws.

Black's Law Dictionary
   Henry Campbell Black. Revised by the Publisher's Editorial Staff. St. Paul, MN: West Publishing Co., 1979. Fifth edition.
   Another guide through the legal labyrinth, *Black's* has long been standard. A bit legalistic for the researcher who doesn't know a tort from a tart, this volume is nonetheless useful.

Immigration Law and Practice
   Jack Wasserman. Philadelphia: American Law Institute, 1979.
   This handbook on immigration law in the United States is considerably easier to work through than its full-fledged counterparts, such as Charles Gordon's multi-volume *Immigration Law and Procedure*.

Sports

Encyclopedia of Sports
   Frank G. Menke. New York: A.S. Barnes, 1978. Sixth revised edition.
   This book covers the history, rules, and records of sports ranging from baseball down to those that are relatively obscure. It also makes for good browsing.

Guinness Book of Sports Records Winners and Champions
   Norris McWhirter et al. New York: Sterling Publishing Co., 1982. Revised edition.
   Like its parent volume, the *Guinness Book of World Records*, this book provides many pages of records, anecdotes, and pictures. Here, for example, one can learn that on August 23, 1973, Dr. Allan V. Abbott bicycled 140.5 miles per hour behind a car equipped with a windscreen.

The Sporting News National Football Guide

Edited by Joe Marcin. St. Louis: The Sporting News (Times Mirror), 1979. New edition.

The Sporting News Football Register St. Louis: The Sporting News (Times Mirror), 1966–

These books give the reader everything but a personal autograph from each player. There are massive amounts of data on players, managers, and teams. The *Register*, for example, gives nicknames, high school and college attended, weight, height, and much more.

As for baseball, almost nothing is left out of *The Sporting News Official Baseball Guide* and *The Sporting News Official Baseball Register* (St. Louis: The Sporting News/Times Mirror, 1984). The *Register* offers a forest of statistics on baseball, in which the avid sportsman can hunt elusive facts. For those with even more pronounced obsessions about the sport, there is *The Baseball Encyclopedia* (Joseph L. Reichler, editor. New York: Macmillan, 1985, sixth edition). It provides over 2,700 pages of data—enough to put almost any baseball fan into a statistics stupor.

The Sporting News Official NBA Guide
Edited by Alex Sachare and Dave Sloan. St. Louis: The Sporting News (Times Mirror), 1982. 1982-83 edition.

As the perceptive reader may have guessed, this volume, like its baseball and football counterparts, can give the researcher virtually any detail about the sport—except, perhaps, the average number of numbers in each of *The Sporting News* guides. One of the few topics it neglects is the history of the sport, a gap that is neatly filled in by *The Modern Encyclopedia of Basketball* (edited by Zander Hollander. New York: Four Winds Press, 1973).

EXERCISES

1. Practice developing a research strategy for research questions. How would you look up the following questions? Come up with at least three specific questions that would help answer the larger question.
   a. Could the U.S. Post Office be run more efficiently?
   b. What has the impact been on consumers of the breakdown of IT&T?
   c. It is difficult to immigrate to the United States compared with other countries?
   d. Have Rupert Murdoch's publishing companies made significant changes in newspapers in Great Britain?
   e. Are quartz dial watches more dependable than digital watches?
   Alternatively, you can use a research question that you are currently working on for any class; substitute it for one of the questions above.

2. Choose two of the research questions in Exercise 1 and list sources in Chapters 6 and 7 that would help you answer the specific questions you devised in developing a research strategy.

3. Local libraries are invaluable for learning about your city and the local government. To become familiar with how to use the library for such information, answer the following questions:

   a. How is your city's government organized?

   b. How does the city elect its mayor?

   c. How many people are on its board of supervisors or town council, and what are their names?

Alternatively, you can learn how the administration is organized in your college. Who is the president or chancellor? How many different departments are in the administration? How many people are on the board of trustees, and where do they work?

4. To become familiar with abstracts, try writing one. Look in *Social Sciences Abstracts* or another abstract service for examples. Then take one of your own papers—or one of the essays you used for the exercises in Chapter 3—and write an abstract for it. It should be 100 words or less, and it should sum up the main points of the paper.

5. Be sure you are familiar with the difference between primary and secondary sources and how to use them.

   a. Which of the following are primary sources? (Hint: You may have to define what kind of information is to be used from the sources.)

     -A dictionary

     -The Constitution of the United States

     -A first-person account of the dropping of the atomic bomb on Hiroshima, ghost-written by a journalist.

     -A series of photographs of a county fair.

     -A book written by a "new journalist" such as Hunter Thompson, George Plimpton, or Gay Talese.

   b. What primary and/or secondary sources might you consult to answer the following questions?

     -Does an anaconda have bad breath?

     -What are some of the best ways to get a two-year-old to go to sleep?

     -How can you make cheese at home?

     -How do you saddle a horse?

6. When you are assigned to write a paper, first make a list of the sources you are going to consult. Time the procedure during which you look for the sources. Then bring your list to a librarian, and ask him or her the quickest way to find these sources. Write a short paper that will contrast your method with that of the librarian.

8

Observing _____

In 1973 the scientific community found itself baffled by a young Israeli named Uri Geller. Investigated by trained scientists in controlled experiments, Geller was demonstrating remarkable powers: He could affect the readings of a Geiger counter, make compass needles move, and bend metal forks and spoons—seemingly by the power of his mind alone.

The scientists were determined to be objective in their investigations. They succeeded instead in being duped. Geller was a magician.

PERCEPTUAL PROCESSES

> Appearances to the mind are of four kinds: Things either are what they appear to be; or they neither are, nor appear to be; or they are, and do not appear to be; or they are not, and yet appear to be.
>
> —Epictetus

As with the scientists who evaluated Geller, our training—and even more, our culture—make us blind to the obvious. Often our expectations, stereotypes, and prejudices "see" for us.

Walter Lippmann made the point explicitly in a famous essay that explains how "stereotypes" shape our view of the world: "For the most part we do not see first, then define; we define first and then see. In the great blooming, buzzing confusion of the outer world we pick out what our culture has already defined for us, and we tend to perceive that which we have picked out in the form stereotyped."[1]

We thus tend to see only a vague outline of nearly everything around us. Moreover, we usually tend to see in a way that our language and culture have shaped for us.

This matter of clear observation is of great importance to any conscientious researcher, for observation is the foundation of research. When Copernicus discerned that the earth moves around the sun and not vice versa, he did so on the basis of observation: He saw that the earth's movement did not square with the theory—derived from a certain human egotism—that the earth was the center of the universe. Keen observation led to the more accurate theory. When a psychologist runs an experiment on the behavior of rats under a certain stimulus, the psychologist bases the conclusions on observation. Just as experimentation depends on observation, so does sharp description. When Mark Twain wanted to get across the "feel" of the city of Istanbul in *The Innocents Abroad*, he described the dogs of Istanbul—too disspirited even to snap at flies, let alone saunter across the street to chase a cat. It was a lively way for Twain to accomplish his purpose.

Observation, then, is the basis of research. Yet because we have so many built-in blind spots and biases, it is extremely difficult to observe well. While clear observation reveals the truth of a situation, poor observation clouds it.

The blindness of the scientists investigating Geller is a case in point. They were tripped up by their conception of their roles as scientists, convinced that their observational powers were better than those of the general public. They considered themselves "objective" and were convinced that their methods were applicable, even infallible, in all situations. One editorial suggests how scientists viewed their role. "In medieval times it was priests, later it was noblemen, in Victorian times businessmen and now scientists who are the arbiters of acceptability and correctness," intoned the editors of *Nature*, a respected British journal. ". . . while this duty falls to the scientist he has a great responsibility to be utterly objective and entirely open."[2]

In their efforts to be "utterly objective and entirely open," the scientists who evaluated Geller ignored reports that Geller had been debunked in Israel and had left the country in disgrace. They also discounted the fact that a professional magician, James Randi, was offering Geller $10,000 to perform any wonders that he, Randi, could not duplicate.[3] The scientists remained imprisoned in their scientific method, while the magician could see the tricks of his fellow magician.

In their book *Individual in Society*, David Krech, Richard Crutchfield, and Egerton Ballachey show how we assign people to predefined categories.

Because so many Americans ascribe a *stereotyped* set of personality traits to such groups as Jews, Negroes, Catholics, or Russians, judgments of individual members of these groups often show typical and stereotyped biases.

Thus, many Americans . . . tend to overestimate the shrewdness of a particular Jew, or the inscrutability of a somewhat reticent Russian—because they believe Jews to be shrewd and Russians to be inscrutable. Through contrast, they tend to overestimate the intelligence of an intelligent Negro and to overestimate the liberalism of a Catholic who is liberal in some of his religious views. Again, the reason appears to be due to the stereotyped notion that Negroes are stupid and that Catholics hold extremely conservative religious beliefs.[4]

The scientists would have done well to read Krech, Crutchfield, and Ballachey's book. The authors go on to say, "The critical point to remember is that this bias in perceiving people is not a fault found only among the prejudiced many. It is found in all men and is due to the very nature of our perceptual processes."[4]

Our perceptual processes affect not only what we notice, but what we accept. We tend to explain away, even ignore, evidence that conflicts with our predetermined views of the world.

The point was demonstrated over 35 years ago in an experiment conducted by Mason Haire and Willa Grunes. They gave two groups of students two descriptions of a "certain working man":

To Group I: "Works in a factory, reads a newspaper, goes to movies, average height, cracks jokes, intelligent, strong, active." To Group II: "Works in a factory, reads a newspaper, goes to movies, average height, cracks jokes, strong, active."

The descriptions were identical except that the students in Group I were told that the worker was intelligent.

Then the students were asked to describe the worker in a paragraph. The typical description by students in Group II was summarized by the investigators:

Virtually every description would fit into the pattern of the typical American Joe: likable and well-liked, mildly sociable, healthy, happy, uncomplicated and well-adjusted, in a sort of earthy way; not very intelligent, but trying to keep abreast of current trends, interested in sports and finding his pleasures in simple, undistinguished activities.

Group I had trouble. The students could not reconcile their stereotype of a factory worker with "intelligent." They solved the problem in a variety of ways:

He is intelligent, but not too much so, since he works in a factory.

He is intelligent, but doesn't possess initiative to rise above the group.

The traits seem to be conflicting. . . . Most factory workers I have heard about aren't too intelligent.

Several students who were incapable of ascribing intelligence to a factory worker simply made him a foreman.[5]

The result of our biases is that we were sometimes pathetically poor observers. In the story titled "The Red Headed League," Sherlock Holmes remarks about a client he has met only a few minutes before, "Beyond the obvious facts that he has at some time done manual labor, that he is a freemason, that he has been in China, and that he has done a considerable amount of writing lately, I can deduce nothing." He had deduced enough, of course, to startle the impressionable Dr. Watson. Then Holmes reeled off the observations that led to his deductions. The man had once done manual labor, Holmes concluded, because his right hand was a size larger than his left. He wore a breastpin that signaled Freemasonry. A tattoo of a fish on the right wrist could only have been done in China (Holmes had contributed to the literature of tattoo marks), and besides, a Chinese coin dangled from the man's watch-chain. Because the man's right sleeve cuff was shiny for five inches, and the left exhibited a smooth patch near the elbow where it had probably been rested on the desk, Holmes concluded the man had been writing recently.

Perhaps all this evidence should have been quite elementary for anyone who observes well. Arthur Conan Doyle, author of the Sherlock Holmes stories, patterned his detective on one of his teachers in medical school, Dr. Joseph Bell, a diagnostician with highly developed powers of observation and deduction. For most of us, though, observation seems to be the *least* developed power. In a series of experiments in Geneva, a group of students proved themselves incapable of describing the entrance hall of their own university.

We need only read the work of an extraordinary observer such as Annie Dillard, author of *Pilgrim at Tinker Creek*, to become aware of how little we see. In an article in *Harper's* magazine, she wrote:

> Often I slop some creek water in a jar, and when I get home I dump it in a white china bowl. After the silt settles I return and see tracings of minute snails on the bottom, a planarian or two winding round the rim of water, roundworms shimmying frantically, and finally, when my eyes have adjusted to these dimensions, amoebae. At first the amoebae look like *muscae volitantes*, those curled moving spots you seem to see in your eyes when you stare at a distant wall. Then I see the amoebae as drops of water congealed, bluish, translucent, like chips of sky in the bowl.[6]

We are not accustomed to that kind of seeing, partly because focusing so sharply is hard work for most of us and partly because there is so *much* to see all around us that focusing on one object requires ignoring others. And what is observed or ignored depends on the observer.

Margaret Mead, for example, remembers a senior year dance she attended with her fiancé by writing that they "danced all night and in the damp dawn, which took all the curl out of my small ostrich feather fan, we walked along Riverside Drive, watching the sky brighten over the river." Years later Mead's fiancé remarked dryly that "I should think that she'd have remembered more than the curl going out of the fan."[7]

Often a sharp focus on some details to the exclusion of others is necessary. A man who drives a car properly does not focus on the myriad details that are open to his view. Indeed, avoiding accidents depends on seeing only essential features: the road ahead, other cars, pedestrians, and traffic signals. Moreover, the driver ordinarily does no more than *notice*; he does not observe in a way that would enable him to recall even these features accurately. But such habits can make us mentally lazy. Getting away from selective observation takes work.

It must be pointed out that many stereotypes are valuable. Knowing that someone is a factory worker, we are probably correct in assuming that he is more interested in discussing labor and management issues than in discussing foreign policy, that he probably prefers popular music to classical, that he is more likely to watch sports on television than either Shakespearean plays or soap operas. Such assumptions may be wrong. How could anyone guess, for example, that one of the most respected American poets of the twentieth century, the late Wallace Stevens, was an insurance executive? But our stereotype of the worker *and* the executive are useful; interactions with either are likely to be smoother if we rely to some degree on what we know about most factory workers and most business executives.

Stereotypes, then, are helpful as well as injurious. One should be aware of the dangers and correct distortions by recognizing those that usually afflict observers.

COMMON DISTORTIONS

Quoting: The act of repeating erroneously the words of another.

—Ambrose Bierce

On more than forty occasions, Gordon Allport and Leo Postman used college students, Army trainees, members of community forums, teachers, hospital patients, and police officials in experiments that analyzed the basic psychology of rumor.

They began with a simple but imaginative test of observation. A slide showing a semi-dramatic picture was flashed on a screen before an audience. Six or seven subjects who had not seen the picture waited in another room. Then one of them entered and stood so that he could not see the slide. The picture was described to him in about twenty details. A second subject then entered the room and also took a position where he could not see the screen. The first subject, who was instructed to report as "accurately as possible what you have heard," attempted to describe the picture to the second. Then a third subject entered, stood with his back to the picture, and heard it described by the second. The process was repeated until all the subjects had attempted to describe the picture. The members of the audience, of course, were able to see the picture while they listened to the descriptions.

The presence of the audience helped to assure that the subjects' reports were likely to be more accurate than most rumors. A subject was certain to be more cautious in his description before an audience that knew the facts than he would be in spreading rumors. Similarly, the effect of the instructions was to maximize accuracy and induce caution. In everyday life, no critical experimenter looms over one's shoulder. The likelihood that the reports would be accurate was also enhanced by the time factor, the lapse of time between the hearing and the telling was short in the experiment and is usually much longer in life. Most important, the subjects were struggling for absolute accuracy. Their hates, fears, and wishes were not likely to be as strongly involved in the experiment as in life.

Despite these factors, the resemblance between the pictures and the descriptions deteriorated rapidly. First, the descriptions became more concise, simpler, and related to one another. After five or six retellings, the story had lost 70 percent of the details. As the descriptions became shorter, they also became more selective, fixed on some details to the exclusion of others. When one subject said, "There is a boy stealing and a man remonstrating with him," *all* the other subjects remembered the unusual word "remonstrating" and passed the sentence along without change.

The most important changes resulted from the subjects' attempts to reconcile the pictures with their personal views of reality. Although one of the pictures showed a Red Cross truck loaded with explosives—and it was so described to the first subject—the storytellers changed the cargo to medical supplies, which is, of course, what we have come to believe a Red Cross truck should carry. Similarly, the same picture, a battle scene, showed a black civilian. He gradually became a soldier—no doubt because most people in battle scenes are soldiers. A drugstore, quite clearly described as situated in the middle of a block, became "a corner drugstore"—we are accustomed to thinking of corner drugstores.

Other distortions were also revealing. When police officers were subjects and a picture involving police was shown, the subjects identified immediately with the pictured police to the exclusion of the other people in the picture, and the nightstick was greatly sharpened as a focus of the picture. Describing a picture that included a black person, a black subject said the man "is being maltreated?" (which *may* have been the message of the picture, but an equally plausible interpretation was that he was a rioter about to be arrested). The most sobering distortion involved a picture that showed a white man holding a razor and accosting a black man. In more than half the experiments involving white subjects, as the descriptions moved from one subject to another, the razor shifted from the hand of the white man to the hand of the black man.[8]

Three steps occurred, then, as the subjects passed along their descriptions of the slides: Each simplified the description, selected some details at the expense of others, and then interpreted the details to fit their views of reality. These three processes—simplify, select, and interpret—Allport and Postman termed *leveling*, *sharpening*, and *embedding*. These processes occur simultaneously and represent an effort to reduce a large amount of information to a simply and meaningful structure.

Although this analysis pertains more to rumor than to observation, the effects are the same. Other experiments indicate that the three-pronged process is basic in all remembering[9]. What we bring to a visual experience helps to shape what we see.

A college teacher, H.H. Kelley, once demonstrated how an experience can be distorted by giving his students written descriptions of a guest lecturer. The descriptions were alike with one exception: one group of students read that the lecturer was "rather cold"; the other group read that the lecturer was "very warm." The students did not know that the descriptions varied. After the lecture, the students were asked to rate the guest. Those who had read the "warm" description rated him as more considerate of others, more informed, more sociable, more popular, better natured, more humorous, and more humane than did the students who had received the "cold" description. Also, 56 percent of the students who had read the "warm" description engaged in discussion with the lecturer; only 32 percent of those who had read the "cold" description did so.[10]

The students were misled, of course, but perhaps no more than everyone is misled by public figures and their detractors. In effect, nearly all public figures act publicly in a way that they hope will show them as "very warm"; their detractors are usually trying to show them as "rather cold."

Distorted perception is also common among those who suppose that their observations are accurate because they were *there*; at a battle, a political convention, or some other event. Maurice Bloch, a noted historian, has pointed up this error by imagining that a military commander is trying to describe a victory won on a battlefield of a size so limited that he has been able to see the entire conflict.

> Nevertheless, we cannot doubt that, in more than one essential episode, he will be forced to refer to the reports of his lieutenants. In acting thus as narrator, he would only be behaving as he had a few hours before in the action. Then as commander, regulating the movements of his troops to the swaying tide of battle, what sort of information shall we think to have served him best? Was it the rather confused reports brought in hot haste by the couriers and aides-de-camp? Seldom can a leader of troops be his own observer.[11]

Nor, of course, can any other participant fully observe all the action.

Few distortions are taken for granted so much as those of photography. The human eye takes in an angle of about 120 degrees, but a typical 50-millimeter camera lens takes in only about 25, and a typical telephoto lens takes in only 5 degrees. As Karl Wieck has remarked, much that meets the eye does not meet the lens. And because lenses also foreshorten perspective, especially telephoto lenses, people who are actually standing quite far apart are made to seem a closely packed mass.

Subtle distortions by camera are common. It makes a difference how a cameraman who is filming a person moves his focus along the body. Movement from head to toe is "looking him over" and is likely to be derogatory. Movement from toe to head implies appreciation. A camera held low and pointed up lends importance to the subject; held high, the camera makes the subject insignificant.[12]

Most of the distortions of perception that are common to particular groups are predictable. Not surprisingly, researchers have found that those who strongly desire a small car see a Volkswagen as physically smaller than do those who have no such desire, and that poor children see quarters as larger than they actually are while rich children see them as smaller.

Nor should it be surprising that political partisans see larger crowds gather to hear their candidate than are actually there. "Crowdsmanship," publicizing inflated figures for political advantage, has been commonplace since court bards flattered their kings by exaggerating victories in battle. But there is evidence that, partisan or not, almost everyone overestimates the size of a large crowd, perhaps because the sight of packed masses is so unusual as to be awe-inspiring. Herbert Jacobs, a retired professor who once worked as a journalist and has studied such distortions, tells of an occasion when a plane carrying Richard Nixon landed at the Milwaukee airport.

A Republican Party official estimated the crowd at 12,000. The police estimate was 8,000. A reporter present said there were 5,000. Skeptical editors of the *Milwaukee Journal* enlarged a general crowd picture and counted heads. The number was 2,300.[13]

The mere presence of researchers, even if they are not known as researchers, may affect a group's actions in some way, if only by adding to its numbers. (It is often said that the Communist Party in the United States seems larger than it is because so many undercover FBI agents are in the Party.)

Take the case of four psychologists who want to study a small secret group that was preparing for the end of the world. They tried to avoid distortion by joining the group, not as observers but as full participants. They were rebuffed at first because the group required that its members have had a "psychic experience." The psychologists had one—or said they had—and were accepted. The method was not entirely successful, for reasons the investigators explained:

> There is little doubt that the addition of four new people to a fairly small group within ten days had an effect on the state of conviction among the existing members, especially since the four seem to have appeared when public apathy to the belief systems was great . . . . Most important of all, perhaps, is that the four observers could not be traced through any mutual friends or acquaintances to existing group members and thus the most common and expected channel of recruitment was evidently not responsible for their appearance.[14]

Obviously, this is a special case; observers have been able to participate unobtrusively in groups less sensitive to new members.

DISTORTIONS CAUSED BY OBSERVERS

The first rule is the first rule in life: see everything yourself.

—Richard Melba

In the 1930s Elton Mayo conducted an experiment that would help change American businesses' views of management.

"Scientific management" had become something of a sensation in the business world. By analyzing the movements of shovelers in a Bethlehem Steel plant to see how they could work most efficiently, Frederick Taylor had helped the company improve productivity dramatically at the turn of the century. Following Taylor's footsteps, Frank Bunker Gilbreth and Lillian Gilbreth (of *Cheaper by the Dozen* fame) were carrying on experiments of "motion study."

The Mayo experiment began along the same lines as did other "scientific management" studies. Elton Mayo observed six telephone assemblers in a Chicago plant to discover what factors—heat, light, sleep—affected their productivity. The assemblers were aware that they were being observed, and over the thirteen weeks of the experiment their productivity continued to rise for no discernible reason. Finally, Mayo concluded that it was the concern for the workers, and the boost in their morale, that made the difference.[15] In short, their observer affected their behavior, exactly as it did in studies of the Hawthorne effect described in Chapter 2. Fortunately for Mayo, however, he achieved what he had hoped to do—improve productivity in the factory. Those who research human behavior for the sake of research alone find such manifestations of the Hawthorne effect much more troublesome.

Observers do indeed affect the behavior of those they observe. A dean who sits in on a class session to learn whether a young instructor is an effective teacher confounds his or her own effort to observe a typical classroom performance; the presence of the dean alters the situation. The alteration is not equal in impact in all situations, of course. Few soldiers in action will behave much differently because a reporter is on the battle scene; the stress of combat is far too great to make the observer an important element. An actress who hopes to promote a favorable image is more likely to alter her actions to influence a movie columnist than to influence, say, the waitress at the diner across the street from the agency that negotiates her roles.

UNDETECTED OBSERVATION

You see, but you do not observe.

—Arthur Conan Doyle

Undetected observation has one tremendous advantage: The subjects behave normally because they are unaware that they are being watched. However attractive undetected observation may be, though, it raises questions of ethics.

Part of the question is the extent to which the observer manipulates those who are being observed, and to what extent the observation invades their privacy or subjects them to stress. For example, a researcher might sit in a corner of a shopping mall and observe passers-by without threatening their well-being and anonymity. Some field experiments, on the other hand, have used the unsuspecting public as experimental subjects. For example, in one study a young passenger with a cane on a New York subway seemed to lose his grasp, staggered a few feet, then collapsed. He lay staring at the ceiling of the subway car until a few of the other passengers helped him to a sitting position. A few days later the same young man boarded the subway carrying not a cane but a bottle and smelling strongly of alcohol. He collapsed again. His fellow passengers were less sympathetic and helpful this time. Only when the train stopped was he helped to his feet by a student. Still later, he returned with the cane, sober, and repeated his first performance as a cripple. Then again he performed as a drunk. He repeated the act so often—sometimes as a cripple, sometimes as a drunk—that eventually more than four thousand subway riders had seen it. They did not know, of course, that he was a student, unobtrusively accompanied by another student who sometimes helped him in order to give the other subway riders the idea. Two female accomplices were always in the crowd, taking notes on the reactions of the passengers.

Ethical questions must be resolved according to a reasonable standard. It is doubtful that such a standard would rule out the kind of observation made by the students on the subway. Indeed, when those who are being observed are not personally embarrassed or injured by an experiment or a report of an experiment, ingenious research is in order.

Today such experiments may or may not be considered acceptable by watchdog organizations like the Office for Protection from Research Risks, part of the U.S. Government's Department of Health and Human Services. Government-funded research must be reviewed for such elements as risk to the subject, confidentiality, and the extent to which the field experiment violates the rights and welfare of the subjects. Where any such matters are in doubt, the researcher is required to obtain the informed consent of the experimental subject—which, of course, transforms the experiment into a laboratory study rather than a field experiment.

On the other hand, observing unobtrusively, even through "participant observation," is still widely practiced. Reporters have joined adolescent gangs, dressed themselves as street people, and joined religious cults to get stories.

Participant observation does bring danger of distortion. When one who participates is *known* to be an observer, the other participants usually react much as they do in the presence of an observer who is not a participant: Their initial behavior is likely to be self-conscious and even secretive. Except in unusual instances, awareness of the outsider tends to diminish in time, but it may not disappear unless the observer's actions are so compatible with those of the other participants that they come to think of him as one of them. Gerald Berreman, an anthropologist, has written of his study of a village in India: "It was six months after my arrival before animal sacrifices and attendant rituals were performed in my presence although they had been performed in my absence or without my knowledge throughout my residence in the village."[16]

The compatible observer may begin participation already sharing the goals of the group he or she joins, or the observer may come to share them over time. This suggests a deep pitfall: To what degree is the individual a participant, to what degree an observer? The psychologists who joined the end-of-the world society were clearly more observers than participants. But one who shares the goals and values of the participants may be a bad observer for that reason—or, in any case, he or she will not perceive as an outside observer would. What is gained by participation may be more than overbalanced by the loss of a more detached view.

"New journalists" like Thomas Wolfe, Hunter S. Thompson, George Plimpton, and Norman Mailer have solved the problem rather neatly. Rather than pretending to be objective, they make themselves part of the story. Plimpton, for example, joined a professional football team to write *Paper Lion*. Such a technique sidesteps the question of how much the observer influences what he sees; the observer makes the extent of his participation quite clear. Nor does the reporter necessarily lay claim to objectivity. The subjective reporting style of the "new journalism" is less well suited to news reporting than to entertainment writing and commentary. Consequently, anyone who attempts to report objectively from the perspective of a participant observer should first pose this question: *Why* am I a participant observer—to participate or to observe and report? Then the individual must evaluate the consequences of the answer and try to provide a balance between participation and observation.

When participant observation lasts for an extended period, one may be able to restore balance through discussions with outsiders during that period. While conducting research for his famous book *Street Corner Society*, William Whyte so immersed himself in the life of his subjects that he did not know how he had changed until a friend came to visit him:

> . . . When John Howard first came down from Harvard to join me in the Cornerville, study, he noticed at once that I talked in Cornerville in a manner far different from that which I used at Harvard. This was not a matter of the use of profanity or obscenity, nor did I affect the use of ungrammatical expressions. I talked in the way that seemed natural to me, but what was natural in Cornerville was different from what was natural at Harvard . . . . When I was most deeply involved in Cornerville, I found myself rather tongue-tied in my visits to Harvard.[17]

Whyte found that when he finally left Cornerville he lost most of the manner that it had imposed on him, which suggests that participant observers should try to arrange for a lapse of time after they leave the milieu they are observing before reporting their findings.

The susceptibility of the participant observer should never be lightly regarded. Two scientific observers of audience behavior at a Billy Graham crusade in New York left their posts at the end of Graham's sermon and went to the altar to make *their* "Decision for Christ"![18]

Observers can help themselves to counter distortions by realizing how often and in what ways their presence distorts what they see. To fit the Heisenberg uncertainty principle (see page 21) to this subject: The act of observing changes what is observed.

However, there are limits to the changes that the presence of any observer *can* make. The presence of a reporter is unlikely to cause a coward to become a hero. Nor can an authoritarian teacher become an adaptable or permissive one—or not very persuasively—merely because a dean is watching. As one researcher has pointed out:

> One cannot completely set aside on a moment's notice the attitudes and patterns of social behavior which have been developed and practiced for years in favor of other, unnatural forms of behavior fancied to be more acceptable.[19]

The pivotal element in nearly all cases in which the observer makes a difference is *time*. Those who can put on a facade that covers their attitudes and behavior—or are caused to do so involuntarily by the stress of being observed— cannot maintain their pose. How long does the dean observe the teacher? How long does the reporter stay with the soldiers? How long does the columnist watch the actress? Virtually every study of the degree to which an observer's presence changes behavior emphasizes that the effect diminishes over time, and in many cases the observer is forgotten. Consciousness of being observed is strongest, then, at the beginning.

This phenomenon suggests important questions that an observer must consider: How does the subject behave when he or she is most conscious of being observed? How does the subject behave later?

GUIDELINES FOR OBSERVING

Our most important sights are those which contradict our emotions.

—Paul Valery

Being aware of the pitfalls of observing enables one to prepare strategies for avoiding them. Consider the following guidelines.

Know Thyself

Anyone who sets out to play the role of observer or record the memories of those who have observed should remember the central human failings of observation. As Allport and Postman demonstrated, we tend to simplify what we see, select the details we will notice, and interpret events to suit our views of reality. These processes are largely unavoidable; one *must* simplify and select because human powers are not infinite, and one's deeply embedded habits, interests, and sentiments inevitably affect the way one takes in new information.

But the process of maturing is largely learning from new experiences; opening oneself to a wide variety of experiences is valuable. Remembering the processes of perception will help anyone guard against the strongest effects of the most evident kind of distortion. At the very least, recognizing the distortions will make one less certain of one's certainties.

Recall Emotional States

The influence of emotional states has been recognized at least since the time of Aristotle, who wrote:

> Under the influence of strong feeling we are easily deceived regarding our sensations, different persons in different ways, as, e.g., the coward under the influence of fear and the lover under that of love have such illusions that the former owing to a trifling resemblance thinks he sees an enemy and the latter his beloved. And the more impressionable the person is, the less the resemblance required. Similarly, everybody is easily deceived when in anger or influenced by any strong desire, and the more subject one is to these feelings the more one is deceived.[20]

An observer can also learn to question his certainties by judging his emotional state at the time they were formed. Most of us learn to discount some unfounded impressions, usually angry ones, and dismiss them with, "Well, I guess I was pretty emotional at the time." This ability is useful in trying to recall observations. What mood heightened my impression of this facet and obscured that one?

Moreover, because study after study has shown what most of us could have guessed, that memory deteriorates rapidly over time, it is clear that the most accurate observations are likely to be those recounted immediately after an event. But if the event places emotional stress on the observer, he is more subject to distortion caused by emotions. This dilemma can be resolved in many cases if impressions of an event are recorded immediately after it occurs in order to capture details that might be forgotten. Later, the observer can assess his first account when he is more tranquil and can evaluate his emotional state at the earlier time.

Concentrate on Significant Details

Bruce Bliven, one of the most accomplished of modern journalists, had the good fortune early in his career to work under Fremont Older, a demanding editor who, Bliven said, "had a personality so vigorous you could feel his presence through a brick wall." How Older taught young reporters to observe is illustrated by an incident. Despairing of an unobservant young reporter who wrote with little flavor, Older decided that the man would be able to write compellingly only if he immersed himself in the life of his subject. Older assigned him to spend three weeks playing and singing hymns with the Salvation Army, which was then a familiar sight on San Francisco street corners. But the reporter's effort to breathe life into his story of the Army was a failure. "Didn't you observe anything?" Older bellowed. "At night, for instance, *where did they hang the bass drum?*" The reporter did not know, and he was fired. Older recounted this incident for years to push young reporters into becoming sensitive observers. Fifty years after his own experiences with Older, Bliven still said, "After I meet someone, I ask myself questions about his personal appearance, to make sure I really saw him."

This is not to say that the observer should lose sight of the forest in order to count the leaves on the trees. Find *significant* details—and don't lose sight of the main focus of research. Just as a driver must ignore the roadside scenery, an observer who attends, say, a political convention has a hopeless task if he does not have in mind or on paper what he expects to focus on. He should be guided, through not bound, by his plans. Then he must train himself to concentrate on what is significant for him. The ability, or the will, to concentrate varies, that is the primary reason some football coaches are better than others at scouting upcoming opponents and picking out small but crucial details of interior line play while nearly everyone else in the stadium is watching the ball. Everyone with vision, however, can train himself to concentrate it.

Remembering the Distortions of Perspective

Consider a hypothetical scene on a college campus. Several students and faculty members are holding a noon rally. A reporter stands only fifteen feet from the principal speaker. He is close enough to observe the speaker's vigorous little gestures and rubs elbows with the speaker's lieutenants and chief supporters, who move about excitedly and fill the pauses in the speech with applause and cheers. Twenty-five feet away, in a good position to hear every word of the speech but not close enough to feel and see the excitement among the speaker's supporters or to hear *their* words, stands another reporter. He is ringed about by students who have merely stopped by on their way to classes. Some of the listeners in *his* area mutter insults, others yawn. If the first reporter is persuaded by his senses to write that the rally demonstrated considerable support for the speaker, and if the second writes that the rally demonstrated little support, who can blame either? Anyone should. The situation is a simple illustration of limited perspectives. The reporter, or any other researcher, who allows himself to be limited by such narrow perspectives will never come within shouting distance of probable truth.

If the problems of perspective were no more acute than this example suggests, solving them, or at least devising methods to reduce their effects, would be simple. Perspective is much more complicated, however.

In 1951, when President Harry Truman relieved General Douglas MacArthur of his command in the Far East, MacArthur came home to crowd-lined streets in many American cities. Kurt and Gladys Lang decided to study "MacArthur day" in Chicago by stationing 31 observers along the parade route and using other observers to monitor the television reports of the parade.[21] A typical account by one of the observers along the parade route was:

> I had expected to hear much political talk, especially anti-Communist and against the Truman administration . . . . I was amazed that I did not once hear Truman criticized, Acheson [Secretary of State under Truman] mentioned, or as much as an allusion to the Communists . . . . I had expected roaring, excited mobs; instead, there were quiet, well ordered, dignified people.

In sharp contrast were the impressions of television viewers. The camera followed MacArthur, and the viewer focused on the interplay between heroic figure and enthusiastic crowd. The cheering seemed constant, and even seemed to reach its crest as the telecast ended. Meanwhile, the reality along the streets was much less exciting. The spectators caught a brief glimpse of General MacArthur, and that was all.

How can an observer avoid the distortion caused by perspective? The most obvious and direct method is to recognize that any single perspective is necessarily limited and must be supplemented with others. A careful researcher is usually quick to realize that he must consider other perspectives when he is weighing another observer's report, but he is often not so quick to supplement his own observations. Nearly everyone is all too ready to trust the evidence he has seen. Wilbur Schramm often arranged to have another researcher accompany him for observing and interviewing, especially in developing countries. He learned that checking one impression against another often yields surprising and useful results.

Deciding whose impression to accept is not always easy, but a guideline used in courts is helpful. The law asks not only whether a witness was actually present and whether his or her vision was adequate, but also whether the witness was *competent*. Many scholars who study Henry James believe that some of the literary figures who talked with James and recalled that he stuttered and hemmed and hawed were probably wrong. Elizabeth Jordon, who had been trained in speech and who also spoke with James, was so entranced by his extraordinary manner of speaking that she wrote down one of his characteristic sentences. It became clear from her description that James was neither a stutterer nor a hesitant speaker but chose to repeat his words variously, "instinctively bringing out the perfect sentence the first time; repeating it more deliberately to test every word the second time; accepting it as satisfactory the third time, and triumphantly sending it forth as produced by Henry James."[22] In such cases, the judgment of an expert is usually accepted.

Seek Other Evidence

Considering perspectives of other observers is usually valuable, but even that kind of cross-checking must often yield to physical evidence. William L. Prosser, a professor of law, has observed, "There is still no man who would not accept dog tracks in the mud against the testimony of a hundred eye-witnesses that no dog had passed by."[23]

Before he retired, Herbert Jacobs taught at the University of California at Berkeley during the period when protest rallies drew large crowds. Distressed by the varying published estimates of the sizes of crowds in Sproul Plaza, he used photographs, density counts, and blueprints of the plaza to devise a formula: If a crowd seems fairly loosely composed—if spectators can be seen moving in and out of the middle—multiply the sum of the length and width of the area they occupy by seven. If the crowd seems compact and there is little movement within it, multiply by ten. Thus, a crowd in an area that measures 100 by 150 feet—a sum of 250 feet—contains about 1,750 people if it is loosely composed, about 2,500 if compact.[24]

The authors of *Unobtrusive Measures*[25] tell how much can be learned from other kinds of physical evidence. They report on research techniques that range from judging reading habits by examining the wear and tear on library books to counting noseprints on the glass that encloses exhibits. One researcher whose work they describe estimated liquor consumption in a "dry" city by counting liquor bottles in garbage cans.

Study Nonverbal Communication

Another way to corroborate one's observations is to back them with an informed understanding of nonverbal communication.

Albert Mehrabian of the University of California at Los Angeles once reported research indicating that what a person says in words is only 7 percent of what he communicates when he talks; 38 percent is conveyed by his manner of speech and 55 percent by his facial expressions and body movements.[26] Ray Birdwhistell of the University of Pennsylvania has said that in an average two-person conversation the verbal components carry less than 35 percent of the social meaning of the situation; more than 65 percent is nonverbal.[27] These analyses are not contradictory despite the differences in percentages; Mehrabian and Birdwhistell are reporting on different speech situations. We may doubt that research of that kind can be so precise, but we receive so many *wordless* messages—from hitchikers, sports fans brought to their feet by actions on the field, frustrated motorists kicking flat tires, students sleeping in class—that recalling them should persuade us that much (if not most) communication is nonverbal.

If reflection is not persuasive, consider the true story of a horse that was bought in Berlin in 1900 by a German named von Osten. The horse, Hans, was taught to count by tapping his front hoof. He learned fast and was taught to add, subtract, multiply, and divide. Eventually, he learned to tell time, use a calendar, and perform other feats, all of which he demonstrated by tapping his hoof. Exhibited to the public, Hans would count the crowd and the number wearing eyeglasses.

Hans became so famous that he was examined by an investigating committee made up of professors of psychology and physiology, cavalry officers, veterinarians, a director of a circus, and the director of the Berlin Zoological Garden. Von Osten was not present during the examination, but there was no change in his horse's apparent intelligence. The committee announced that Hans actually was able to perform as advertised, that no trickery had been involved.

But then a second investigating committee was established. One of the examiners told von Osten to whisper a number in one of Hans's ears while another examiner whispered another number in the other ear. Then Hans was told to add them. He could not. Similar tests revealed why he failed: Hans could see no one who knew the answer. The secret of his remarkable feats became clear. When the horse was asked a question, anyone who knew the answer unwittingly became tense and assumed an expectant posture. When Hans's hoof taps reached the right answer, the onlooker would unwittingly relax and make a slight head movement. That was the signal to Hans to stop tapping.[28]

Even though Hans did not perform feats that proved high intelligence, his feat of observation was remarkable enough. It hints at how much we say without speaking. But it is only a hint, for in recent years researchers have begun to uncover a vast field of nonverbal communication that includes body language but is not limited to it. One researcher, Mark L. Knapp, defines the field by placing the many studies in seven classes.

1. Body motion (also known as "kinesic behavior") includes gestures, movements of the body, limbs, hands, head, and feet, facial expressions, eye behavior, and posture.
2. Physical characteristics include physique or body shape, general attractiveness, body or breath odors, height, weight, hair, and skin color or tone.
3. Touching behavior includes stroking, hitting, greetings and farewells, holding, and guiding another's movements.
4. Paralanguage deals with *how* something is said rather than what is said—voice qualities and vocalizations such as laughing, crying, sighing, whispering, and heavily marked inhaling or exhaling.
5. Proxemics is the study of one's use and perception of one's social and personal space—how people use and respond to small-group settings, crowds, and the like.

6. Artifacts include use and manipulation of objects such as perfume, clothes, lipstick, eyeglasses, wigs and other hairpieces, false eyelashes, and the entire repertoire of personal aids and falsifications.

7. Environmental factors are different from all the others in that they are not concerned with personal appearance and behavior. They include furniture, interior decoration, lighting conditions, smells, colors, temperatures, and added noises or music. [29]

So much has been learned about how we communicate without words—and nonverbally in conjunction with words—that it defies summary. A few findings seem to be no more than analyses of the obvious, such as one reporting that many attractive students use their good looks to get better grades than they deserve. [30] A few findings are presented with dubious precision, such as an analysis of the "courtship dance" of the American adolescent, which is reported as consisting of exactly 24 steps between the initial contact of the young male and female and the coitional act. [31] But many of the research reports are convincing, and useful to anyone who hopes to observe accurately.

The experience of Don Dodson shows how body language helps us understand what people mean when they speak. Interviewing in Nigeria in 1971, he took notes and made tape recordings. He discovered when he returned to the United States that his rather sketchy notes were more valuable than the recordings. Although the tapes provided a full record of what had been said and could be used in interpreting paralanguage (*how* something is said), they were divorced from facial expressions, movements, gestures, general appearance, and surroundings. The notes did not include these factors either, but Dodson discovered that he had been influenced by such factors in taking his notes. In many instances, he had been able to note exactly what he needed because the notes were part of the nonverbal experience in a way that the recordings were not.

There is a danger, however, in trying consciously to apply what one has learned about nonverbal communication. Like those who read Freud's *Interpretation of Dreams* and consider themselves instant experts on dream states, many are so taken with the ideas and insights of nonverbal theory that they try too quickly to move from theory to practice, or try to interpret almost any noticeable movement, tone, facial expression or gesture as highly significant. Beginners are not alone in being over enthusiastic about the traces of nonverbal communication they observe. In an otherwise excellent book entitled *Word Play*, Peter Farb proclaims that "Pupil performance does not depend so much upon a school's audiovisual equipment or new textbooks or enriching trips to museums as it does upon teachers whose body language communicates high expectations." [32] Farb may be right, but other theorists doubt that a teacher's body language is as important as Farb makes it seem.

A researcher can avoid much of the danger by testing his observations over time. He might focus almost exclusively on nonverbal rather than verbal language in the first of several interviews with one interviewee. Does the interviewee inhale and exhale markedly? Does he laugh nervously? Does his clothing seem to be highly individual? These or other traits are likely to seem pronounced to a researcher who looks primarily for them. In later interviews, however, the researcher is likely to find that he was misled in at least one particular *because* he was looking for traits. Such an exercise helps place observation in perspective.

No research strategy can transform a fallible human into a faultless observer, but one who is armed with knowledge of the many pitfalls and with strategies for avoiding them has taken a long step toward observing truly.

EXERCISES

Learning to observe accurately requires practice in observing details dispassionately. The following series of exercises will help you to develop observation skills.

Read the following passages from Mark Twain's *Life on the Mississippi*, in which Twain writes about the way two different viewers would describe the surface of the water on the same stretch of river. The passenger or untrained riverboat pilot would see merely a beautiful red sunset at a wooded river's edge, with a drifting log. A pilot's view of the scene would be much different:

> This sun means that we are going to have wind tomorrow; that floating log means that the river is rising, small thanks to it; that slanting mark on the water refers to a bluff reef which is going to kill somebody's steamboat one of these nights, if it keeps on stretching out like that; those tumbling 'boils' show a dissolving bar and a changing channel there; the lines and circles in the slick water over yonder are a warning that that troublesome place is shoaling up dangerously; that silver streak in the shadow of the forest is the 'break' from a new snag, and he has located himself in the very best place he could have found to fish for steamboats . . .[33]

Twain has illustrated how one's training affects one's observation.

Now do the following exercises:

1. Find a scene that is small enough to describe, such as your desk, the entrance to the library, or a small aquarium. Write a list of things you notice about the scene—colors, shapes, locations, movement. Stay away from interpretation, as in "The fish is swimming as if it is looking for food." You don't know whether the fish is looking for anything; stick with "The fish is swimming along the glass, bouncing its mouth against it." Write down details for 30 minutes; there should be plenty of material. This exercise will hone your observation skills by showing you how much there is to notice.

2. Take the list of items you noticed and pick out the seven or eight most telling details from your perspective. Then pick out the seven or eight most significant details as your mother might choose them, as an urchin from the ghetto might see them, as an Indian from the forests of Brazil might see them. For example, you might notice the different kinds of fish in the tank—this angelfish is a different kind from that angelfish, one of the fish frequently swims through the plant in the corner, and so on. Your mother might describe the state of the algae on the sides of the tank and the fact that the catfish is not nibbling at it so much as resting on the bottom of the tank. The ghetto child might notice the colors of the fish.

3. Now choose two of the three sets of significant details and write them into two four-paragraph descriptions of the scene. The two descriptions should show how bias turns up in the details chosen.

4. Finally, trade papers with a classmate and see if you can tell from each others' descriptions who it is that is looking at the scene.

5. Observe one of your instructors when he or she conducts lectures. What gestures are used frequently? What pet phrases does the instructor have? Does the instructor pace in the classroom? What is the facial expression when he or she is seemingly in high spirits? What does your instructor do when pondering something? Write a 200-word paragraph to describe your instructor.

6. If possible, attend a wedding ceremony. What kind of dress do the bride and groom wear? How do most of the guests dress? How many people attend the ceremony? Are they mostly old, middle-aged, or young? Write a short report, describing the scene and the atmosphere.

9

Interviewing ⎯⎯⎯

Interviewing has definite disadvantages as a research technique. Psychologists David Weiss and Rene Dawis once wrote that "it is indefensible to assume the validity of purportedly factual data obtained by interviews."[1] Journalist Thomas Morgan once said, "*I* want the truth; *they* want to be beautiful." Irving Wallace, novelist and magazine writer, noted, "You wouldn't really know what goes on in my head and heart, because I wouldn't tell you, even if *I* understood. We all have protective devices out of necessity, because a living man must possess a private self, for without it he is only half alive."[2]

There is much support for these judgments. Researchers have found that mothers report childrearing practices that are different from what they actually did; mothers whose infants have difficulties immediately after delivery tend to forget that fact, though they remember accurately other events surrounding the delivery. Similarly, homeowners report incorrectly on household repairs, hospitalized patients report their preoperative anxieties inaccurately—the list of discrepancies increases with nearly every careful investigation by social scientists.[3]

Fallible memories are one problem; personal interest is another. Using less methodical techniques than those of the social scientists, journalists find again and again that what they are told often differs from the truth. Some of them may reflect ruefully on a judgment published in *The Nation* in 1869, when formal interviewing was not common in journalism: "The 'interview,' as at present managed, is generally the joint product of some humbug of a hack politician and another humbug of a reporter."[4]

If the interview is so error-prone, why use it? The primary answer is suggested by the title of an excellent monograph by two social psychologists, Eugene J. Webb and Jerry R. Salancik, *The Interview, or The Only Wheel in Town*.[5] The title comes from an anecdote familiar to gamblers:

FIRST GAMBLER, *arriving in town*:   Any action around?
SECOND GAMBLER: Roulette.
FIRST GAMBLER: You play?
SECOND GAMBLER: Yes.
FIRST GAMBLER: Is the wheel straight?
SECOND GAMBLER: No.
FIRST GAMBLER: Why do you play?
SECOND GAMBLER: It's the only wheel in town.

A reporter may find interviews to be the only wheel in town for breaking stories, but the interview is not really the only wheel for most research. It is an important one nonetheless. Interviewing yields opinions, fresh observations, and perspective on the research topic. An interview subject can clarify a topic and suggest further directions for research. An interview can also provide the human interest that is vital for making reports interesting and readable.

Interviewing, despite its failings, is an important vehicle for fact-finding as well. There is a basic defense for interviewing, one that tempers the gloomiest judgments: The more we learn about the inaccuracies that frequently crop up in interviews, the more we know about what kinds of questions are likely to be answered inaccurately—and what kinds we can trust.

Because they have relied for so long on interviews and conducted so many, both journalists and social scientists have developed a large body of useful techniques. The full panoply of survey research methods is not essential in all interviewing of course, but applying the insights of the social scientists to the interview style of the journalist yields lessons for almost any researcher.

The Journalist's and Social Scientist's Interviews

There are differences between the interview methods of a journalist and those of a social scientist. Researchers who conduct opinion surveys have learned to engineer questions and prepare interviewers to get the least biased sample possible. They interview many subjects to arrive at a generalization, and they try to make all interviews alike. Journalists, on the other hand, have learned to delve deeply into individual interview subjects, ferreting out information and opinions and taking the problems of bias and possible inaccuracies in stride. For them, a free-flowing interview often works best.

The difference between the two methods is reflected in the ways that interview subjects are asked to interact with the researcher. Consider:

- Most often journalists are welcome and their questions answered eagerly. Because they sometimes assume the role of adversary to those in power, especially politicians, some journalists' *questions* may be distasteful to the subject. But the mass media are usually considered to confer status on those whose opinions are quoted and whose experiences are related. In general, then, the natural role of the journalists is one of power because most of those they interview want to have their views quoted in print or on radio or TV.
- The favors that social scientists can confer on interview subjects are seldom so immediate, so direct, or so obviously beneficial. The subjects are not likely to have their opinions or experiences publicized tomorrow or next week, and they probably will not receive *any* personal publicity; little social research singles out individuals. There is another, usually weaker, lure for the interview subject: the possibility that they are contributing in a small way to important findings. Many social scientists emphasize this contribution with satisfying results. It is also true that so few in any society are ever asked to offer their opinions or relate their experiences that many who are asked for interviews—especially by people of high status—are flattered and cooperative.

To contrast the positions: the *journalists* are often *offering* favors when they interview; *social scientists* are often *receiving* a favor. What these generalizations say about the usual role of the different interviewers should be obvious.

Note that the student who interviews for campus publications often shares the favorable position of the professional journalist, and the student who interviews for a project supervised by social scientists usually shares their status and can make appeals for the same cooperation. But the student who seeks interviews for, say, a term paper is usually in the unfortunate position of requesting cooperation for his own purposes. Fortunately, many who are asked for interviews by students are willing to help. Nevertheless, the role of the student is nearly always that of the supplicant, which limits his ability to ask questions that the interview subject is likely to consider abrasive or embarrassing.

Psychologists Eleanor and Nathan Maccoby point out in their chapter on interviewing in *The Handbook of Social Psychology* that concepts of role are central: "The interviewer must occupy some role, whether he wishes it or not, and therefore the research worker must be conscious of the various roles possible . . . and attempt to establish the role which will best further the purposes of the study."[6] This is excellent advice, and almost any researcher can adapt his or her role to some degree depending on circumstances—and, of course, depending on the role the interview subject establishes for him or herself.

TIPS FROM THE SOCIAL SCIENTISTS

The important thing is not to stop questioning.

—Albert Einstein

The Single-Interview Error

Social scientists would not dream of adopting the technique of the fabled naturalist who published an astonishing report on the behavior of rats after observing just one rat. Journalists and student researchers can endorse the social scientists: Multiple interviews are helpful and, for the same reason, a lengthy interview is often better than a short one. More information yields a more rounded, and more accurate, picture of the subject.

Ricardo Diaz, a documentary filmmaker, tells of interviewing a young American race-car driver who sought the world's land speed record, which was then held by a foreigner. When Diaz asked him, early in the interview, why he was in such a dangerous occupation, the young man spoke grandly of the challenge of speed and the need to bring the world's record home to the United States. Much later, when they had covered many other subjects and were less formal with each other, Diaz asked him again why he drove for a world record. The driver then admitted that, as one with little education and a taste for splendor, he saw no other path for himself. Perhaps the real answer combined elements of the first and second—and more. In any event, the pitfalls of a single brief interview are obvious.

By the same token, it is usually absurd to expect to picture a person or relate his or her purposes or policies adequately by interviewing just that subject. To do so is to invite imprisonment in the subject's perspective. "The reporter has to talk to enough people so that he can reduce the degree to which he is misled," Joseph and Stewart Alsop have written.[7] Lyndon Johnson's prime technique was to overwhelm the reporter with rhetoric and activity; other public figures have developed different and equally successful ways of manipulating interviewers. The interviewer must counter such techniques by learning more than the interview subject tells. Additional interviews and careful research in documents enable the reporter to compare what all the sources say to arrive at the probable truth.

The truth will not always emerge neatly. A reporter once wrote an article on Congressman John J. Rooney of New York, who was the chairman of a congressional committee that was pivotal in deciding the budget for the U.S. Department of State. Year after year Rooney would present his committee's budget recommendations to the House of Representatives and verbally attack the State Department at the same time. He consistently called "representation allowances"—money that enabled U.S. missions to make small expenditures for entertaining—"booze money for those striped-pants cookie-pushers." The allowances for such major embassies as those in England and France were always too small for the entertaining that had long been traditional. As a result, only wealthy men who could pay entertainment bills out of their own pockets could afford to represent the United States there. But a high official of the State Department assured the reporter that Congressman Rooney was actually the best friend the Department had. He explained that most congressmen were contemptuous of the State Department. By attacking it, Congressman Rooney seemed to be their ally, when in fact he always presented a budget that was larger than Congress would have approved had Rooney not attacked. Given the known attitude toward the State Department of many congressmen, this theory seemed plausible. But checking budget records over several years and conducting other interviews—especially with retired State Department officials who no longer had anything to gain or lose from Congressman Rooney's actions—persuaded the reporter that it was not true. The weight of all the evidence caused him to judge that the congressman's attacks were sincere—but the possibility that the State Department official was right led the reporter to report that theory as well.

Social scientists, as well as historians and biographers who interview, have also learned that they cannot rely on a single source. Many social scientists ask questions that can be checked against records (When asked, "Do you have a library card?" many who do not have cards report that they do, because using a library lends status). They also ask questions of friends and relatives of the interview subject. Any competent historian or biographer uses much the same techniques for checking accuracy.

Appearance and Manner of the Interviewer

Interviewers are often distorted before they begin. Studies show that the interviewer's race, religion, sex, and even age influence response. Most counter-measures are aimed at reducing the social distance between the interviewer and the subject. In a few cases, a vast social distance is useful, as the success of journalist Tom Wolfe, whose dress is usually bizarre, has shown. Most often, though, a great distance causes distortion. Many respondents in social science research will answer questions in a way that they believe will meet the interviewer's approval, if the interviewer seems to represent a higher social class than that to which the respondent belongs. Other respondents may resent an interviewer who seems to be of a higher social class. In short, the appearance and manner of the interviewer influences the interview. For that reason, some editors have recommended—even ordered—reporters to dress to match the occasion of an interview.

The Way Questions Are Worded and Delivered

One of survey researchers' biggest concerns is question wording. Most do extensive pretesting to ensure that the questions are free from bias, are not "loaded" or leading, and follow a progression that does not influence the respondents' answers. Nevertheless interviewers are still prone to framing questions thoughtlessly.

A classic case of sloppy wording occurred in the summer of 1972, when an obnoxious young American named Bobby Fischer was playing a Russian, Boris Spassky, for the chess championship of the world. Fischer was behaving so abominably that the editors of the *Sacramento Union* thought may of their readers might favor the Russian. They printed a small ballot that asked: "Are you pulling for Fischer or Boris Spassky to win? Yes ——————. No ——————."

Some differences in question wording that can affect respondents' answers can be quite subtle. For example, "Do you think the United States should allow public speeches against democracy?" would seem to be the opposite of "Do you think the United States should forbid public speeches against democracy?" One would expect opposite percentages when matched samples of respondents are asked these questions. Instead, these were the results:

First Question	*Second Question*
Should allow 21%	Should not forbid 39%
Should not allow 62%	Should forbid 46%
No opinion 17%	No opinion 15%

Clearly, there is something forbidding about "forbid." People will more readily say that an act should not be allowed than say it should be forbidden.[8]

Although it is fairly easy to avoid loaded questions in writing interview schedules and questionnaires (constant evaluation is essential, however), it is not so easy to avoid them in free-flowing interviews. More distortions may spring from questions that lead respondents down the interviewer's path than from any other source. Note how this respondent is pulled by the interviewer:

Q: What kind of writers are left in television then?
A: Those who are still around are trained in the taboos of the business . . . .
Q: Again this stems from the commercial exigencies of television, doesn't it?
A: It comes from the commercial nature. I don't want to be unfair to the businessman but . . . .
Q. But all these purposes—artistic, commercial, etc.—are at war with each other.
A: Continually at war. The thing I object to is that the world of commerce is using the resources of the theatre, of all our culture, for sales purposes.
Q: On a medium that belongs to the public.
A: Yes, I think that is short-sighted and foolish . . . .
Q: What can a governmental regulatory agency do in this regard? The Federal Communications Commission has been a rather toothless organization in recent years, hasn't it?
A: Until the last few months, the FCC has been an utter disaster as far as making its influence felt.[9]

Some journalists have developed aggressive interviewing styles in which they goad subjects to respond. Most often, however, the interviewer should ask questions in a way that indicates that there are no right or wrong answers. He or she should not show surprise at an answer and should not agree or disagree. Perhaps the model for the unemotional interviewer was Dr. Albert Kinsey, who undertook his research at a time when sexual behavior was seldom openly discussed. "The interviewer should not make it easy for a subject to deny his participation in any form of sexual activity," Dr. Kinsey wrote. "We always begin by asking when they first engaged in such activity."[10] When a subject admitted an unusual sex act, Kinsey would ask in a matter-of-fact tone, "How many times?"

Of course, an interviewer *does* have opinions and attitudes. In a free-flowing interview, the interviewer may be challenged to express them in order to keep the interview moving forward. In that case, it is usually best to use Benjamin Franklin's technique for argument:

> I made it a rule to forebear all direct contradiction to the sentiments of others, and all positive assertions of my own. I even forbid myself the use of every word in the language that imported a fixed opinion, such as certainly, undoubtedly, etc., and I

adopted instead of them, *I conceive, I apprehend, I imagine a thing to be so and so, or so it appears to me at the present.* When another asserted something that I thought to be an error, I denied myself the pleasure of contradicting him abruptly, and of showing immediately some absurdity in his proposition; and in answering I began by observing that in certain cases or circumstances his opinion would be right, but in the present case there appeared or seemed to me some difference, etc. I soon found the advantage of this change in my manners; the conversations I engaged in went on more pleasantly. The modest way in which I proposed my opinions procured them a readier reception and less contradiction; I had less mortification when I was found to be in the wrong; and I more easily prevailed with others to give up their mistakes and join with me when I happened to be right.

Interviewers should avoid arguments, but Franklin's *manner* is a model when they cannot.

The Interviewer's Attitudes

Just as the interviewer who reveals his own attitudes may influence response, the interviewer who seems to expect certain responses may receive them for that reason. In one of the earliest investigations of this kind of distortion, Stuart Rice found that welfare recipients blamed their plight on causes that they thought would square with the interviewer's values: an interviewer who identified himself as a Prohibitionist obtained three times as many answers blaming alcohol as did another interviewer who described himself as a socialist; the socialist obtained twice as many answers blaming industrial factors as did the Prohibitionist.[11]

The interviewer can indicate his expectations much more subtly, as Collins points out:

The interviewer may use facial expressions, gestures or sounds that encourage a respondent in a particular line of comment which he might not otherwise follow. Many laboratory studies have shown that if the interviewer smiles, leans forward, or says "mm-hmm" or "good" when the respondent uses particular words or phrases, the respondent will tend to use those expressions even more often. The same things happen if these encouraging signals are given when a particular attitude is expressed; it comes to be expressed even more often and strongly.[12]

GUIDELINES FOR INTERVIEWING

Judge a man by his questions rather than by his answers.

—Voltaire

The social scientist's and the journalist's interviews are far different, but most student research interviews will more closely resemble the journalist's. The interview is usually best handled if it is free-flowing, so that the interviewer draws out the subject, guiding the interview so that all the research topics are covered.

One who has never conducted a formal interview and knows little or nothing about techniques may in fact be a better interviewer than one who has conducted many interviews and has studied in depth the insights and experiences of professional interviewers. Interviewing has a highly personal character, and curiosity, intelligence, and warmth are extremely valuable. Those who study interviewing techniques, however, can certainly improve their interviewing style.

Preparing in Advance

To obtain a good interview, there is one cardinal rule: Prepare in advance. An interviewer should always learn as much as possible about the subject before the appointment. Subjects who are not actually incensed by an interviewer's ignorance are likely to be uncomfortable with one who demonstrates a lack of preparation. Doing the homework—learning at least the basic facts about the interview subject—is complimentary and encourages response. John Gunther, the late author of a series of books based in part on interviews, warned, "One thing is never, never, never to ask a man about his own first name, job, or title. These the interviewer should know beforehand." And, of course, much more.

The late A.J. Liebling, who was one of the most accomplished writers for the *New Yorker,* described the value of preparations, or "preps," thus:

> One of the best preps I ever did was for a profile of Eddie Arcaro, the jockey. When I interviewed him, the *first question* I asked was, "How many holes longer do you keep your left stirrup than your right?" That started him talking easily and after an hour, during which I had put in about twelve words, he said, "I can see you've been around riders a lot."[13]

For lengthy and important interviews, journalists customarily prepare lists of questions. They do not feel bound to ask all of them, however, and they frame new questions during the interview. They argue that an interview is a human, not a bookkeeping, situation. Growth and continuity in an interview spring from conversation. Transitions should be natural; questions should grow logically from the discussion, one answer suggesting another question. One who plans exactly what he or she will ask may miss the opportunity to pose a question that occurs during an interview. Some journalists believe so strongly in promoting a free-flowing discussion that they seldom do more than jot down a few key words prior to interviewing—but even they are likely to advise beginners to write questions in a notebook and leave spaces to record answers. Attempting to move immediately into the smooth discourse of the professional interviewer leads to floundering—and to forgetting important questions.

The Free-Flowing Interview

Only when interviewing busy and abrupt people—and those who are merely suffering the interview—should the interviewer begin questions abruptly. Small talk at the beginning is usually designed to encourage the later conversation. This does not mean that the interviewer should make an obvious and awkward effort to chitchat, so that a stumbling leap to the real subject will be required. The usual prelude to questioning a politician about his candidacy is not the weather, but politics in general.

William Ryan, Sterling Green, Saul Pett, and Peter Arnett, all of the Associated Press, once discussed the value of various interview beginnings:

RYAN: . . . I like to work up gradually to major questions.

GREEN: I generally do it quite the opposite. I like to land on him with a hard one right at the start and show him that we mean business and get away from any idea that "This is a puff piece." There's considerable benefit in this because it puts him on his mettle and he begins to answer responsively from the start.

PETT: I think it depends on the kind of story. If it's a hard news spot interview, we can't really fool around too much. If it's a personality type interview, you almost have to. On an interview with Mayor Lindsay, I knew that he had a good sense of humor. So I prefaced my first question by saying, "I have something terribly serious to ask you. I hope you'll be frank in your answer." And I could see him straighten up and get ready for this tough question. And then the question was: "Would you want your daughter to marry a mayor of New York?" Well, we got along fine after that. But, I cite that only as an example of work put into questions in advance.

ARNETT: Much of my work has been in the foreign field, where I interviewed people who were not very familiar with English and used an interpreter. In that case I went right into the biggest question first. However, with others familiar with English, I prefer the small talk approach.[14]

Usually the ideal is halfway between monologue and dialogue. If the subject talks in an endless monologue, leading points may be ignored. Most subjects must be steered. On the other hand, if the interview is a real dialogue, with the interviewer doing half the talking, the interviewer is probably showing off and perhaps irritating the subject.

The most delicate point in journalistic interviewing may be the need for the interviewer to comment appropriately on an answer and develop the next question without seeming to dominate the interview. A comment is important in connection with at least a few questions, for an interviewer usually invites a full response by making it clear, modestly, that he or she is knowledgeable. The subject usually speaks freely, reasoning that the responses will be recorded in a meaningful context. It is a cardinal error, however, for an interviewer to fail to ask questions because of a fear of exposing ignorance. If the interviewer knew *everything*, there would be no reason for an interview. On some occasions, though, usually in digging up hidden information, a journalist pretends to know more than he or she actually knows. The pretense ordinarily suggests: "Because I know three-quarters of the story, you might as well give me the rest so I can come out with the full story rather than a distorted version of it." This sometimes works, even if the journalist has only a vague tip.

Often, an interviewer must adapt to the interview subject. Saul Pett, a veteran Associated Press feature writer, has related two experiences that indicate how adaptable an interviewer must be. His most difficult interview subject was Dr. Albert Kinsey, the sex researcher, who was himself a practiced—and no-nonsense—interviewer. Kinsey met Pett for their appointment at precisely the agreed-upon minute, pulled out a travel alarm clock, wound it, set the alarm, set a coffee table between himself and Pett, checked the clock against his wristwatch, and, finally looking up, said, "Yes." It was obviously no time for small talk.

Pett's best interview subject was a writer, Dorothy Parker. When he went to interview her shortly after her seventieth birthday, she opened the door and asked, "Are you married, my dear?" "Yes, I am," he answered. "Well, in that case," she said, "you won't mind zipping me up."

Inevitably, there are awful occasions when a bored subject answers in mono-syllables: "Yes." "No." "Who knows?" transforming those deadly situations is difficult, but it can sometimes be accomplished with a simple question: "Why?" Although the subject can answer most direct questions with a simple positive or negative, it is quite another thing to give the *why* of an answer in one syllable. The real aim, of course, is to inspire interest, to ask the interview subject to explore the depths of his or her own point of view. Writer John Gunther has commented: "One thing I have found out is that almost any person will talk freely—such is human frailty—if you will ask him the measure of his own accomplishment."

Probing

How strongly an interviewer pursues a line of questioning, or how strongly the interviewer "probes," varies widely with purposes and situations. When a researcher is conducting one of many interviews in a sample, the object is to make each interview as much like all the others as possible. Uneven probing can distort results.

Journalists, especially those who report politics, often ask questions the interview subjects consider challenging and abrasive. Such questions *may* grow out of a journalist's own opinions, but it is a mistake to assume that they always do. Many politicians find it useful for their own purposes to charge that reporters are, in effect, political opponents. After they retire, however, most politicians admit that asking tough questions is the journalist's job.

Students will probably be relieved to hear that tough questions are sometimes not even necessary with skillful probing. For example, simply remaining silent for five seconds or so may be enough to encourage an otherwise unhelpful interview subject to speak.

Dan Rather of CBS News offered several lessons in skillful probing during an hour-long interview with President Nixon on January 2, 1972. Nixon had not then announced whether he would seek reelection. Rather asked, "May we assume you are a candidate for reelection?" Nixon answered that he would have to decide by January 14, the date for filing for the New Hampshire presidential primary: "I will be making a decision and I will be announcing it by the fourteenth."

Not satisfied, Rather posed the question another way, asking whether Attorney General John Mitchell, who had managed Nixon's 1968 campaign, would resign soon to prepare the new campaign. Nixon responded:

> Well, you're getting me right into the question that I just refused to answer, but I understand that. If I make the decision to become a candidate—and there is, of course, good reason to think that I might make the decision in that direction . . . .[15]

Rather asked two more questions relating to reelection: "Mr. President, under what circumstances would you *not* be a candidate for reelection?" and "Mr. President, can you give us assurances, categorically and unequivocally, that if you are a candidate, that you want to run again with Vice President Agnew and that he will be your running mate if you have anything to do with it?" When Nixon had answered these questions, no one needed to wait until January 14 to be aware that he would run for reelection. And no one had to wait until July, when Nixon formally announced his choice of a running mate, to be aware that he would again run with Agnew.

Student researchers may find that the purposes of their interviews may not require probing. Also, as was mentioned previously in this chapter, a student may lack the clout to probe as effectively or as deeply as a journalist. Nonetheless, students, like journalists, must be prepared to probe if necessary. Just as the effectiveness of a free-flowing interview depends in part on good preparation for the interview, so good preparation is essential for asking tough questions of the interview subject.

Respecting Confidences

Anyone who conducts many interviews is certain to be asked at some point to keep information confidential. Although the request is most often made for only part of the information divulged, journalists have been surprised to be asked at the end of an interview to keep *everything* secret. This occurs most often because the source suddenly decides that he has been indiscreet. Some journalists refuse such requests, holding rightly that an agreement should have been reached at the beginning. In ideal circumstances, the interviewer and his subject stipulate at the beginning what kind of information can be reported and what kind will be disclosed only to give the journalist a broad understanding.

Agreements are now frequently made that allow disclosing all or part of an interview but that require cloaking the name of the source. Washington correspondents and government officials have established fairly explicit ground rules for attributing information. "Off the record" means that information is disclosed only to widen the journalist's general understanding and is not to be reported in any form. "Background only" means that information may be reported but not attributed to its source—which is why so many news reports from Washington are attributed to "congressional spokesmen," "informed sources," and "White House officials" rather than to specific persons. Journalists helped frame these rules because some information could not be obtained without protection for the source. A member of Congress who has information about another member of Congress or an administration official, or an official who has information about another official or about a member of Congress might not disclose it if he or she must be identified as the informant. Julius Frandsen, former Washington Bureau Chief of United Press International, has said that "A lot of skulduggery in government would never come to light if everything had to be attributed."

Confidential information is thus sometimes complicated, and guidelines may be confusing. But there are two clear necessities: Ground rules must be established, and an agreement to keep confidences must be respected.

All rules and rules-of-thumb must, of course, be adapted to interview situations, and some interviewers are by nature better than others.

Taking Notes and Taping Interviews

Journalists are so divided among themselves whether to take notes, use a tape recorder, or take notes *and* use a recorder that generalizing is dangerous. But this rule-of-thumb may be useful: Take notes freely or use a recorder, or do both, in interviewing those who are accustomed to speaking for publication or broadcast (politicians, civic leaders, and entertainers). There are, of course, exceptions. Vladimir Nabokov, author of *Lolita* and other acclaimed novels (and a notable punster), told an interviewer, "No, tape recorders are out. No speaking off the Nabocuff. When I see one of those machines, I start hemming and hawing . . . hemming and hawing. Hemmingwaying all over the place." It may be significant that Nabokov was in his seventies at the time. In any case, younger celebrities are more likely to be accustomed to such gadgetry.

Young or old, many of those who are not used to speaking for publication or broadcast are likely to become self-conscious in the presence of notetaking or a tape recorder. Some actually freeze, but many soon relax and forget that their words are being recorded. This is especially likely to happen in group interviews; the interplay of conversation leads to a focus on the other individuals and away from devices.

All this points to the other side of the journalist's rule of thumb: Be careful in introducing a notebook or a recorder into an interview with those who are not accustomed to being quoted.

W.H. Crockford of the Richmond (Virginia) *Times-Dispatch* says, "Flipping out the notebook the minute you flush the quarry has never worked too well for me. It scares some subjects. The best excuse I find for breaking out the pad is a bit of blue-eyed admiration for some happy observation they've just made. I may try, 'Say, that's good. I want to be sure I get that down just right.' And write. The notebook now spells reassurance."

As for the mechanics of notetaking, most researchers devise their own shorthand: *imp*, for *important*, *w/* for *with*, *w/o* for *without*. One journalist's technique for winning time to record an important answer without causing an awkward silence is to ask another, minor question immediately. While the subject is responding to the second, the journalist records the answer to the first.

Truman Capote, the late author of *In Cold Blood* and many other books, was part of the small minority against using notes or tape recordings:

> If you write down or tape what people say, it makes them feel inhibited and self-conscious. It makes them say what they think you *expect* them to say . . . . Long before I started *In Cold Blood*, I taught myself to be my own tape recorder. It wasn't as hard as it might sound. What I'd do was have a friend talk or read for a set length of time, tape what he was saying, and meanwhile listen to him as intently as I could. Then I'd go and write down what he had said as I remembered it, and later compare what I had with the tape . . . . Finally, when I got to be about 97 per cent accurate, I felt ready to take on this book. [16]

Recorders are not infallible, and neither are the interviewers who use them. Nothing is more frustrating than ending a long tape-recorded interview and finding that the recording is just yards of blank tape. Even when recorders operate without error, the interviewer must interpret, selecting the telling and appropriate points from an often unwieldy mass of information. It is time-consuming to transcribe (or even to hear) all of it, and it is frustrating to know that a few valuable words are submerged somewhere in what seems to be miles of tape. For this reason, many reporters both tape and take notes, relying on the tape to check quotations. No note-taking interview comes close to a full and faithful record of an interview; on the other hand, a tape alone fails to record visual cues such as body language and gestures or the interviewer's impressions of the subject.

Another reason for keeping a taped record is for verification in case of disputes. When a former automobile dealer, Douglas McKay, was appointed Secretary of the Interior in a Republican administration, his first words during an important speech to the Chamber of Commerce of the United States were, "Well, we're here in the saddle as an Administration representative of business and industry." An Associated Press reporter, Sterling Green, published the statement. The Democrats leaped on it, charging that the administration represented only one segment of society. McKay denied making the statement—a taped record showed that Green's report was accurate. "In a difficult, disputatious situation," Green said later, "a tape is a good thing to have going, even if you're not planning to use it at all for the purposes of your story."[17]

IN A NUTSHELL

Skepticism, like chastity, should not be relinquished too readily.

—George Santayana

The experience of social scientists and journalists, taken together, yields valuable insights into using interviews for research. Multiple interviews, interviews of several different subjects, and careful attention to the interviewer's appearance and manner—and the wording of questions—all help to counter the inaccuracies inherent in the interview as a research tool.

A student researcher, who often must get information from just a few interview subjects, does well in taking the advice of experienced journalists—preparing for the interview, planning to be adaptable, knowing when and how to probe, and being prepared to take notes and tape the interview. The least experienced interviewer may be as effective as a seasoned interviewer, but all interviewers can learn from each other's insights.

EXERCISES

1. Prepare for an interview with the president or chancellor of your university. Write a list of questions you would like to ask. Compare your list with those of your classmates.
2. It has been said that within every person there is a central question that characterizes

that human being. Interview a classmate for 20 to 30 minutes, then write a description of the person that centers around that question.

3. Read some of the interviews that Studs Terkel reported in *Working* or any of his other books. Do the interviews seem to reflect the interview subjects accurately? What techniques did Terkel use to get his interviewees to "speak for themselves"?

4. Interview at least one person for the next research paper you do. Interview the person *after* you have completed most of the research, and follow the guidelines for preparation that have been given in this chapter. Turn in your notes with comments on the following things:
   a. Was my list of questions adequate? Was it too extensive?
   b. Was my approach fairly effective for my interview subject?
   c. Did I hold back on any questions or forget any questions?
   d. Did the interview flow nicely? How could it have been better?
   e. Did I take adequate notes?

5. As part of your interview, include at least one open-ended and one closed-ended question—for example: Open-ended questions such as "Why did you choose to study this or that topic?" or "What happened when you visited this or that country?" and closed questions such as "When did you study that?" and "Where exactly did you go?" Note the difference between the kinds of answers each question draws.

Notes

CHAPTER 1

[1]Frank Maloy Anderson, *The Mystery of a Public Man* (Minneapolis: U of Minneapolis P, 1948).

[2]T.S. Eliot, *The Rock* (New York: Harcourt, 1934).

[3]Richard D. Altick, *The Art of Literary Research*, 3rd ed. (New York: Norton, 1981) 6.

[4]Altick 58.

[5]Richard D. Altick, *The Scholar Adventurers* (New York: Macmillan, 1950) 15.

[6]Harold D. Lasswell, *The Future of Political Science* (New York: Atherton, 1963) 160.

[7]Carl L. Becker, "Everyman His Own Historian," *American Historical Review* Jan. 1932: 221-36.

[8]A. Kent MacDougall, "Radical Historians Get Growing Following, Dispute 'Myths' of Past," *Wall Street Journal* 19 Oct. 1971: 1.

[9]David Hackett Fischer, *Historians' Fallacies* (New York: Harper, 1970).

[10]James B. Conant, *Science and Common Sense* (New Haven: Yale UP, 1950) 50.

[11]Quoted in Morris R. Cohen and Ernest Nagel, *An Introduction to Logic and Scientific Method* (New York: Harcourt, 1934) 398-99.

[12]Clark L. Hull, "A Primary Social Science Law," *The Scientific Monthly* Oct. 1950: 225.

[13]S. M. Lipset, The Psychology of Voting: "An Analysis of Political Behavior," 5 ed., *Handbook of Social Psychology*, ed. G. Lindsey, (Reading, MA: Addison-Wesley, 1954), 2: 1124-75.

[14]Eugene J. Webb et al., *Unobtrusive Measures: Nonreactive Research in the Social Sciences*

(Chicago: Rand McNally, 1966).

[5]Abraham Kaplan, *The Conduct of Inquiry* (Scranton, PA: Chandler, 1964).

CHAPTER 2

[1]Otto Friedrich. " 'Shall I Die? Shall I Fly . . .' " *Time* 9 Dec. 1985: 76.

[2]James Fallows. "America's Changing Economic Landscape," *The Atlantic Monthly* March 1985: 47-68, 61.

[3]Lester Markel, "Interpretation of Interpretation," *Nieman Reports*, Spring 1971: 10.

[4]Ray Mungo, *Famous Long Ago* (Boston: Beacon, 1970) 75-76.

[5]Quoted in Edward P. Thompson, *The Making of the English Working Class* (New York: Pantheon, 1964) 210.

[6]Robert J. Donovan, "The Rules Have Changed," *Nieman Reports*, March 1970: 10.

[7]Alden Vaughan, *The New England Frontier* (Boston: Little, Brown, 1965) 62.

[8]Quoted in Cong. Rec. 18 July 1972: S11111.

[9]Julius Duscha, "Your Friendly Finance Company and Its Friends on Capitol Hill," *Harper's* Oct. 1962: 76.

[10]Associated Press, "VIPS Meet the GIs—A Muddy Dialogue," *San Francisco Chronicle* 8 June 1970: 1.

[11]Stephen Isaacs, "The Pitfalls of Polling," *Columbia Journalism Review* May-June 1972: 13.

CHAPTER 3

[1]Jacques Barzun and Henry F. Graff, *The Modern Researcher* (New York: Harcourt, 1957) 19.

CHAPTER 4

[1]Seán O'Faoláin, "Speaking of Books: Facts of Life," *The New York Times Book Review* 18 April 1965: 2.

CHAPTER 5

[1]G. Naber, "Online Versus Manual Literature Retrieval," *Database* Feb. 1985: 20-24.

[2]Robert E. Skinner, "Searching the History of Social Sciences Online," *Database* Feb. 1985: 28-34.

[3]Stephen Hess, quoted in Steven Weinberg, "The Paper Trail," *Washington Journalism Review* August 1985: 10.

[4]Carol Tenopir, *Online Review* 9. 2 (1985): 150+.

CHAPTER 8

[1]Walter Lippman, *Public Opinion* (New York: Macmillan, 1922) 81.

[2]"Challenge to Scientists," *Nature* 7 December 1973.

[3]James Randi, "Geller is a Fake!" *Science Digest* April 1975: 63.

[4]David Krech, Richard Crutchfield, and Egerton Ballachey, *Individual in Society* (New York: McGraw-Hill, 1962) 31.

[5]Mason Haire and Willa Grunes, "Perceptual Defenses: Our Processes Protecting an Original Perception of Another Personality," *Human Relations* 3 (1950): 403-12.

[6]Annie Dillard, "Sight Into Insight," *Harper's* February 1974: 44.

[7]Quoted in Jane Howard, *Margaret Mead, A Life* (New York: Fawcett-Crest, 1985) 43.

[8]Gordon Allport and Leo Postman, "The Basic Psychology of Rumor," *The Process and Effects of Mass Communication*, ed. Wilbur Schramm, 1st ed. (Urbana: U of Illinois, 1960) 141-55.

[9]See especially K. Koffka, *Principles of Gestalt Psychology* (New York: Harcourt, 1935) and F.C. Bartlett, *Remembering* (Cambridge: Cambridge UP, 1932).

[10]Quoted in Krech, Crutchfield, and Ballachey, *Individual* 53.

[11]Maurice Bloch, *The Historian's Craft* (New York: Vintage, 1956) 49.

[12]Karl Wieck, "Systematic Observational Methods," *The Handbook of Social Psychology*, ed. Gardner Lindzey, 2nd ed., 5 vols. (Reading, MA: Addison-Wesley, 1968) vol. 2.

[13]Herbert Jacobs, "How Big WAS the Crowd?" paper presented at the California Journalism Conference, Sacramento, 24 February 1967.

[14]Leon Festinger, H.W. Reichen, and S. Schacter, *When Prophecy Fails* (Minneapolis: U of Minnesota P, 1956) 240.

[15]Daniel Boorstin, *The Americans: The Democratic Experience* (New York: Random House, 1973).

[16]Gerald Berreman, *Behind Many Masks*, Monograph No. 4 (Ithaca, NY: Cornell University Society for Applied Anthropology 1962) 8.

[17]William F. Whyte, *Street Corner Society*, 2nd ed. (Chicago: U of Chicago P, 1955) 304.

[18]Kurt and Gladys Lang, "Decisions for Christ: Billy Graham in New York City," *Identity and Anxiety*, ed. M. Stein, A.J. Vidich, and D.M. White, (Glencoe, IL: Free Press, 1960).

[19]Schoggen, "Environmental Forces in the Everyday Lives of Children with Physical Disabilities," unpublished manuscript, 1969, 56.

[20]Aristotle, *Aristotle's Psychology: A Treatise on the Principle of Life*, trans. William A. Hammond (London: Swan Sonnenschein, 1902) 239.

[21]Kurt and Gladys Lang, "The Unique Perspective of Television and Its Effect: A Pilot Study," *Mass Communications*, ed. Wilbur Schramm, 2nd ed. (Urbana: U of Illinois P, 1960) 544-60.

[22]Elizabeth Jordan, quoted in S. Nowell-Smith, *The Legend of the Master* (New York: Harper, 1948) 16.

[23]William L. Prosser, *Handbook of the Law of Torts* (St. Paul: West Publishing, 1964) 216.

[24]Jacobs, "How Big WAS the Crowd?" 9.

[25]Eugene J. Webb, Donald T. Campbell, Richard D. Schwartz, and Lee Sechrest, *Unobtrusive Measures* (Chicago: Rand McNally, 1966).

[26]Joyce Brothers, "The President and the Press," *TV Guide* 23 Sept. 1972: 7.

[27]Quoted in Mark L. Knapp, *Nonverbal Communication in Human Interaction* (New York: Holt, Rinehart and Winston, 1972) 12.

[28]O. Pfungst, *Clever Hans, The Horse of Mr. Von Osten* (New York: Holt, Rinehart & Winston, 1911).

[29]Knapp, *Nonverbal Communication* 12.

[30]Knapp 64.

[31]Knapp 18.

[32]Peter Farb, *Word Play* (New York: Knopf, 1974).

[33]Mark Twain, *Life on the Mississippi* (Boston: J.R. Osgood and Company, 1883), 88.

CHAPTER 9

[1]David J. Weiss and Rene V. Dawis, "An Objective Validation of Factual Interview Data,"

Journal of Applied Psychology 44 (1960): 381-85.

[2]Kirk Polking, "An Exclusive Tape-Recorded Interview with Irving Wallace," *Writer's Yearbook*, 1966: 86.

[3]A summary of many studies may be found in Charles F. Carrel and Robert L. Kahn, "Interviewing," *The Handbook of Social Psychology*, ed. Gardner Lindzey and Elliot Aronson, 5 (Reading, MA: Addison-Wesley) 2: 526-95.

[4]Quoted in Daniel J. Boorstin, *The Image, or What Happened to the American Dream* (New York: Atheneum, 1962) 15.

[5]Eugene J. Webb and Jerry R. Salancik, *The Interview, or The Only Wheel in Town*, Journalism Monographs (Austin: U of Texas).

[6]Eleanor and Nathan Maccoby, "The Interview: A Tool of Social Science," *The Handbook of Social Psychology*, ed. Gardner Lindzey, 5 (Reading, MA: Addison-Wesley, 1954) 1: 453.

[7]Joseph and Stewart Alsop, *The Reporter's Trade* (New York: Reynal, 1958).

[8]Stanley L. Payne, *The Art of Asking Questions* (Princeton: Princeton UP, 1951) 8-9, 57.

[9]Webb and Salancik, *The Interview* 29.

[10]Alfred C. Kinsey, Wardell Pomeroy, and Clyde Martin, *Sexual Behavior in the Human Male* (Philadelphia: Saunders, 1948) 53.

[11]Stuart A. Rice,"Contagious Bias in the Interview: A Methodological Note," *American Journal of Sociology* 35 (1929): 420-23.

[12]Andrew Collins, *The Interview: An Educational Research Tool*," an occasional paper issued by the ERIC Clearinghouse on Educational Media and Technology (1972) 9.

[13]A.J. Liebling, *The Most of A.J. Liebling* (New York: Simon and Schuster, 1963) 157.

[14]Associated Press, "The Art of the Interview," *AP World* (Summer 1972): 19.

[15]Transcript of "A Conversation With President Nixon," CBS Television, 2 Jan. 1972: 1-2.

[16]Jane Howard, "A Six-Year Literary Vigil," *Life* 7 Jan. 1966: 71.

[17]Associated Press, "Art of the Interview" 22.

INDEX